This Broken Archipelago

Provincelands: the cascading dunes swallow the forest.

THIS BROKEN ARCHIPELAGO

Cape Cod and the Islands, Amphibians and Reptiles

James D. Lazell, Jr.

Photographs by Martin C. Michener

A DEMETER PRESS BOOK

Quadrangle / The New York Times Book Co.

BOOK DESIGN: VINCENT TORRE

Library of Congress Cataloging in Publication Data

Lazell, James D
  This broken archipelago.

  "A Demeter Press book."
  Bibliography: p.
  Includes index.
    1. Reptiles—Massachusetts—Cape Cod region.
  2. Amphibians—Massachusetts—Cape Cod region.
  I. Title.
QL653.M4L39 1976   598.1'09744'92   75-36270
ISBN 0-8129-0605-5

A hook of land hewn from New England encloses the southwestern terminus of the Gulf of Maine. Below it are some coastal islands: the chain of the Elizabeths, stringing out to westward, Martha's Vineyard, Nantucket to the south, and many others much smaller. Strange animals live on this hook of land, and on these islands. The sea makes the climate insulated, equable, cool in summer, mild in winter.

This hook of land, and these islands, are not at all like the rest of the world. They are unique: each bit different from the others; the sum distinct from all the planet earth.

What a succession of chances, or what changes of level have been brought into play, thus to spread these small animals throughout this broken archipelago!

CHARLES DARWIN

CONTENTS

Contents

PREFACE

THIS BOOK has been written in jumps and hunks. I have lots of facts about some subjects, lots of opinions about others, variable amounts of both about most. I have abandoned the idea of equitable species accounts. I know almost nothing about some species and (relatively) a good deal about others. Standardized species accounts could only have been achieved on the bed of Procrustes.

Vertebrate animals are arranged in classes: Amphibia is one, Reptilia another. There are also Mammalia (mammals), Aves (birds), Agnatha (jawless fishes), and several others. Classes are divided into orders. Orders are divided into Families, Families are divided into Genera (one genus, two genera). Within each genus, complementing the same first (generic) name, are the species. If an animal has three names, the last is the subspecies, or geographic race. Lots of species break up into recognizable geographic races, and lots do not. I write as though everyone understood all of that perfectly.

Literally hundreds of people have contributed to this work. I live in trepidation that I will leave out someone of importance in any attempt to write up acknowledgments. But I can explain how people have contributed most signally by explaining my methods. I have two file card boxes before me, containing a combined total of over 1000 three-by-five cards. Each card represents a firsthand identification, by me, of from one to several hundred specimens (the latter especially of choruses of calling frogs). On each card is the basic data available, or as much as handily fits: locality; date; collector (if not me); whether the specimens were released or pickled; if pickled; where they are now; often individual characteristics of the animals like sex, size, etc.; often weather data; and lastly a citation to additional information, such as an original field catalog entry.

For more than ten years I have kept field notes and catalogs on travels through the Cape and Islands (as well as others) and specimens collected there.

To compile the card files I have examined specimens in a number of museums: United States National Museum of Natural History (USNM), part of the Smithsonian Institution; the American Museum of Natural History in New York (AMNH); the Academy of Natural Sciences in Philadelphia (ANSP); the Museum of Comparative Zoology at Harvard (MCZ); and a few others. I am indebted to the curators of these collections for permission to examine and report on their material.

The MCZ, being the nearest large museum, has been by far the most important. I have deposited there all the specimens I collected.

Most of the cards in the file do *not* represent pickled carcasses. I have chosen to pickle and deposit in the MCZ only representative individuals from (a) the different islands, or (b) extreme localities on the Cape. I do not enjoy, or see much point to, executing animals of well-known taxonomic status—as our species usually are. However, the importance of a representative, or voucher, specimen cannot be underestimated. Initially, I was mortified to note how few actual museum specimens there were from the whole Cape-Islands region. No one, it seems, had ever even bothered to pickle a Fowler's toad from Provincetown, at the tip of the Cape, or a garter snake from No Mans Land, our southernmost bit of land. I have had to collect a hundred or more voucher specimens. Only an actual specimen will *prove*, to some other scientist, that the species really occurs on some island or extreme of land.

Most of the cards, then, represent animals I identified in the field and did not collect. Many of the collected specimens were caught by my colleagues, students, and other friends: the cards, and their museum data, indicate the collector.

I have also considered firsthand inclusions based on photographs. I carded them (and their photographer) whenever (a) there was no question in my mind as to the identity of the species, and (b) there were accurate data on the photograph.

For eight years I taught, and headed the science department, at the Palfrey Street School in Watertown, Massachusetts. Dr. Martin C. Michener—Marty, in this work—still teaches photography and science there. Marty provided the photographs for this book. The most useful known collecting device on earth is a thing called *student*. Although the student does require feeding, it can be obtained, often in fairly large quantities, free of charge. After feeding, it is provided with an assortment of collecting bags and released in the areas from which specimens are desired. The results are often amazing. Primary examples I have used in the preparation of this work are: Terry Aladjem, Annie Downes, Paul Elias, Nick Howell, Peter Lynch,

Mark Merrill, Peter Rabinowitz, Connie Rinaldo, Sarah Robey, Cary Sheldon, and Numi Spitzer, and others to a lesser extent. Many of them have written or will write their own works of primary biological literature.

The Children's School of Science provided me a most profitable summer's employment at Woods Hole, Falmouth; I am especially indebted to Carolyn Miller and Betty Metcalf.

Educational Expeditions International, of Belmont, Massachusetts, fielded three very able assistants for me in 1973: Bob Beckham, Bruce McIntosh, and Rich Rothman. In 1975 EEI sponsored three assistants, Christine Werme, Nick Howell, and George Peabody, plus eight students: Maureen Cieplak, Ann Brown, Mark Ferrari, Sebastian Bell, Eileen Barber, Carrie Kroehler, Jim Whitehurst, and Laura Brophy.

A number of professional biologists, conservationists, and naturalists have contributed heavily; their names and locations will be of help to future workers: Lee Davis, Barnstable; Wallace Bailey and Betty Andersen, Wellfleet; Dick Cunningham, Paul Godfrey, and Warren Perry, Cape Cod National Seashore; Woody Mills, Ashumet Holly Reservation; Soo Whiting, Gus Ben David and Bob Woodruff, all of Martha's Vineyard; Ollie Brazier and Hoima Cherau on Naushon; Julie Perkins, and Edith and Clint Andrews on Nantucket; Jim Baird for Monomoy; and Ian Nisbet for Muskeget. All of these, and often their sons and daughters, are just a few of many contributors.

Dr. John A. (Jack) Musick, now at Virginia Institute of Marine Science, was a graduate student working at Woods Hole when he caught for me a big adult black racer which he found up and active on 16 November 1966. I thought that sufficiently amazing to begin compiling notes on Cape and Islands reptiles and amphibians. I certainly was naive.

Ed Gruson, of Demeter Press, really made this book possible because he loves both natural history and a good story.

If you do not find your name listed above, by all means read this book: in the tales and anecdotes that follow you may well yet appear. If you don't, then wait for the first revision. I have many stories yet to tell, although after ten years, considering all the questions I would like the answers to, I realize that I know almost nothing at all about the subject.

The publishers of several periodicals—*Massachusetts Audubon*, *Man and Nature*, and *Aquasphere*—have kindly granted permission to reprint passages from articles I have written over the years.

This Broken Archipelago

Herpetology

H ERPETOLOGY is the study of amphibians and reptiles. Amphibians are animals that lead two lives; the name comes from the ancient Greek *amphi,* for two, and *bios,* for lives. Their two lives are the tadpole larva and the metamorphosed adult. The name amphibian has nothing whatever to do with "going both on land and in the water"—a misconception foisted upon us by the military-industrial complex. The amphibians are indeed an ancient group, going back some 350 million years to a dim, distant time of trilobites, pteridosperms, and lepidodendrons in a period called the Devonian. No doubt you can scarcely remember them in that time, and I have trouble myself.

Some ancient amphibians were huge, cumbersome creatures, but all still living today are relatively small. There are three living groups: the frogs (including toads, spadefoots, and other tailless creatures), the salamanders, and the caecilians (a tropical group of legless burrowers that need not concern New Englanders).

The distinguished herpetologist Dr. H. G. Dowling has commented that reptile enthusiasts insist on keeping the amphibians within the study of herpetology simply because then we can always catch *something.* It is surely true that amphibians are often easier to find in this area than reptiles, usually easier to catch, and are available during more months of the year. Snake hunts in New England can be frustrating and fruitless, but one can *always* find a salamander.

Reptiles too are an old group, going back about 300 million years to the Carboniferous—the time when huge forests flourished, forests now left to us as seams of coal. For a period beginning about 250 million years ago and lasting for about 150 million years, reptiles ruled the earth. There were vast radiations of orders and families. Dinosaurs flew in the air, swam in the seas, and trembled the earth beneath their feet—the heaviest creatures that have ever walked on land.

From the great age of reptiles only the turtles have marched ever forward, virtually unchanged, to haunt us with their story of unequivocal success. Other living reptiles include the snakes, the lizards, the tuatara (a peculiar creature found on a few islands off New Zealand), and the crocodilians (including alligators, caimans, and gavials). The latter group is really far more closely related to birds than to any of the other living reptiles.

Turtles are not related to anything that lives today or can be demonstrated to have ever lived at all. They are reptiles by definition only; their ancestry remains unknown.

All reptiles and amphibians are vertebrate animals—just like people, goldfish, and canaries. The vertebrates—all the fishes, amphibians, reptiles, birds, and mammals—belong to a group called the phylum Chordata, including sea peaches, lancets, and acorn worms. All of us have in common three major features: a dorso-tubular nerve cord (called the spinal cord in people), a notochord (a gristle rod in the back that is completely replaced in adult people, reptiles, amphibians, etc.) and gill clefts. You may not think you have gill clefts, but—just to begin with—there's the eustachian tube to your middle ear, the crypt in which your tonsils sit (or sat), the pockets of your parathyroid and thyroid glands, and so on. The gill clefts on a shark are pretty obvious; those on baby salamanders only slightly less so.

Vertebrates all have backbones, and reptiles share with birds and mammals many other features: a basically similar heart, lungs, the same sort of kidneys, and strong membranes that surround the developing embryo and protect it from its environment. Amphibians are far more similar to fishes. They have hearts, stomachs, intestines, etc., rather like ours, but their kidneys are of a totally different sort. Some have lungs, some have gills, some have both, and some have neither. None have protective embryonic membranes, so they must either lay their eggs in water or devise some clever way to prevent their eggs from drying up on land.

Considering the vast distinction between amphibians and reptiles, it is puzzling to herpetologists that so many people confuse, for example, salamanders (amphibians) with lizards (reptiles). Needless to say, they are utterly unrelated. People are forever calling what I do "lizard hunting," despite the fact that there are no lizards on the Cape or Islands, and no evidence that there ever were any. There probably are no lizards living in the wild anywhere in Massachusetts, though three specimens were collected in the last century. The only lizard known to occur in New England at all is the five-lined, or blue-tailed, skink. It is incredibly rare this far north, but common in the southeast.

Reptiles and amphibians are ubiquitous and amazingly abundant. There are more species of these two groups, taken together, than there are of either birds or mammals. But herpetology, in the main, is the study of small creatures. The great dinosaurs are gone these millions of years, and what few genuinely large reptiles remain on earth are mostly found far out at sea or in remote corners of the warmer climes. Some of these migrate regularly to the Cape and Islands and have earned their place in this book. As a general rule, though, if you want to know the reptiles and amphibians of any part of New England first-hand, you will have to learn to notice small things, and look in small places. A moldering stump, a rusting can—this is where the physiography of the herpetologist's world begins. You will have to learn to see green snakes amid green grass and brown toads in the brown earth. You will have to go out in the rain in the middle of a March night and walk in the cold, cold water. And you will have to walk miles over the heath and dunes in the midsummer sun.

Who, you ask, would consider doing this for a glimpse into the lives of the slimy, the slithering, and the snapping? Few indeed. For those few of us, however, there are cherished secrets. Reptiles and amphibians, though not all small, are cryptic; they lead lives largely hidden from our view. Only a few of us know that snakes are abundant in downtown Boston, that monstrous reptiles as heavy as a three-year-old child lurk beneath the scum of the Charles River, or that magnificent yellow-orange and jet-black salamanders prowl in numbers beneath suburban lawns. I wonder how many vacationing housewives would drive so unconcernedly over to one of my favorite dumps to unload the family refuse if they knew that dump to be a focal point of the serpentine world. There are over a hundred snakes per acre—some of them longer than I am tall.

And how many people have ever seen a spring peeper, or pinkletink, one of the most abundant vertebrate animals in North America?

Surely everyone has heard them, though perhaps without knowing it. If I tell you that the creature which emits the shrill piping of the early spring is globular, eyeless, bright green, eight-legged and that it makes its noise by flatulence vibrating its wiry tail, how many of you could really be sure that I am wrong?

Well, you may not want to go out in a driving sleet storm and crawl on your hands and knees through six inches of swamp water over two feet of mud; I will do it for you. I am a herpetologist. I walk through the same world as everyone else, but I see it differently. I too see trees and marshes, rusting hulks of old cars and rotting tar paper, the rocks, the beaches, and the sea. I see all this in my strange perspective, through my peculiar eyes. You may read this work out of curiosity or even revulsion and, if I succeed, may finish with a fascination, perhaps a fondness, and at least a glimmering of respect for creatures you never liked, and never knew, before.

Herpetologists are basically hunters, like their ancestors of a million years ago. Moderately large animals with stereoscopic vision, good hand and eye coordination, and a relatively advanced brain capable of devising and utilizing natural objects as aids, we grovel about in the brush and under stones, logs, old hubcaps, and the like, searching for our tiny, stupid, primitive, and seemingly near-helpless prey. Sometimes we find them. This book is about some of the ones I have found.

6

1

The Land

It takes a prodigious imagination to visualize the proportions of the glacial phenomenon of the Pleistocene.

COUNT GIBSON

A MILLION years ago the world was different, but not astoundingly so. The dinosaurs had been gone nearly a hundred million years, and close approximations of today's familiar bison, elephants, horses, and camels roamed the land. All of the families of reptiles and amphibians we know today were present, and probably all the basic generic sorts as well. But at least some of the species we see now were not yet evolved, and man himself was still confined to the old world tropics. The coast of southern New England was smoother; there was no Cape Cod, no Islands.

Then the ice came. It came down across Canada, creaking, groaning, slowly flowing southward and eastward, ripping, rending, and crushing all that stood in its inexorable path. The ice ripped Cape Cod and the Islands from the mountains of Maine and New Hampshire; the ice gouged Falmouth and Chatham and Chilmark and Siasconset from the hills and valleys of upland New England and dumped them where you find them today.

7

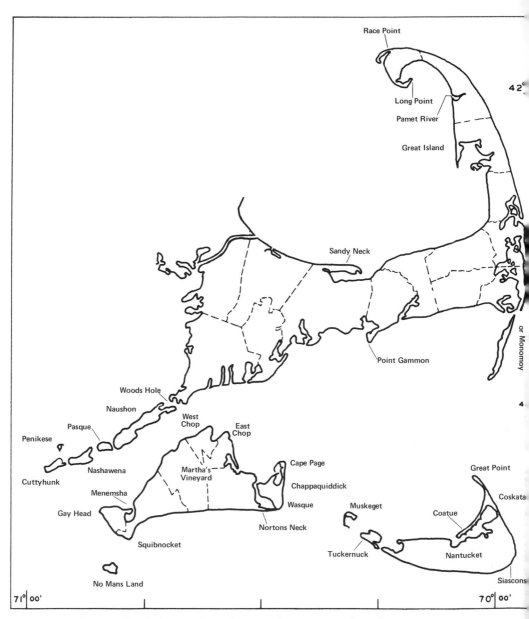

Race Point

42°

Long Point
Pamet River

Great Island

Sandy Neck

or Monomoy

Point Gammon

Woods Hole
Naushon
West
Chop
East
Chop
Pasque
Penikese
Nashawena
Martha's
Vineyard
Cape Page
Great Point
Cuttyhunk
Coskata
Menemsha
Chappaquiddick
Muskeget
Coatue
Gay Head
Wasque
Nantucket
Squibnocket
Nortons Neck
Tuckernuck
Siascons

No Mans Land

71° 00'   70° 00'

Cape Cod and the islands, with some place names indicated.

The ice came four times, and after each advance it retreated. We live today in a period of retreat, called an interglacial. Whether the ice will go on melting, and sea level go on rising, or whether the ice will come onward again cannot be certainly decided now, but man's own pollution of his thin envelope of atmosphere will surely be a major factor. The first time the ice came it pushed far to the south;

8

its more northern works were subsequently covered, but we still have No Mans Land and Squibnocket to attest its journey. The second and third times the ice brought most of the rest of Martha's Vineyard, Chappaquiddick, Tuckernuck, and Nantucket. The fourth and last time, the ice may have reached the Vineyard briefly, but it fell back and left us most of Cape Cod and the Elizabeth Islands. During that last great period of glaciers—the one we know the most about—the ice at its maximum lay 10,000 feet thick. Its countless billions of tons accounted for so much of the earth's water that sea levels were reduced as much as 300 feet from what they are today. Presumably the earlier glacial maxima were basically similar.

During each interglacial period the climate warmed dramatically,

Salamander country: the Provincelands, Cape Cod.

A focal point of the snake hunter's world: Provincetown dump.

and plants and animals of cold climate tolerance moved northward, staying close to the retreating ice. Plants and animals of the warm south moved northward too, but at a distance. The northward movements of opossums, cardinals, titmice, and mockingbirds within recorded time (and still continuing) are examples of this interglacial phenomenon.

At the times of great glacial maxima the southern border of the ice was scalloped into huge lobes. The lobes stretched into the warmer climates as far as they could go, and across their faces they melted away. But more snow fell than melted in the north. It packed to new ice and pushed outward—south and east. Anything that stuck up above the surface of the land, like mountain tops, or was attached to it loosely, like soil, was imbedded in the ice or pushed forward by it. Huge rocks were ground to cobbles, cobbles to pebbles, and pebbles to sand. Deep sediments of clay and silt were scooped out by the advancing ice and pushed before it. But when the burden of debris reached the melt lines across the faces of the lobes, the ice could carry it no further. There, in huge crescentic ridges called *terminal moraines*, the wreckage of the land's surface came to rest.

The glaciers seem to have retreated rapidly. Over all the land to the north and west traversed by lobes, they unceremoniously dumped their loads of rock and pebbles. Hills of this material are called *knobs*. The glaciers left behind scattered blocks of ice imbedded in the moraines and sunk in the land behind them. The melting ice formed huge lakes behind the dikes of the terminal moraines, but as the ice melted more and more to water, the moraines could not hold it all.

The meltwater broke through the moraines and carried tons of light material—mud, clay, sand, and pebbles—with it. The meltwater formed great rivers rushing southward to the sea, depositing their solid sediments of mud and sand as they went. The holes between the islands, like Woods Hole and Robinsons Hole, are where the water broke through the moraine. The great ponds and long ponds of the southern Vineyard, Nantucket, and the Cape from Falmouth to Chatham are the heads of those once-great rivers.

As the ice melted, sea levels rose. The rivers became estuaries, and then, when the ice was gone, stopped flowing. The valleys of these extinct rivers are called *pamets*. The sea's waves broke through the moraines at many points where holes are or were. The waves carried the sand and brought more of it; their actions smoothed the ragged coasts, filling in with sea sand a hollow here, smoothing off by erosion a headland there. The new land made of sea sand was built on the skeleton of the old land made by ice.

The scattered blocks of ice sunk in the moraines melted and left holes called *kettles*. Many of them hold fresh water today, and whether temporary (drying up each summer) or permanent, these kettle ponds form the basis of the freshwater biology of the Cape and Islands.

Cape Cod and the Islands, therefore, consist of three basic kinds of land: the moraines, the outwash plains, and the seaborne drift sand.

The moraines make the high land and all the land of the "knob and kettle" country. Here are rocks, large and small, some as big as

Herpetologist at work: Chilmark, Martha's Vineyard.

the cottage I live in—a jumble of objects too heavy to wash out across the plains to the south. Because these rocks are not native to the area where we now find them, they are called glacial *erratics*. The smaller material—gravel and pebbles—is called *till*. A thousand or more years ago the moraines supported vast, magnificent forests of American beech, *Fagus grandifolia*, the climax forest type of southern New England. Man, beginning with the fire-prone Indians, and culminating in the incredible Sandwich glass works, destroyed those forests. The trees at their finest were a hundred feet tall and two-and-a-half feet in diameter. There is only one place in all New England where that forest remains. One small island escaped the Indians' fire and white man's axe. Because it is private property, because it is posted against all trespass, and because it is carefully patrolled, the forest is still there today. This tiny remnant of virgin wilderness can never be opened to the public. Consideration of it would be a contradiction in terms. With the coming of masses of humanity the wilderness no longer exists. The island must be kept isolated. That way there will always be a bit of the primeval forest, a glimpse of the way the world used to be.

The outwash plains are composed of fine-grained material: sand, mud, and a little gravel. As they extended southward from the moraines toward the sea, their climax beech forests would have given way to subclimax ecological stages: white pine (*Pinus strobus*), bayberry (*Myrica pennsylvanica*), and eventually marsh grasses of the genus *Spartina*. Today the beech climax is largely gone and the white pine virtually extinct. Black and red oaks (genus *Quercus*) and pitch pines (*Pinus rigida*) predominate as the woodland types of both moraine and outwash plains. The long ponds and great ponds of the outwash plains vary from salt to fresh, depending on their openings to the sea along their southern edges. Most are brackish most of the time. Nearly impenetrable jungles of scrubby oaks, bayberry, and catbriar extend across great areas of the outwash plains. Because they are so flat, a wanderer can easily get lost, and on a cloudy day, with no obvious directional indicators, things can get serious.

The sand, drifted by the waves and blown by the winds, accounts for great areas of Cape and Islands terrain. The entire land area north of Pilgrim Heights—all of Provincetown and the Provincelands —is made of sea sand. All of Monomoy and Muskeget are sand—the former strung out by longshore current, the latter founded on submerged moraine. Sweeping into Cape Cod Bay, the current drags the sand out across Barnstable Bay and has thus made Sandy Neck. From Truro the sand still carries southward inside the Cape to bridge Wellfleet's islands south to wave-washed Billingsgate. Outside, the sand is swept southward to form Nauset Light Beach, across Nauset Harbor, and Nauset Beach, across Pleasant Bay. The sand streams off the end of Nauset Beach to form Monomoy, and then on across the Sound to make Great Point on Nantucket, and Cape Poge on Chappaquiddick. The sand streams south and west from Great Point to make Coatue, founded on a moraine visible above the sand only in the Coskata woodlands, and westward to make most of Eel Point, Smith Point, the beaches of Tuckernuck, and all of Muskeget. From Cape Poge on Chappaquiddick, the sand streams southward to the corner at Norton's Point; it streams across the south shore of Martha's Vineyard, closing off great ponds as it goes. Along the Elizabeth Islands the sand carries, smoothing the coasts and forming barriers across coves to make ponds, to Cuttyhunk.

Wherever an island, or almost-island, is connected to other land by drifting sea sand a *tombolo* is formed. The tombolos of Monomoy, Great Point, and Cape Poge are primary examples.

Sandy Neck: looking eastward along the tombolo. Here beach grass (*Ammophila*) holds the dunes in their early stages.

Most people who visit the Cape and Islands do not realize that they have entered a wonderland of knobs and kettles, erratics and pamets, till and tombolos—one of the most fascinating geological regions on earth.

Because sand has formed such large land areas, the greatest ecological diversity and the clearest picture of ecological processes can be seen in it. At its interface with the sea, between the tide lines, lies a classical *ecotone*. An ecotone is a region between two utterly different ecological regions—in this case the land and the sea—which is quite unlike either, or any combination of the two. In the beach ecotone we find a diversity of organisms, mostly tiny, that can live nowhere else. The crustaceans, mollusks, worms, protists, and other forms of life adapted to the surf and sand could not live on land or in the deep waters just off shore. Above the breakers is a region of bare sand. Beginning here we can trace the development of land ecology from bare ground to climax forest. A small stand of beech forest still survives in the heart of the Provincelands. It is not virgin, but is nevertheless primary forest, the climax type of our region.

What happens as one goes from bare ground to climax forest is called *ecological succession*. Briefly stated, the theory of ecological succession is that any given land area goes through a series of well-defined plant and animal communities, called *seral stages*, on its way toward the ultimate climax community. Ecological succession, according to the theory, works just as well in time as in space. That is, if you clear the climax forest to bare ground, the same seral stages will occur over the years as occur between the beach and the climax forest when one makes a traverse today. In practice, just as one might expect, ecological succession is far from perfect. Because of differing conditions of soil, salinity, acidity, alkalinity, available moisture, etc., some stages are skipped or added on moraine land, others skipped or added on sand. Then, too, some seral stages are remarkably tenacious, refusing to give way to the next stage for one reason or another. A classical example is the "pine barrens" stage, in which the primary, obvious life form is *Pinus rigida*, the pitch pine.

Barnstable, Cape Cod: drift sand invades the pitch pine and bear oak woodland.

A whole community of plants and animals, abundantly associated in areas of pitch pine dominance, are rare or absent from other stages. The pitch pine community is forest-fire-adapted and forest-fire-dependent. The continuation of the pitch pine community—at least over the large areas it now occupies—depends on fire. The pine is not killed by forest fire and neither are its associated plants and small animals. The latter often survive excellently just below the surface in burrows and tunnels; the former are often untouched because the fire roars through the tops of the trees. Because pitch pine burns explosively, the pine barrens have their own built-in maintenance system: you can hardly prevent pine barrens from burning, and burning keeps the land in pine barrens. A seral ecological community of this sort is so stable that it is often called a *subclimax*. It is one of the richest herpetological areas imaginable.

The only reptiles regularly present in the open North Atlantic

Vast sediments of clay all askew, pushed up on their edges by the force of glacial ice, form the famous cliffs of Gay Head, Martha's Vineyard. Relentlessly, the sea cuts them back and erodes away this ancient land. Great rocks—glacial erratics—attest the former position of the moraine. Scale is indicated by the telephone pole on the beach in the foreground.

Long Beach on Gay Head: even as the sea cuts away the old land, it builds the new. If the dune grass, salt-spray rose, and beach peas can hold these dunes, new ones will form to seaward.

Ocean are the sea turtles. In the cool gloom of climax forest are a salamander and two snakes, on a regular basis. All other reptiles and amphibians, including those of the climax forest, utilize the seral stages and subclimax communities as their habitat. Plants are the ecological markers of their respective communities; if one would seek out the reptiles and amphibians, it would be good to know a bit about those plants.

Beginning at the land-sea interface, a variably wide zone extends inland in which the predominant life forms are grasses. Along the beach, the grass is *Ammophila breviligulata*, called simply beach grass or dune grass. On bay and estuarine shores, where the interface between land and sea is less violent, the grasses grow in shallow water and may form huge salt marshes. Here, the predominant grasses are species of *Spartina*. The *Spartina* marshes are, of course, an ecotone. Lest one tend to dismiss the ecotone as an interesting but trivial phenomenon, let me stress that the salt marsh is the richest and most biologically productive region on earth. It has been

Pitch pine invading, vinelike, succeeds the bear-berry. Truro, Cape Cod.

fairly stated that the entire earth ecosystem—all life as we know it—
depends, directly or indirectly, on the salt marshes of the world. If
that statement seems preposterous, or even unlikely, just start reading
up on the subject. Teal & Teal (1969) is a good place to begin. You
will not have to read much about the salt marsh before conceding
the point. It is by the grace of the grass *Spartina* that we live.

Once above water on ocean or bay side, the sand dries and by its
very nature begins to shift before the wind. The sand blows into
dunes. Left to their own devices, the dunes will march inland,
inundating all before them. It is delicate *Ammophila* which must
first stop the blowing, cascading sand. The stems and leaves of the
grass form tiny windbreaks; the roots interlace to hold the dunes.
If the grass can hold the sand a short year or two, larger herbaceous
plants succeed it—the members of *Artemisia*, wormwood and dusty
miller; *Lathyrus*, the beach pea; the lovely species of *Rosa*; salt-spray
and Virginia roses; the tough *Euphorbia* called seaside spurge; and,
of course, *Rhus radicans*, poison ivy.

18

Dusty miller (*Artemesia stelleriana*) establishes a foothold in the beach grass
(*Ammophila breviligulata*).

Resplendent in lovely purples, scarlets, russets, ochres, and greens, growing first as a ground trailing vine, then low herbage, then as dense shrubbery, and someday even attaining the character of small trees, poison ivy is the finest and most wonderful of all our plants. Poison ivy holds the shifting sands; it shades and shelters the birds and animals; its berries richly augment the complex ecological food chain; best of all, poison ivy keeps the people off the land. It is the trouncing, trampling feet of man that crush and kill the fragile plants of the dunes, and set the sand to blowing mercilessly inland.

The poisoning agent of *Rhus radicans* is an organic chemical of the phenol group called *urushiol*, a yellowish oil found in every part of the plant. To quote the U.S. Department of Agriculture (*Farmer's Bulletin* 1972, published in 1958):

> Poisoning is usually caused by contact with some part of the plant. A very small quantity of the poisonous substance is capable of producing severe inflammation of the skin and can easily be transferred from one object to another. Clothing may become contaminated and is often a source of prolonged infection. . . . Dogs and cats frequently touch the plants and transmit the poison to unsuspecting persons. . . . The itching sensation and subsequent inflammation, which usually develops into water blisters under the skin, may continue for several days from a single contamination. . . . Severe infection may produce more serious symptoms, which result in much pain through abscesses, enlarged glands, fever, or complicated constitutional malfunction. Secondary infections are always a possibility in any break in the skin, such as is produced by breaking vesicles that have formed as large water blisters.

Secondary infections may lead to blood poisoning, gangrene, and death. This publication also points out: ". . . absolute immunity to the toxic principle apparently does not exist." For your own safety, remain in your car or travel only on the specified footpaths. Nature can be evil and is blessedly filled with poison ivy.

With stability, the dunes develop a carpet of bearberry (*Arctostaphylos*) and springy clumps of poverty grasses (*Hudsonia*). This gives way to a shrub stage of beach plum (*Prunus maritima*), shadbush (*Amelanchier*), and bayberry (*Myrica pennsylvanica*). Bear oak (*Quercus ilicifolia*) eventually succeeds the bayberry. Then comes the pitch pine stage noted above. Ideally, young oak trees of the hard core unidentifiables (red, black, and white oaks, with all their combinations and permutations) should grow up among the pines and eventually shade them out. Then, as the oak forest matures to moist shadiness—if the world went by the book—tiny beech seedlings would insidiously sprout up from the woodland floor. As the beeches grew taller, they would fight the oaks for light. Gaining height and strength, they would win, and the oaks, shaded beneath a towering canopy, would dwindle and die. At the edges of the beech forest one could always walk through the seral stages to the sea. Over most of the land, though, there would be only the dark, silent forest again. There would be no pitch pines, no bayberry, no poverty grass. And, of course, no people. Otherwise all this would not have come to pass.

I have noted only a few of the commonest plants in the parade of ecological succession. If you know their relatives and compatriots well, it becomes fascinating to wander over the land and speculate on its history. Not all of it was cleared in one fell swoop. Some of it was never clothed in climax forest. The plants, and the animals that move through them, can reveal the story of an acre here and a woodlot there. At places like Ashumet Holly Reservation in Falmouth and Pilgrim Heights in Truro, you can see many of these plants and the seral communities they represent. At the Lowell Holly Reservation, in Mashpee, there is a superb stand of old forest. The

Sandy Neck: ghost forest. Here the wind exposes land once covered by trees. A once rich soil shows as dark in the blowing drift sand.

Sandy Neck: habitat destruction. Here dune buggies have cut through the delicate *Hudsonia* "poverty grass" that holds the dunes. These tracks are more than two years old.

oaks are straining now to keep up with the beeches; all is headed toward the climax.

In working on the herpetology of Cape Cod and the Islands, separating the land areas into four major regions has proved most useful: (1) Cape Cod and its adjacent Monomoy Island, (2) the Elizabeth Islands, (3) Martha's Vineyard and its adjacent islets of No Mans Land and Chappaquiddick, and (4) Nantucket and its adjacent islets of Tuckernuck and Muskeget.

Cape Cod and Monomoy

On 29 July 1914 the Army Corps of Engineers opened the Cape Cod Canal and made Cape Cod an island. Since that date, any land animal gaining access to any area covered by this work has had to cross salt water. Prior to that date, land animals could have come to Cape Cod proper over land without flying over, swimming through, or floating across sea water.

The island of Cape Cod is entirely included within Barnstable County. A small strip of Barnstable County, including a good portion of the town of Bourne and a corner of the town of Sandwich, lies on the mainland north of the Cape Cod Canal. That area is not included in this work. At the widest span across its base, from Woods Hole in Falmouth to Sagamore in Sandwich, the island of Cape Cod measures just less than twenty miles. Across its base in an east-west direction, from Wings Neck in Buzzards Bay to the outer edge of Nauset Beach in Chatham, the island of the Cape stretches less than forty miles. The average width of the base of the Cape, say at the level of the town of Dennis, is about seven miles. From the south tip of Nauset Beach, Chatham, the great hook of the outer Cape curves northwest for thirty-three miles to Race Point, above Provincetown. Depending on which ponds you count and which you call bays, and whether the tide is high or low, the entire island of Cape Cod amounts to not much more than 350 square miles.

There are a number of small islets, and things called islands, around Cape Cod. For the sake of sanity, I have elected not to give separate consideration here to *included* islands. An included island I define as one surrounded on at least three sides by Cape mainland. This eliminates Toby's, Basset, Amrita (Scraggy Neck), and such in Buzzards Bay; the several islands (Sampson Head, Sipson, Little Sipson, Strong, and Tern) in Pleasant Bay; Lieutenant Island in Wellfleet Bay; and others even less noticeable. Great Island, along with Great Beach Hill and Jeremy Point, all extending southward to enclose Wellfleet Bay on the west, are not really islands at all: the drifting sand spans them with walkable land and marsh. Billingsgate goes under at high tide.

The only island in Barnstable County that I have deemed worthy of separate consideration is Monomoy. It is included within the limits of the town of Chatham and extends southward for nearly nine miles. Monomoy was long a National Wildlife Refuge, but has now become a National Wilderness Area. It is as inviolate and safe from human destruction as federal law can make it. The Massachusetts Audubon Society owns the lighthouse, and a small plot of land, near the southern end. On the Sound side, Monomoy is a vast *Spartina* salt marsh: the home of countless millions of sea creatures and a paradise for waterfowl. Made of drift sand, Monomoy is nowhere wide enough to have ever provided the land area needed

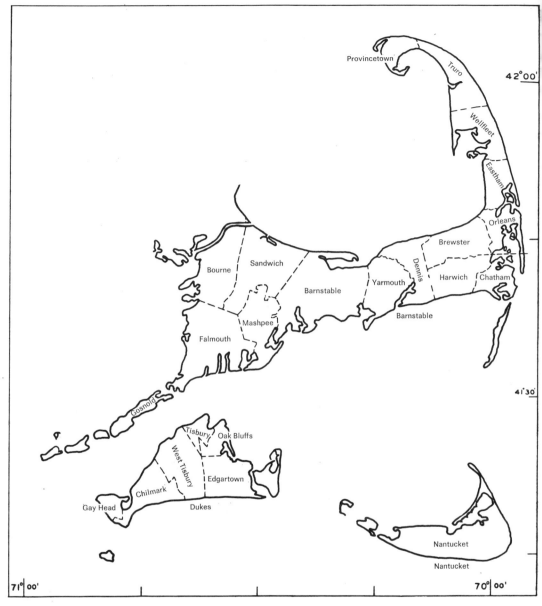

Cape Cod and the Islands, indicating the boundaries of counties and towns. (Modified from map 70–9, Commonwealth of Massachusetts, Department of Community Affairs.)

for ecological succession to proceed to climax forest. It is an excellent place to observe the seral stages.

Cape Cod is divided into fourteen separate towns: Bourne and Sandwich have portions on the Cape; the other twelve—Falmouth, Barnstable, Mashpee, Yarmouth, Brewster, Dennis, Harwich, Chatham, Orleans, Eastham, Truro, and Provincetown—make up the rest. For people (like me) not originally from Massachusetts, a strange fact is apparent: there is not one square foot of land in the Commonwealth that is not in some town or another. In Massachusetts, you literally cannot get out of town, except by going into another one. Barnstable County, with its fourteen towns, is the largest and most complex county of the three making up the Cape and Islands. If you are not accustomed to the Massachusetts arrangement of towns, things can get awfully confusing.

First, remember that our towns are land areas, not clusters of buildings. The clusters of buildings within a given town may have names not at all relevant to or reminiscent of the real name of the town. Thus, some of the most famous Cape Cod place names, like Woods Hole and Hyannis, are not towns at all; they are places within the towns of Falmouth and Barnstable, respectively.

Let us invent for consideration the typical and hypothetical Massachusetts town of Addlepate. Within Addlepate is a cluster of buildings actually called Addlepate—or Addlepate Center. This is to distinguish it from North Addlepate, South Addlepate, East Addlepate, West Addlepate, Addlepateton, and Addlepateville. All those are part of the town of Addlepate, too. Also, there are apt to be other clusters of buildings in the town with historical (or historical sounding) names like Rourke's Mills and Heathcliff. Last of all, there are a few more places with Indian-sounding names, like Poakawissetpong and Squawbun. That's a typical Massachusetts town.

Not all towns have all those components; some have even more. When you get to Martha's Vineyard, the whole system goes to hell in a handbasket, as I shall explain in due time.

Aside from the separate island of Monomoy, Cape Cod is divided into two important zoogeographic subdivisions: the base of the Cape, from the Canal eastward to Orleans, and the Outer or Lower Cape which is the forearm north to Provincetown. In colonial times, a salt creek cut right through from Cape Cod Bay to Town Cove, Nauset Harbor, making the Outer Cape a separate island. This creek, known as Jeremiah's Gutter, was navigable for small craft. Jeremiah's Gutter and its flanking *Spartina* marshes made a barrier to the dispersal of some species of reptiles and amphibians northward onto the Outer Cape. Thus, for a time, the Outer Cape was isolated from the mainland Cape, just as the Elizabeth Islands are today. It is most instructive to compare the Outer Cape and the Elizabeth Islands in the light of this similarity. That comparison is more appropriate than one to Monomoy, because the Outer Cape and the Elizabeths are

Sandy Neck: salt damage. Ditches dug with the intent of controlling mosquitoes allow storm tides to bring salt in. The result kills plants in areas already along the way toward a forest stage of succession.

similar in habitat diversity, whereas Monomoy is relatively de-pauperate.

Jeremiah's Gutter is said to have been closed by drifting sand about a hundred years ago. Today the Orleans rotary at the junction of Routes 6 and 28 is built on what was Jeremiah's Gutter. For a century land has been available for northward dispersal of the fauna.

Similar, but less complete, breaks occur through the Outer Cape at Pamet River and Pilgrim Lake. The latter was salt water in colonial times and was artificially closed. The water has now gone fresh, because fresh water is less dense than salt water and, in a land-locked system, floats on the salt water, eventually pushing it outward and away. Thus, what was once a barrier to those intolerant of salt is now a seemingly hospitable freshwater marshland.

Jeremiah's Gutter and Pilgrim Lake are examples of areas the sea has lost. In general, the trend has been the other way, and the sea has claimed more than it has given up. Sea level is rising. It has been rising ever since the beginning of the retreat of the last great glacial maximum: the Wurm (or Wisconsin). The Wurm's great moraines became the skeleton of Cape Cod.

As the ice retreated, animals could colonize the new (and newly exposed) land. Of course, in the early stages of ice retreat sea level was much lower, so all of the Cape and Islands region was united. However, it was much colder. The only animals that could take advantage of the land by walking to what are today islands like Nantucket would presumably be those best able to stand cold weather. As the ice retreated farther, the sea level rose and the climate warmed. Today, the Cape and Islands are the warmest part of Massachusetts, and warm climate animals can thrive. However, the most recent arrivals showed up too late to walk across to the Elizabeth Islands, the Vineyard, or Nantucket. On Cape Cod we expect to find populations of the most warm-weather-adapted species in the state. However, we should not be surprised when we fail to find them on the Islands. They arrived too late.

Elizabeth Islands

In wildness is the preservation of the world.
HENRY DAVID THOREAU

The Elizabeth Islands begin just across the currents of Woods Hole from Lands End, Penzance, Cape Cod. Initially, there are a cluster of small islets and peninsulas: Uncatena, Nonamesset, Veckatimest, and more. These are all connected by causeways to Naushon, the largest island of the group and the third largest of all our coastal islands (after Martha's Vineyard and Nantucket, but followed closely by Chappaquiddick). I have often caught reptiles and amphibians on the causeways, so I do not regard the cluster of islets at the east end of Naushon as faunally separate. Next come Pasque, Nashawena, and Cuttyhunk, the nethermost of the chain. Also there is Penikese, just inside Buzzards Bay, between Nashawena and Cuttyhunk.

All of the Elizabeth Islands together constitute the town of Gosnold, in Dukes County. (The rest of Dukes County is all Martha's Vineyard, Chappaquiddick, and No Mans Land.) There is no cluster of buildings in Gosnold called Gosnold, so Gosnold immediately departs from the scheme described for the typical town. Town meeting for the town of Gosnold is held in Cuttyhunk. This is appropriate, for Cuttyhunk is the only island in the Elizabeths open to the public.

Penikese is a Wildlife Refuge, closed except to scientists, because of its importance as a seabird nesting ground. (The Commonwealth administers it, and now uses it as a school for boys. I hope this will not affect its herpetology.) All the rest of the Elizabeths are private property, posted, patrolled, and administered by trustees.

In this day of socialized, organized hue and cry, we biologists sit in quiet trepidation, all our hopes pinned on those trustees who control that private property. The Department of the Interior, National Park Service, visited the islands a few years back. They reported that there was nothing they could do to enforce isolation of the area. No available status could be granted to save those islands. Even as a National Wilderness Area, they would be open to the public, and that would be the end.

The people, with the power of the masses, have burned and chopped and paved and populated quite enough. Until some governmental arrangement can be made to preserve Naushon, Pasque, and Nashawena, these islands must remain private and unmolested. Naushon is the only place in the Cape-Islands region not cleared

A massive monument to the might of the ice of the Wurm glaciation: Naushon, Elizabeth Islands.

The way it used to be: American beech forest, Naushon, Elizabeth Islands. This is private property, patrolled against trespass.

of timber. The Sandwich glass works folded before their axes reached Naushon. Here is the last place remaining almost as it was before we came. Imported plants like scotch broom do grow on the knobs, and chestnuts are virtually gone from the forests, but still the magnificent beeches live on in pure stands, still attaining over a hundred feet in height and two or three feet in diameter. Storms have topped them out and even blown many down, but that is a natural process. In patches, the forest is still virgin.

Little Pasque did not fare so well. It was clear-cut and today supports only shrubby vegetation and a clump of imported, exotic pine trees. It has a series of little kettle ponds down its middle and fine salt marshes.

Nashawena, though clear-cut, has proceeded in ecological succession to the oak stage. Beeches are now growing in parts of the oak woodlands, and climax forest may one day be attained again. Nashawena has extensive pastures and a prosperous farm.

Cuttyhunk, the islet where Captain Gosnold and his men built their little colony of a few weeks' duration, similarly has oak woodlands, kettle ponds, and salt marshes.

On Penikese are a couple of small ponds, but no woods and few shrubs. This open heap of morainal debris, a big kame, supports numerous nesting seabirds, including such rarities as Leach's petrel and Manx shearwater. I am most apprehensive about the Commonwealth's decision to use it for a boys' school; I believe it should have been left a sanctuary. It was on Penikese, in 1873, that Jean Louis Rodolphe Agassiz founded his little institute, the antecedent of the great Marine Biological Laboratory in Woods Hole.

It is difficult today to assess what effect the cutting of the forests had on the smaller Elizabeths. Their fauna are notably less than Naushon's, but this may be a natural reflection of their greater propensity for storm damage and less stable ground temperatures, both functions of their smaller size.

Martha's Vineyard, Chappaquiddick, and No Mans Land

Nowhere else in this country do I know anything like the variety of scenic effect that is exhibited in this hundred or so square miles.
NATHANIEL SOUTHGATE SHALER

The island called Martha's Vineyard today is obviously misnamed. The marginal inscription in Brereton's chronicle of Captain Gosnold's voyage appears beside a description that fits No Mans Land like a glove, and cannot possibly—in terms of size alone—be stretched to fit an island a hundred times larger. It is clear, to me at least, that Gosnold regarded what we call the Vineyard as part of the mainland.

It is also clear that he sailed from his "Marthae's Vineyard"—No Mans Land—across to Cuttyhunk and established his brief colony right on the island in the pond (open to the sea) where his monument stands today.

A lot of people have disagreed with Brereton's account of what Gosnold did, or at least that flagrantly obvious reading of it. For example, Mr. Harold C. Wilson, author of a little book on the Elizabeths called *Those Pearly Isles,* is convinced that Gosnold's island should be in West End Pond, on Naushon. West End Pond is a classic kettle hole, formed by the melting of a large block of ice imbedded in the morainal ridge that makes all of Naushon (except the sand beaches). The idea of an island in West End Pond is preposterous. Supposing the island to have been a bit of high ground in the swamps to the west is equally ridiculous. Brereton said it was an island, surrounded by water, not wooded swamp. Anyway, sea level was lower in 1602, and what is swamp today was probably drier then, and better forested.

A more imposing critic of the obvious is the late Charles Edward Banks, author of *The History of Martha's Vineyard,* a scholarly three-volume work. Banks decided Brereton lied about the size of the island to deliberately throw competitors off the scent and rejected No Mans Land because it lacks lakes of fresh water. Banks was misinformed. If he had ever *been* to No Mans Land, he would have seen lovely big lakes of fresh water, just as can be seen on any other piece of morainal land. If he didn't go to No Mans Land, he shouldn't have claimed knowledge of it.

In general, Banks can be faulted throughout for poor natural history. He found Brereton's "beares" laughable, but the joke is on him. Dr. Joseph Waters identified *Ursus americanus* (black bear) bones in Indian midden remains (Ritchie, 1969). There certainly *were* bears.

Banks goes on to note that penguins occur today only in the southern hemisphere. Brereton was obviously talking about the native great auk, a large, flightless water bird now extinct by the hand of man. Further, Banks lists less than forty sorts of birds, including the imaginary golden-winged woodpecker. Banks, like many old New Englanders, thought everything was just exactly as it should be, and the way God created it, when he was a boy. He could admit changes in his lifetime, but not before. He was determined to see his Martha's Vineyard as Gosnold's Marthae's Vineyard, but he was wrong.

Gosnold's island is called variously Nomans, Nomans Land, and No Mans Land. None is grammatical. The U.S. Coast and Geodetic

Till of the Gunz glaciation and sea-borne drift sand form Long Beach, Gay Head, Martha's Vineyard.

Survey gives No Mans Land, which will do as solidly official. No Man's Land is what they meant to say, of course, but they got close enough for government work.

No Mans Land is a square mile of the oldest of the four great glacial moraines: the Gunz. Once forested, it was clear-cut for the Sandwich glass works; thereafter it was used for sheep raising until the Navy took it over in 1954. It is now a government boondoggle. It is supposed to be, or become, a wildlife refuge, but the Navy still uses it as a bombing target. There has been much ado about bombing the island, but that is nearly irrelevant to the native wildlife. The bombs that hit at all strike the extreme western tip most of the time. The few that hit the main part of the island may wipe out a few of the introduced rabbits and feral geese, but who cares? It was the deforestation of No Man's Land that wiped out the wildlife. Only three reptiles—the nearly ubiquitous garter snake, the painted turtle, and the snapper—survive there. Once there must have been amphibians, but we can find none today. What the devastation of the woods didn't do, aerial insecticide spraying probably did. Toads might have survived the former, but not the latter.

It has been twenty years since No Mans Land was cultivated in that remarkably destructive way that sheep raising requires. The vegetation is coming back in scrubby oaks and introduced white poplars, but nothing will ever repair the damage done by sheep grazing.

Chappaquiddick lies just to the east of the Vineyard. The separation between "Chappy" and the Vineyard is a narrow channel of the sea that was once a river pouring through the glacial moraine. If the moraine were higher, this channel would not go all the way, and its southern portion would be a great pond like those along the southern Vineyard to the west. As it is, Norton's Neck tombolo frequently spans the southern edge temporarily, or forms a moving stepping stone between the two islands. Right in downtown Edgartown, on the Vineyard side, the channel bends in a sideways U-shape, with the bottom of the U at the ferry dock. On the Chappaquiddick side a peninsula juts out to meet the incoming ferry.

Chappaquiddick is made of two major lumps of morainal knob-and-kettle country: one central to the main portion of the island, presumably of mostly Mindel and Riss (second and third glacial maxima) material, and the other at Cape Poge to the north, made of the most recent, or Wurm, material. Cape Poge is connected by a tombolo that, on reaching the northern tip, curves in a great circle westward, then southward, then eastward to encircle Little Neck. The clams of the Little Neck sand bar and adjoining flats were so popular a generation ago that many people still call all steamer clams "little necks."

The main morainal mound of Chappaquiddick picks up across the narrow channel of Edgartown and curves northwestward to form Oak Bluffs. At this point, between two vast lobes of ice, the moraine was breached by a mighty river that today is visible only as Lagoon Pond. The second lobal moraine curves away again, west and south, to terminate eventually at Gay Head. The great central delta of the Vineyard is a spectacular outwash plain with fossil river beds and their flooded lower reaches, the great ponds.

The Vineyard and its two satellite islands are all of Dukes County, except for the Elizabeths described above. There are five more towns. Of these, Oak Bluffs is fairly straightforward. Edgartown is complicated by the fact that the satellite island of Chappaquiddick is all part of it. Chilmark is more complicated, because the geographically

The vast sedimentary deposits of the ancient sea bottom yielded to the force of the ice. Today, forced upward, askew, they form the cliffs of Gay Head, Martha's Vineyard.

remote satellite of No Mans Land belongs to it. Closer to No Mans Land is Gay Head, probably the only town in the Commonwealth lacking a post office or zip code. Gay Headers get their mail in Chilmark.

Then come the real problems: nowhere in all the town of Tisbury is there such a place as Tisbury. The whole town is just about filled up by the collection of buildings called Vineyard Haven. There is a West Tisbury, but it is a separate town, not part of Tisbury at all. (It is largely south, not west, of Tisbury, anyway.) If it were not for West Tisbury, this would be a dull book, for West Tisbury is the richest herpetological area anywhere among the Islands.

Nantucket, Tuckernuck, and Muskeget

> . . . we desire to conserve nature in many instances for unabashed aesthetic reasons and hold that these are basic, necessary and do indeed define the nature of man on a par with economics, energetics or any other reason.
>
> WETHERBEE, COPPINGER, AND WALSH

Nantucket is The Island. No other place in Massachusetts can rightfully be referred to in that way. Vineyarders refer to the Vineyard and Chappy; the Cape is the Cape to be sure; but when a man says he is going to The Island, he means Nantucket. Unique in the Commonwealth, its county and town limits are coterminous; there are no towns in Nantucket County except Nantucket.

The Island forms a rough crescent, being mainly the same moraines of Mindel and Riss that made Chappy and the skeletal eastern Vineyard. These moraines are also responsible for Tuckernuck and Muskeget, to the west of the main island.

Way to the north, connected by a tombolo, is Great Point—a bit of Wurm moraine. The Coatue peninsula, scalloped in a series of points on the inside southern edge, swings away from Great Point, southwest in a grand arc almost right into the center of town. If the harbor were not constantly dredged, Coatue would close it off. Then the harbor would slowly go fresh, succession would begin, and a vast new land area would ultimately be part of Nantucket.

At the southwest tip, Smith Point tombolo stretches toward and occasionally reaches Tuckernuck, a modest extension of the major moraines. Tuckernuck has the head of one of the prettiest little fossil rivers I know of slicing right down its middle. Of course mainland Nantucket has a number of larger ones, with their attendant ponds at the southern ends.

The tiny islet of Muskeget, virtually awash in the sea between the great islands of Nantucket and Martha's Vineyard, is surely the most remarkable bit of land along our entire Atlantic coast. The plant associations and ecology of Muskeget are unique and quite unlike those of seemingly similar land areas in the rest of the Cape-Islands region. On Muskeget's bars breed huge grey seals (*Halichoerus grypus*), the southernmost known colony. Amid Muskeget's beach grass dwells the big, pale, peculiar *Microtus breweri*, a vole found nowhere else on earth, and defiantly distinct from the common *Microtus pennsylvanicus* of all the neighboring islands. On Muskeget big, brown, transversely barred garter snakes in one generation prey upon, and in another become prey to, thousands of nesting larid seabirds.

Changes over time on the island of Muskeget have been excellently documented in close ecological detail by Wetherbee, Coppinger, and Walsh (1972) in the Muskeget Railroad Survey Report.

There is one point on which I disagree with Wetherbee, Coppinger, and Walsh. They believe Muskeget was a much larger, wooded, morainal island just 300 years ago. Surely Muskeget is founded on moraine, and some till is exposed on its shoals and bars, but the real morainal debris of Muskeget lies, I believe, well below the sea-borne sand. Muskeget, I claim, has been throughout historical times like a buoy on an anchor. The moraine is the anchor and the sand moves around and about the surface at the whimsy of the waves.

Wetherbee, Coppinger, and Walsh interpret the eighteenth century map of Southhack as showing Nantucket, then inhabited Tuckernuck, then wooded and inhabited Sturgeon Island—today's Muskeget—and then a fourth, uninhabited isle to the northwest. I interpret the same map as showing Nantucket, the Smith Point island—separated as it often is from Nantucket—then wooded Tuckernuck. Their unnamed islet to the northwest is then logically the real Muskeget.

Sea level has risen and continues to rise. However, in a couple of centuries it has only come up a foot or two at best. The various low islands, like the Middle Ground in Vineyard Sound and Skiffs Island just east of Chappy, no doubt did support beach grass—and so, briefly, sheep farming—not long ago. They are shallow shoals today. But reduction of a large, wooded island to dunes and 'sandbars in so short a time is too much to believe. Muskeget is getting smaller, changing shape, and moving around, but it is not all that different today than it was when Europeans first saw it. If larid seabirds do, in fact, undergo cyclic changes in species composition on their nesting islands, then Muskeget may well return to something quite like what it was.

36

2

The Sea

━━━━━━━━━━━━━━
━━━━━━━━━━━━━━

*We went to see the Ocean, and that is probably
the best place of all our coast to go to.*
HENRY DAVID THOREAU, *Cape Cod*

IT IS THE SEA, I have said, that makes the Cape and Islands
unique—the sea that mitigates temperature extremes, that isolates
populations, that controls vegetation, that builds land, that takes
land away. But the arrangement is reciprocal, for the land—perhaps
more dramatically here than in any other area of comparable size—
controls and modifies the sea.

Fluid, restless, lovely, and wicked, the sea is impeded, directed,
piled up, deflected, warmed, cooled, and nourished by the land. The
mighty arm built by glacial ice juts out to change the sea herself.
The first of the great elbow capes of Atlantic America, Cape Cod
divides two of the most different and more important water masses
on earth: the Mid-Atlantic Bight and the Gulf of Maine.

It is remarkable that my father, who was born on the Gulf of
Maine, never heard its name until he heard it from me. People see
the world from the land, even though two-thirds of the world's

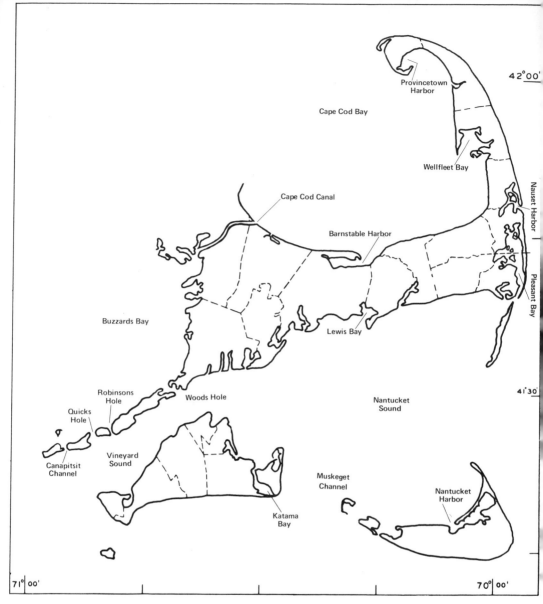

The waters of the Cape-Islands region, showing names for the principal bodies.

surface is the sea. The volume of the seas is more than three times that of the land above sea level.

Take a map of eastern North America and rotate it clockwise, so that the land is on top and the bottom is all ocean. You will note there is a great curve inward between Cape Hatteras and Cape Cod. Such a curve is called a *bight*. Cape Cod encircles the near end of another water mass; Georges Bank (slightly under water, it may not show on your map) nearly spans the entrance; and Nova Scotia juts out to barricade the far end. Such a body of water, nearly enclosed, is properly a *gulf*. Farther north above Nova Scotia is another gulf; the Gulf of St. Lawrence.

The most striking feature of the sea is that it is in perpetual motion. Actually, there are many distinct sorts of motions in the sea. If we are ever to have the remotest inclination to understand the life of the huge leatherback of the open ocean, or the tiny four-toed salamander in the sphagnum of Naushon, just for examples, we must come to an understanding of the motions of the sea.

The first and most obvious motion of the sea is tide. In a rhythmic pattern, the tide *floods* to a relative high and *ebbs* back again to a relative low. This is primarily caused by the gravitational attraction of the moon. The solid materials of earth yield little to the moon's pull, but the fluid is drawn dramatically. A remarkable change takes place in the extent of flood and ebb, correlated to the phases of the moon. As the moon waxes to full, the tidal floods and ebbs become more and more extreme. At full moon the highest high tides and lowest lows are achieved. These are called *spring* tides (which have nothing to do with the spring of the year). Next, as the moon wanes to half, the tidal floods and ebbs fade in extent. At half moon we have the lowest highs and the highest lows, and therefore the least difference between them. These are called *neap* tides.

The sun causes the apparent phases of the moon, and the sun's gravitational pull causes spring and neap tides. The amount of gravitational pull one object exerts on another is directly related to the size of the object, and indirectly, or inversely, related to the distance between the objects. So, big objects pull harder than little ones, but distant objects pull more weakly than close ones. In fact, gravitational pull is inversely proportional to the *square* of the distance, so as the distance increases the pull decreases most spectacularly. Thus, though the sun is millions of times bigger than the moon, it is also hundreds of times farther away and can exert only about one quarter the gravitational pull.

Th moon looks full to us because we are in line between the sun and the moon. The sun's light illuminates the entire visible face of the moon. In this arrangement, the gravitational pulls of both moon and sun work in concert on the earth's waters.

When the moon wanes to half, it is in a position at a right angle to the line from earth to sun. In this position the gravitational pulls of moon and sun are antagonistic; they detract from each other's influence on the earth's waters.

Let us carry the moon's cycle out. The moon continues to wane past half until it is dark, or new. In this position the moon is in line between the earth and the sun; its illuminated face is towards the sun and we cannot see it. In the dark of the moon the two gravitational pulls are once more in concert and spring tides occur. As the moon waxes from new to half, it moves into a position at a right angle again to the line from sun to earth. In this position we can see only half of its face. The moon and the sun are once again pulling antagonistically and neap tides occur.

If the moon would just stand still, and if you would just stand still, things would work out fine. The earth turns all the way around on its axis once in twenty-four hours. The moon would be right back again, directly overhead, in the same spot at the same time every night. It would then be high tide once every twelve hours, and low tide once every twelve hours, and exactly six hours between high and low.

But the wretched moon will *not* stand still. It pokes around the earth: all the way around once in about thirty days. If the earth turns around on its own axis once every twenty-four hours and the moon rotates around the earth once in about thirty days, then by rough arithmetic (mine is always rough as a cob), the moon is going to take about one extra hour getting back directly overhead again. So the poor tides are going to get dragged around late too. It's going to be more like twelve-*and-a-half* hours between high tides, another twelve-*and-a-half* between low tides, and, of course, something like six-*and-a-quarter* hours between high and low.

Well, you want to go see diamondback terrapins in the Great Salt Marsh. The time to see them is just when the morning sun is getting really warm, and they are basking in the sun: just about 10 A.M. should be fine. Of course, you want to go at dead low tide, when the water is least and shallowest; this improves your chances of getting a good look. Let's see, full moon tonight—perfect. The tide table says dead low at 10 A.M.—oops . . . last week's tide table. Well, low tide lags an hour a day; it's been seven days; oh *no*. The whole system is out of phase. *Rats!* What a mess. You might as well hunt snakes at the dump. And this place is socked in fog until noon anyway. (For a fuller, more physically accurate and detailed description of the tidal phenomenon, I strongly recommend Professor Gibson's introductory chapter to his delightful book, *Sea Islands of Georgia*. But it won't do you one bit of good on Vineyard Sound.)

You want to go see a ridley browsing for shellfish on the Middle Grounds. When you went down to the dock about six hours ago it was full high tide, so now should be perfect: dead low, right?

Down to the dock you go *and it's full high tide again.* Oh *come on.*
It's bad enough Lazell and Gibson are both desperate liars and fools
into the bargain, but now the author of the universe has obviously
stuffed his pen and switched to abstract art.

I warned you that the land affects the sea almost as much as
the sea affects the land. I warned you that this Cape and these Islands
are unique—each part different from all the others. I should have
warned you that the parts of the sea are utterly unique too. It is
possible to make sense out of what is going on. Let us repair to the
works of Alfred C. Redfield (1953, 1972, and papers cited therein).
Dr. Redfield, Associate Director Emeritus of Woods Hole Oceanographic Institution, has spent a lifetime studying the marshes and
waters of Cape Cod. Even he, however, has difficulty making the
situation readily explicable.

The rising tide is, quite literally, a ridge of water, elevated above
mean sea level and traveling from mid-ocean toward land. One may
consider the North Atlantic to be rather like a bowl; if you tilt the
right edge of the bowl up, a ridge—or wave—of water travels across
it towards the left side. It tends to strike the whole left (which is
western in the real case) about the same time. That is, it reaches
the nine o'clock position on the rim of the bowl just about when it
reaches the ten o'clock position. Cape Cod and the Islands are just
about at that imagined ten o'clock spot.

But the Cape, the Islands, and Georges Bank severely disrupt the
simple picture of a bowl. The ridge of water is greatly impeded by
the shallow massif of Georges Bank and confined by the stony peri-
meter of the Gulf. The water cannot get into Cape Cod Bay as fast
as it reaches No Mans Land. When it does make the trip, it is greatly
piled up by the shallows of the mouth and restrictions of the rim:
the tide comes late, but very high, in Cape Cod Bay.

The water is not so confined and restricted south of the Cape, at
least initially. At No Mans Land, it rises nearly four hours sooner than
at Provincetown, but it is a much shallower rise. What happens,
however, in the Sounds?

The ridge of rising tide pours into the Sounds between Gay Head
and Cuttyhunk and between Monomoy and Nantucket at about the
same time. Some pours in over the shoals and bars between Chappaquiddick and Muskeget, but this cannot be done quickly because
of the shallow ground. Now the two ridges of water approach each
other from along Vineyard Sound and across Nantucket Sound.
What happens when they meet? *They pass each other and go
right on.*

Dr. Redfield says, "if it is difficult to visualize two waves retaining their identity as they pass in opposite directions along a strait, drop two pebbles into a quiet pool of water. A group of waves will spread as a circle from the points where each pebble falls. When the two circular waves meet, each passes on undisturbed by its encounter with the other."

Given a lofty overview, you could stand on the shore of Vineyard Sound and watch the high tide coming toward you up from the Mid-Atlantic Bight. You could watch the ridge arrive, give you high tide, and pass out into Nantucket Sound. You would also see the high tide coming across Nantucket Sound past Cape Poge; the two ridges would meet and pass. Here would come high tide again—the *other* high tide from the east.

It is interesting to note that, of course, there is no corresponding double *low* tide. A little more than six hours from the temporal midpoint between those double high tides, the water will have ebbed to low. You can now look for your ridleys on the Middle Grounds, but I doubt you will see many in the dark.

The next most obvious of the motions of the sea is current. But currents have many causes and come in many kinds. Of course, the tides cause currents. Whenever the land constricts the sea—whether over shallows or shoals, or through narrow passages like the Holes— tidal currents make spectacular rips. Spring tide rips can be so strong that even massive inboard engines can make scant headway against them. Generally, though, tidal currents only move the same water back and forth. There would be no *net* flow if only the tides caused currents.

Winds also push the water and create currents. At any time of year the wind in the Cape-Islands region blows from the southwest. This is because air, heated in the tropics, rises convectively, cools as it rises, and descends again to earth at about $30°$ N latitude. The descending air pushes outward across the earth's surface, creating a south wind in the northern hemisphere. A westerly component is added to this wind by Coriolis Effect—the deflection of moving masses to the right in the northern hemisphere. As an air mass travels from $30°$ N latitude toward us at more than $40°$ N latitude it is deflected right, or east. Winds are named by the direction they come *from*, so air traveling north and east is called a southwest wind.

During the winter months, however, the southwesterlies are far weaker, though more constant, than the northeasterlies generated by storms over the North Atlantic. The net airflow is altered accordingly to northeast.

Differences in water density also cause currents. Denser water is, by definition, heavier and tends to sink in less dense water. Or, one may say, less dense water tends to float on denser water. There are two major causes of differences in water density: temperature and salt. At least down to about 4° C., water acts like virtually every other chemical and gets denser as it cools. This is because heat supplies the molecules of water with energy to move. The more heat, the more movement; the more movement, the more space a given number of molecules will take up. As the temperature diminishes, the molecules pack closer together. So, cold water—other things being equal—is heavier (denser) than warm water.

But other things are not often equal. Simply put, salt molecules are able to distribute themselves throughout the water molecules, literally between them, without much affecting the spacing of the water molecules relative to each other. So, salty water—other things being equal—is heavier (denser) than fresh water.

What happens when a warm freshwater stream empties into a cold ocean? Naturally, the warm fresh water tends to float far out to sea on top of the cold, salty water. Just the reverse occurs when a frosty-cold, freshwater stream enters a warm sea. The densities are much more nearly equal, and more mixing immediately occurs.

Imagine the complexities that seasonal temperature changes are going to generate. The sea, being fluid and in perpetual motion, varies only a little in temperature. At No Mans Land, for example, the sea varies from a winter low of about 40° F. to a summer high of about 70° F.—about thirty, never more than forty, degrees. Inland, at the sources of our rivers and streams, the surface temperatures vary from below 0° F. in winter to above 90° F. in summer: three times the change of the sea.

Thus, we may assume that winds and densities are going to cause currents that have *net* effects—overall water motion—that will vary from season to season.

The man who knows most about these currents in our area is Dean Bumpus of the Woods Hole Oceanographic Institute. I have listed two of his summary works in the references at the end of this book. Here I will attempt to generalize and paraphrase.

The surface waters of the Cape-Islands region tend to move in three great *gyres*, or circles. The water in the northern part of the Mid-Atlantic Bight circulates clockwise. It moves northeastward toward us, up the coast, and then flows out from Buzzards Bay, along the south shore of the Vineyard, out through Vineyard Sound, through Nantucket Sound, and eastward, out between Nantucket's Great Point and Cape Cod's Monomoy. This gyre seems weak and broad. The net flow comes into Nantucket Sound from the west and south (past Muskeget). A second clockwise gyre centers on Georges Bank, east of Cape Cod. The general motion of this water is northward off the Outer Cape, east around Georges Bank, and south again well out to sea. The last gyre, within the Gulf of Maine, circles counterclockwise. This water generally tends to flow southward from Nova Scotia along the northern, mainland shores of New England, and deflect east and then north at Cape Cod. This is the strongest of the gyres, because it is the most nearly landlocked. Its waters cannot spread out so far and dissipate their current.

Often, littoral sand drift and longshore currents tend to go the opposite way from the gyres. Caused by wind and wave action, this is especially notable on the Outer Cape.

Let us try to understand the causes of the gyres. First, the Gulf Stream, far offshore from New England, is a great flow of warm, light, tropical water floating on the North Atlantic. As it moves northward, Coriolis Effect deflects it right, or eastward, across the Atlantic. Consequently England, on the same latitude as frigid Labrador, has a relatively mild climate. The Gulf Stream makes Europe habitable. Warm, moist air tends to be generated over the Gulf Stream. Warm, moist air is less dense than cold, dry air because (a) it is warmer, of course, and (b) the water molecules in it are lighter than the oxygen, nitrogen, and other common molecules and, unlike salt in water, tend to displace them. Winds circulate around the light, low-pressure air masses, and far to the south of us, tend to push some of the Gulf Stream's water into the Mid-Atlantic Bight. Rivers also pour fresh water into the Bight, and the net effect is that the surface water, either warm from the Gulf Stream or fresh from the rivers, has to get out again. It flows out to the south at Cape Hatteras and out to the east at Cape Cod.

The Gulf of Maine gyre is also easy to explain. The Gulf Stream tends to pile up water in the eastern North Atlantic. Since water seeks its own level, some of it pours back westward in the arctic seas toward Labrador. The great St. Lawrence pours fresh water into the Gulf of St. Lawrence, and it too must seek its own level by flowing out. The current, deflected southward by Newfoundland, picks up more moving water off the Gulf of St. Lawrence and pushes into the Gulf of Maine. In late summer and autumn, when the land has warmed the St. Lawrence, this effect is enhanced and the southward, inshore current of the gyre picks up to as much as ten knots a day.

The Georges Bank gyre probably results simply from the northward flow along the Banks on their northern and western sides. Some water gets moved along with the Gulf waters and must be replaced from the south and east. If you think of the Gulf of Maine gyre as a wheel turning counterclockwise just touching another wheel around Georges Bank, you can see how the Bank gyre is set in motion.

Consider some of the obvious seasonal effects on the gyres. During the spring and summer, when northeasters are infrequent and weak, and when fresh water pouring in is warmest, the southwesterly wind between 30° and 40° N latitude will be able to affect the greatest amount of surface water. The northern and eastern flow out of the Mid-Atlantic Bight will be at its strongest. In winter, the northeasters will nullify the southwesterlies, the colder fresh waters from the land will mix more readily, and the current through our Sounds will be at its weakest. Thus, the effects of the southwesterlies are greatest in spring and summer, least in fall and winter.

Up to the north of us, well outside the zone between 30° and 40° N latitude, the influence of the southwesterlies is never so great. Here, as summer progresses towards autumn, the fresh water from the land gets warmer. The waters of the St. Lawrence mix less well and float better on the ocean. Thus, the current from the north in the Gulf of Maine is enhanced. This current is therefore greatest in late summer and autumn.

There is another sort of gyre in our waters that, while less obviously affecting life, may yet prove to be of colossal importance. This is a circulation in the vertical. The fresh water pouring into the sea tends to float and must displace the water below it. Much of displaced water is forced off the edge of the Continental Shelf, but some of it, closer inshore, pushes in towards the land. Here it is warmed in the shallows in summer and mixed with the fresh water in winter. The result is a very slow circulation of bottom water in toward shore. Nutrients brought in from the rivers may float far out to sea before settling to the bottom. The pokey bottom movement—only tenths of a knot per day—can slowly bring them back to the edge of the sea and thus benefit the huge communities of life there.

I must point out, however, that what the bottom current does for nutrients it does just as well for contaminants or pollutants. Man should be more careful about using the sea bottom as a dump. Our noxious wastes may well come back to haunt us.

The motions of the sea affect the land in ways other than just shaping it, heating it in winter, and cooling it in summer. They also dramatically affect the freshwater table. This is also the result of density. Rain that falls on the Cape and Islands percolates down into the jumbles of boulders, gravel, and sand and sits there. There is no bedrock anywhere near sea level, so no impervious material can deflect it. The porous, pervious land of the Cape and Islands works like a set of giant sponges. The fresh water is less dense than the salt, and the sponges of land mitigate any mixing that wind and waves would do to rainwater falling on the sea. The result is a *lens* of fresh water held within the porous land. The floating fresh water depresses the salt water underneath it, and the salt water forces the fresh up into the sponge. Viewed in vertical section, the fresh water makes a great, bi-convex bubble within the land.

As more rain falls, the fresh water must ultimately seep out the edges of the land. As the tide rises, the pressure of the sea water from below increases. The water in the lens rises too, and the flow out the edges gains strength. The water table of the Cape and Islands is far more dynamic than that of the mainland.

Also, the temperature of the rains affects the temperature of the ground far more in an area with a floating freshwater lens than it ever could over bedrock. The icy cold precipitation of winter can cool the lens and ground. The warm rains of summer can similarly warm the lens and ground. Ground temperature a few feet from the surface where animals hibernate varies hardly at all over bedrock on the mainland. It varies a little more in the interior of a big land mass like Cape Cod, the Vineyard, or Nantucket.

On small islands, like Muskeget, Penikese, or Monomoy, the effect can be major. Seasonal variations in ground temperature can be relatively extreme. It is important to remember that these extremes derive from the fact that the Cape and Islands are underlain *by the sea* rather than by bedrock like the mainland.

You have borne with me through tides, and currents, and densities. You grant that all this matters to the diamondback, the ridley, and great leatherback swimming north to the arctic seas. But what can be the relevance of it all to the tiny four-toed salamander buried deep in his sphagnum home on Naushon?

Imagine it is August. The warm rains of early summer have soaked the ground with the least dense fresh waters of the year. It is long since the last rains; the flow outward to the sea is at a minimum for the year. The land is hot and dry. The sea is warm, too. The difference between saltwater and freshwater densities is at a minimum. A huge tropical low pressure area is coasting towards us from the southwest: a cyclone or hurricane. The moon is dark. The sea pours through the Holes into Buzzards Bay in the full flood of spring tide.

The storm is upon us. The waves crash over the narrow barrier beach. The *Spartina* marshes and the little tidal creeks are utterly drowned. At a hundred knots the hurricane pushes the flooding tide from the southwest. All of Buzzards Bay, augmented by all the Atlantic can give, rises over the low-lying land. Great tree trunks, telephone poles, and boat hulls are thrown about relentlessly, again and again, mighty comber after comber churning, smashing, swirling into the cattails, alders, and red maples. The sea rises five, eight, ten feet over its normal level—ten feet over the sphagnum moss, ten feet over the home of the tiny salamanders.

Why . . . *how* can they be there? I wish I knew.

3

Salamanders, Order Urodela

===============

> A salamander, according to one of Mr. Webster's
> definitions, is "any person or thing that can stand
> great heat." With all due respect to the creator
> of dictionaries, there is probably no greater
> fallacy amid all the welter of nonsensical mis-
> beliefs that plague natural history.
>
> ROGER CONANT

ZOOGEOGRAPHY, the study of the distribution of animals, is a proud science. Although one may claim, with good argument, that Pliny and Aristotle considered zoogeography, or that Marco Polo gave it a real shot in the arm, it was not really until the nineteenth century that zoogeography became a sophisticated study. Darwin and Wallace were the first real zoogeographers. It was animal distribution, in its vagaries and with its puzzling confusions, that provided the fundamental factual base that lead to the understanding of evolution by means of natural selection.

The greatest standard of zoogeography, a classic in the finest sense, is a volume by Philip J. Darlington (1957). Dr. Darlington, an Alexander Agassiz Professor at the Museum of Comparative Zoology, Harvard University, is an incomparable expert on the Carabidae, or ground beetles to you and me. In pursuit of beetles, Darlington has gone practically everywhere. In the process of going practically everywhere, Darlington figured out the broad outlines of animal distribution: where the major groups seem likely to have arisen, and by what routes they appear to have spread. To do this, Darlington had to know not only where animals of each group are today, but where their fossils indicate they used to be. He had to weigh the evidence, make sense of apparent contradictions, and choose between likely alternatives. He did all of that with genius. The results are quite remarkable, and, in the main, unarguable: almost everything originated in the Old World tropics.

Certainly, if one considers the orders of land vertebrates (discount the so-called orders of birds, which are not comparable to real orders and much more like families), it may be said that an Old World tropical origin is the rule. The orders we are here most interested in —the frogs, the turtles, and lizards and snakes—are all from the Old World tropics. It makes good sense; life is far more abundant in the tropics, and the Old World has the vast majority of the tropical land area.

But the salamanders did not originate in the Old World tropics. Unique among the orders Darlington has chronicled, the salamanders seem to have evolved in temperate climes, and—worse—in north temperate climes, and—worst—in the New World. The salamanders, like the dollar, rattlesnakes, and bubblegum, are ours: truly American.

That is not to say that there are no salamanders elsewhere. There are a dozen or so Eurasian species and a couple in northern Africa. A few seem to have spread quite recently into South America. But that is all. There are hundreds of kinds of salamanders in North America. Unlike, for example, bears, there is nothing in the fossil history of salamanders to indicate that they originated elsewhere and then moved here. Salamanders are so much a part of the North American scene that it is hard for me to imagine anyone being unfamiliar with them. Anyone who has ever peered down into a well or spring, or looked under a rock or log in the woods, or walked outdoors in the rain at night has probably seen salamanders. Probably, though, the observer would call them lizards.

Strangely, most people do not seem to know about salamanders. Very few people know where to look for them, and almost no one can identify all the various species. The salamanders, I believe, deserve better recognition.

Here is a good place to introduce two useful terms. Salamanders are *autochthonous* to North America; this is where the group arose. One may say, also, that the Order Caudata—the salamanders—is a North American *autochthon*. Salamanders, however, are no longer *endemic* to North America. Endemic, in its biological rather than medical usage, means confined to one place. Since a few salamanders occur elsewhere, the Order Caudata as a whole is autochthonous in, but not endemic to, North America. Five families of salamanders are endemic to North America: the Sirens, Amphiumas, Mudpuppies, Dusky Salamanders, and Mole Salamanders. The latter has a common and gorgeous representative in our area. Three other families, the Newts, Lungless Salamanders, and Hellbenders, occur here and in the Old World too. One family, the Hynobiidae—closely related to our Mole Salamanders—occurs in Eurasia; there are only a half dozen or so different kinds. A last family is an autochthonous endemic in caverns of southern Europe. There is a single, large, blind, white, eel-like species: the olm, *Proteus anguinus.*

I have glossed over several major issues. First, the Sirens are not regarded as salamanders, but as members of a separate Order, the Trachystomata, by some excellent authorities (like Drs. Goin and Auffenberg). Their points are well taken, and the skeletal features of the Sirens appear to support their point of view. Others believe Sirens are salamanders after all. Since it is not an issue in New England, I will drop it here.

Most authorities do not regard the dusky salamanders (genera *Desmognathus,* abundant in New England, *Leurognathus,* and *Phaeognathus*) as a distinct family. None of them occur in the Cape-Islands region, so I should not involve them here. It seems only fair to report, however, that the argument for the Family Desmognathidae is overwhelming as presented by Soler (1950) and has never been refuted in any meaningful sense by those authors who choose to ignore it. To ignore facts is foolish.

When I was a boy the American mudpuppies and the olm were considered members of the same family: Proteidae. Then Dr. Max Hecht came along and argued—quite convincingly, I thought—that the resemblances were just convergence. So, there were two families. Then Larsen and Guthrie (1974) published one of the most amazing papers in scientific literature, complete with 3-D photographs you have to look at cross-eyed to see. They were for all one family again. I looked cross-eyed, and I saw the 3-D pictures, and I believed them. Then James L. Edwards teamed up with Max Hecht, and they presented a paper at our annual convention (yes, herpetologists have annual conventions, too) in 1975, the upshot of which was that none of anybody's evidence proves anything. That is science. You can take your choice.

The distinction between Hynobiidae and Ambystomatidae (our

own spotted salamander) is really trivial; they should be reduced to subfamilies. Internal (Ambystomatidae) opposed to external fertilization (Hynobiidae) is a small matter when the anatomical resemblance is so close.

I have said one can always find a salamander. I will take on all comers, any time of year, in the Cape and Islands area; I can always find a salamander in the field, alive and well. In times of severe drought, salamanders are hardest to find. They go toward water, which often means straight down below the ground surface. In winter they also go down, but usually remain fairly active, at least where springs bring water near the surface.

Salamanders often retreat into the interiors of decaying logs, either for moisture or insulation against the heat of summer or the frost of winter. It is this habit that has got them—literally—into the fire. When such a log is heaped on the burning hearth, the salamanders must attempt a hasty exit. Sadly, far from being born of the fire, the little fellows will be fried to death by it.

Spotted Salamander

This, the largest and flashiest species in the area covered by this book, is the jet-black and orange-yellow creature I referred to as prowling beneath suburban lawns. The ground color is olive to brownish or dull grey in the gilled larval stage, and the vaguely paler spots first begin to show as mottled or frosted areas on that ground. They give little hint to the black bodied, yellow spotted glory of the five to eight inch adult. The ground color shades to slate or chocolate brown on the sides and lead grey on the belly.

In at least some of the south, like the Cumberland Plateau in Tennessee, spotted salamanders have dark orange spots on the head and pale yellow spots on the body. At present, no one seems to have considered the possibility of different geographic races of *Ambystoma maculatum*. It is a dandy little project for anyone interested and ambitious.

That name, *Ambystoma maculatum*, is now regarded as the official and correct one for this species. It has not always been so. The spotted history of the name of the spotted salamander makes a good object lesson in how taxonomy, the official scientific naming and classification of living things, works. The original name of the genus was given by Tschudi in 1838. His intention was to commemorate the rather short head, and therefore short mouth, characteristic of these salamanders as a group. *Stoma* means mouth. However, *ambly-*, rather than *amby-*, is the correct Greek prefix for short. By leaving out the *l* in *ambly-* in his first printed use, Tschudi cast his error in the matrix of immutable things. No matter what the first published name is, it has to stand forever. You can use real Latin or Greek, or you can invent anything you like. Any latinized form is official when published in print in such a way as to be identified with a particular sort of animal.

Many scientists, familiar with Greek and realizing Tschudi's error, emended the name to *Amblystoma*. They thought they were doing the world a favor. Actually, Tschudi could have named his genus *Absmytsamo*, if he chose, and that would be it: the Law of Priority says the first name stands.

The spotted salamander had originally been named *Lacerta maculata* by Shaw in 1802. Then Spencer Fullerton Baird dug up the name *punctata*. Both *maculata* and *punctata* (feminine) mean spotted in Latin. It wouldn't matter if they meant embedded in peanut brittle. The point is *maculata* is older, so it wins. When the species *maculata* was transferred out of the genus *Salamandra* (feminine) to the genus *Ambystoma* (neuter), the only permissible change was the gender of the species name. Thus, *Ambystoma maculatum* is correct. Dr. Joseph Tihen provides the details of all of this, and the precise references.

When I was in school the biological supply houses sold a creature called *Amblystoma punctatum*. It wasn't really a creature at all. It was a mixture of two: *Ambystoma maculatum* and its relative *Ambystoma tigrinum*. *Ambystoma tigrinum*, the tiger salamander, is also yellow and black, but the yellow spots are so big and run together that the blackish ground color only shows up as wavy stripes. Also, tiger salamanders are much bigger.

Our spotted salamander breeds in woodland temporary ponds, free of fish (egg eaters), and has a short larval life of a few weeks. It must metamorphose into a lung-breathing adult, without gills, before the ponds dry up in late summer or autumn. This is one of our most obvious species for which temporary ponds are absolutely necessary. I will say more about the importance of temporary ponds when I come to the wood frog.

The tiger salamander lays eggs that are more resistant to fish predation; perhaps the taste is unattractive. Anyway, it lays its eggs in deep, permanent ponds. Its larvae keep their gills for a long time— often for years, sometimes throughout life. Tiger salamanders can be

Spotted salamander (*Ambystoma maculatum*), adult male, about 6 inches total length: Mashpee, Cape Cod.

Spotted salamander (*Ambystoma maculatum*): a speculative range is shaded, based on consideration of topography and habitat. Dots indicate localities where specimens (often hundreds) have been examined.

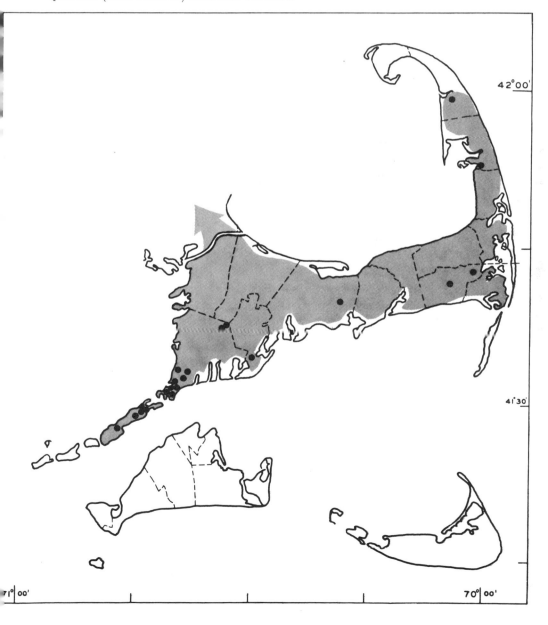

very tolerant of salty water too, and some of the western races and populations occupy very briny lakes. The patterns of growth, development, and the basic physiologies of the two species could hardly be more different.

When the supply houses realized their error, they stopped listing the imaginary *Amblystoma punctatum*. They listed either *Amblystoma tigrinum* or *A. maculatum*, or both, if they had both (both do occur together south of Massachusetts). The result was chaos.

It seems that a wealth of scientific literature was based on experiments on the growth, development, and physiology of *Amblystoma punctatum*. The biologists involved just couldn't carry on without it. It is said that some supply houses switched back, and again sent off lots of the two species mixed. In most cases, though, the physiological researchers just girded their loins and proceeded to call whatever they received *Amblystoma punctatum*. I wouldn't give you much for the experimental data that has resulted.

A lot of people deride the scientific habit of naming things, claiming that "scientists think that giving something a name explains it," and that "taxonomists are just biological stamp collectors." Calling something by a name is the first step toward understanding it. If you can get others to agree on your name for it, then at least it can be identified. If we can't identify it, we can never hope to explain or understand it.

Our spotted salamander populations are pretty much confined to shady woodlands, and are densest along the moraines. They extend out onto the outwash plain of Cape Cod, but I have never found them on sand land.

I have breeding records from 8 March through 8 April on Cape Cod, and 4 to 11 April on Naushon. Larvae metamorphose as early as 22 July, at least, and some are still in the ponds as late as 1 November. Spotted salamanders are abundant on the upper, basal Cape. I have counted more than thirty breeding adults at one pool in Falmouth on a single night. North of Jeremiah's Gutter, on the lower Cape, they are scarcer. I have not located any north of Truro, despite extensive efforts. My northernmost Truro population undergoes wild vicissitudes of reproductive fortune. In 1971 there were just four egg masses laid. Two of these suffered 100 percent mortality before hatching; the other two were over 50 percent dead on 23 April. The next year, 1972, was much wetter. Twenty-seven masses were laid in the same place, and most were healthy. Mortality on 8 April was 50 percent before hatching in the least lucky batches.

On Naushon this species is widespread, but not very common. I have counted no more than six egg masses in ponds five times the size of the Truro puddle, even in good years like 1970.

Dr. Robert Shoop, now at the University of Rhode Island, studied Massachusetts spotted salamanders for years while he was on the faculty at Wellesley College. He found that despite the fact that the eggs are all laid and hatch about the same time, the larvae metamorphose and become land dwellers over quite a long period. The number of eggs laid in a given year does not seem to matter nearly as much in getting out a successful crop of young as does the rate of development and the duration of the temporary pond's life. A good year will be characterized by plenty of water, a long pond duration, and therefore a relatively long larval life. Apparently the bigger and healthier you are before you leave the pond, the better your chances of success on land. On the other hand, long larval life is a gamble. What happens if it is a dry season and the ponds evaporate early? Well, then at least some of those short-term larvae will make it. It seems important to have quite a spread in time of metamorphosis; life is a chancy thing.

Michael Edward Douglas (1975) studied spotted salamanders in Kentucky. He tagged specimens with radioactive needles and thus got the only home range and territory information on the species known to me. Of course, once the adults leave their breeding ponds, they become subterranean burrowers and essentially disappear. Douglas, however, could still locate them with a geiger counter. He found that individuals moved only about 200 meters (six or seven hundred feet) from their breeding ponds and occupied over-winter home stations of only about 300 square centimeters (less than half a square foot). That is a pretty sedentary sort of life, but living underground makes travel difficult. Since worms and other food items are abundant, the spotted salamander need not travel far for groceries. When traveling time comes in the spring—time to return to the breeding ponds—the salamanders come up to the surface and walk overland.

It seems to be the drumming of the first heavy rains of late winter or early spring that stimulates the burrowing spotted salamanders to tunnel to the surface. They start out, cross-country, to their own home pond. Their homing ability is superb, but no one knows how they do it. The males arrive first, usually, and swim around in frenzied excitement. Often, the males litter the pond bottom with their spermatophores—literally, sperm-bearing capsules—before the females arrive. Once in the pond, the females are induced by much nuzzling and petting to pick up a spermatophore between their swollen cloacal lips. The *cloaca*, in all reptiles and amphibians, is the body opening that functions for all purposes of waste removal and reproduction. Thus, although the male lacks a penis or penis-like structure, he does manage to effect internal fertilization.

Once fertilized, the female lays from one to three dozen eggs in a gelatinous glop; this glop absorbs water rapidly, and expands into a blob from five to eight or more inches in diameter. The blob is usually free-floating, but often twigs or pond weeds are enmeshed in it, serving as an anchor.

Spotted salamander egg masses turn quite a lovely shade of light, bright green. This is because an alga takes up residence in the gelatin. Any case where two different species live together can be called *symbiosis*—literally together life. Many symbioses, like a parasite living in the host, are detrimental to the one unlucky species. Our spotted salamanders, developing in their egg mass, and their alga, however, seem to be a case of mutualism—symbiosis beneficial to both parties.

The egg mass provides a home and nutritive materials, like carbon dioxide (a waste product of the salamanders) and protein, for the alga; in turn, the alga provides oxygen, produced far in excess of its own needs, for the growing larvae.

The spotted salamander is certainly a cold-climate adapted form, occurring today hundreds of miles north of Cape Cod, all the way to Cape Breton Island and the Gaspé Peninsula. Why wasn't it able to colonize the areas of Nantucket and the Vineyard before they were separated from the main by rising sea land? Perhaps the spotted salamander did so, but has been extirpated or made invisibly rare on those islands. We can deduce that heavy pesticide spraying wiped out whole populations of amphibians on these islands a few decades ago (see the toads, below, for a discussion of this). We may never know where this lovely creature once lived.

Perhaps it survives on Martha's Vineyard in a condition of extreme localization and rarity like the newt does. I have one reasonable sight record from the Vineyard and anxiously await an actual specimen.

If it has been the drumming of the first heavy rains of late winter or early spring that has brought life and reproduction to the members of *Ambystoma* since long before the Pleistocene, that same rain soon may bring them extinction. Rain, snow, or precipitation in general was, a scant century ago, pretty pure water. It certainly is not today. Now it is worse than *aqua regia*, the hideous poison of the ancients. *Aqua regia* is a mixture of acids, and that is what now falls on us, and on the salamanders, from the heavens.

Drs. Harvey Pough and Richard Wilson, at Cornell, have studied

56

the ghastly acid rain and its effects on spotted salamanders. Their results, reported to the American Society of Ichthyologists and Herpetologists in the spring of 1975, are most depressing. What happens is this: sulfur dioxide and nitrous or nitric oxides are by-products of fossil-fuel combustion. Fossil fuels are coal, oil, gas, and their derivatives. In the atmosphere these sulfur- and nitrogen-containing oxides react with water and oxygen (often as O_3, or ozone) in the presence of electricity (lightning) to form the nitric and sulfuric acids. Without the electricity, they form nitrous and sulfurous acids, which are bad for us (and the salamanders) too, but not as bad. But there seems to be plenty of electricity up there. These acid molecules are *hygroscopic*—they attract and collect water molecules. Pretty soon, down they come as rain. This rain eats up our marble and limestone structures, corrodes our metals, and burns the vegetation. It is even worse for the salamanders.

The rains crucial to the salamanders fall just at that time of year when the sulfur and nitrogen compounds—generated by home heating and industry all winter—are at their highest atmospheric concentrations. And it falls when there is the very least foliage in the forest to take the brunt of its burning and help to neutralize it. It falls on the winter woods, leafless and bare. It flows into the temporary ponds and concentrates there, for these ponds generally lack outlets, at least as the spring progresses. Over the years, the buffering effect of the soil is depleted, for there is only so much of the really good acid neutralizers—like calcium carbonate—and every year more of the acid falls. Already our rainfall is apt to have a pH of less than four. That is pretty strong acid.

The scale used to measure acidity and basicity (or alkalinity), called pH, goes from zero to fourteen. Seven is neutral and zero is as strong as acid can be. Above seven are the bases, or alkalis, and fourteen would be as strong a caustic soda as you could make. A pH of four will dissolve bone. Adult spotted salamanders seem to be able to take it for the brief time they are in the ponds. Their skins are made of living cells, and the cells killed by acid can be replaced. But the developing salamander larvae are not so lucky. Their energies must go into growth, not replacement. And so the acid rain gets to them, and their very source of life becomes their death.

Pity the spotted salamander, for the acid rain is getting worse. But we live here too, and our day will come.

Chilmark, Martha's Vineyard: proceeding north along Meetinghouse Road, up the face of the moraine. At the bottom soils are deep and well watered. At the top soils are shallow and well drained. The vegetation is unprotected from the wind. The road width provides comparative scale.

Meetinghouse Road, halfway up.

Meetinghouse Road, the top.

Newt

Our eastern North American newt, known today by the ponderous name of *Notophthalmus viridescens viridescens,* is the subject of an even more ponderous quantity of scientific literature. None of our species has a life history nearly so complex. In the overview, there are more transformations between egg and adult than in any of our other terrestrial vertebrates; in close detail, a bewildering number of omissions, modifications, and variations are possible and demonstrated.

Fertilization is internal, as in our other species. The courtship consists of a prolonged series of tail fannings and strokings by the male, with concomitant nuzzling with nose and chin, and clasping with the modified hind legs. The male usually clasps the female around the neck or anterior body, and attempts to draw her over the spermatophore he has deposited. Once he has succeeded, the female shortly proceeds to lay a dozen or more eggs in gelatinous strands along underwater plant stems, twigs, or something similar. The eggs hatch into tiny larvae—about four millimeters, or a fifth of an inch long—with big, bushy gills almost as long as they are. Breeding takes place in the spring, and classically the larvae lose their gills, develop lungs, and emerge from the ponds and lakes by the following autumn. They are dull brown at first, but soon become the bright orange-red characteristic of the land-dwelling stage called an eft. For one to several years the red efts live on land, in the woods, under rocks and logs by day, and crawling all over the forest floor by night—especially in the rain. Often, one can find hundreds of red efts on a rainy summer evening in Massachusetts.

The red eft has a peculiarly artificial, rubbery look. Close up, his skin looks dry and grainy. He has a big, toad-like head, and a rather short, but vertically flattened, tail. When surprised, he usually just sits there and curls his tail up along or over his head and body.

One day, feeling grown up, the red eft returns to the lake or pond of his hatching, or perhaps another close by. Another startling color change takes place; the dorsal ground color turns an olive, dull, greenish brown, and the ventral color is a sharply set-off yellow. The only red that remains is a series of spots inside black circles in a row along each side of the back. These red spots inside black circles were there all along, since late in the gilled larval life, but were just less noticeable.

Male newts develop a grand tail, broadly finned above and below.

They also develop a ridge of blackened bumps or ridges along the inside of their enlarged hind legs. Females look rather mundane. Now, as full-fledged newts, they are ready to begin the cycle again.

George Kingsley Noble, late of the American Museum of Natural History and an almost legendary figure in the annals of herpetology, spent a lot of time observing and documenting newt life-histories, especially in coastal New England. William Healy, previously at Holy Cross, Worcester, and now at the University of Michigan, has carried on this work. I have said the variations on basic life history may be bewildering, and I will add some of my own observations to the mess.

In Brewster, at Nickerson State Forest, one may find newt populations that stick pretty much to the book. In some areas to the west of us especially, and maybe on Cape Cod, newts attain the red eft stage and never leave it. This seems to be an adaptation to temporary breeding ponds. Like spotted salamanders, the terrestrial efts return each year to the water to court and lay, but do not transform into fully aquatic newts.

Newts have been studied most extensively by all of us in the town of Falmouth. They are common from Woods Hole in the south to Ashumet in the north. They make two very different departures from the norm. Many individuals, like those at Ashumet, lose their gills at the end of their larval life and become an overall yellow, semi-aquatic, marsh and pond edge salamander, venturing out into the woods like an eft on rainy nights. They aren't real red efts, but they aren't olive newts either.

On down toward Woods Hole, entire populations never leave the water to become efts, or even semi-efts, at all. They never lose their larval gills. They just grow up to be big, dark olive, sexually mature newts with feathery gills on the sides of their necks. Animals that become sexually mature when still ostensibly in a juvenile stage, or larval form, are called *neotenic*. The phenomenon of *neoteny* is a common occurrence in our coastal newt populations.

Newts seem to be very intolerant of salinity. Some solid experimental work to demonstrate just how intolerant they are would certainly be welcome. At least, they never seem to occur very close to the coast, where much salt spray gets to the fresh waters. In coastal areas, one may speculate, dry years and low water levels might concentrate newts in ponds where salinity becomes too high. Being a normal newt would lead to death or debilitation, and so be selected against by natural processes. Being a semi-eft, however, would keep open the option of burrowing down in the soil to a moist depth, like spotted salamanders do. Being free of the water could be a key to survival.

Newt (*Notophthalmus v. viridescens*), adult female, about three inches total length: Falmouth, Cape Cod.

Newt (*Notophthalmus v. viridescens*): a general range is shaded, based on scattered samples and appropriate habitat. Heavy bars are where red efts are known to occur; bold dots are where neotenic adults are known to occur; the black dot indicates where mature, yellow "semi-efts" have been found.

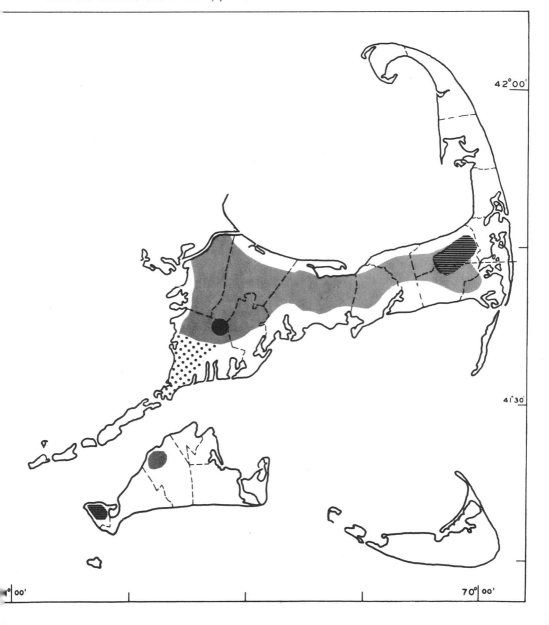

On the other hand, the biggest and deepest ponds might never dry up to the extent that salt concentration becomes a problem. Survival in such ponds or lakes might be increased by retaining gills. Our neotenic newts do develop their normal, adult lungs. They have both gills to absorb dissolved oxygen from the water and lungs to handle air.

In deep, permanent water the newt has one other major problem—predation. Getting eaten by somebody bigger is a problem all newts seem to have handled very well. Their skins secrete chemicals so noxious or downright poisonous that nothing I know of will eat them. I have watched a largemouth bass charge a leisurely swimming newt—mouth agape—only to veer off a few inches away. Was the bass warned by chemical sense? Or do those red porthole spots serve as a warning? *Aposematic*, or warning, coloration is a widespread phenomenon in animals; coral snakes are a classic example. Red is an excellent, natural, aposematic color, meaning "stop" to more species than man.

The newt is a cold-tolerant, but not a salt-tolerant, species. It should, then, have made it out onto continuous land as the Wurm glacier receded, and survived where the land is wide enough to protect it from salt. Thus, it came as a small surprise to discover the existence of old specimens of newts from Martha's Vineyard.

The original Vineyard newts are adults from Seth's Pond, a deep kettle hole in West Tisbury. I went back there and started looking. I looked all over. I looked farther afield; I looked in and under, high and low. I asked all my friends on Martha's Vineyard. They all thought I was nuts. They had never seen a newt anywhere on the island.

The newts had once been there. Had they been exterminated completely by insecticides like Nantucket's toads, or rendered so rare that no normal collecting procedure would reveal them?

Susan Whiting—Soo, to most of us—is a professional biologist who began with botany and has branched out to include most everything, including herpetology. She has often taught summer sessions of "Fern and Feather," a natural history program for kids provided by the Felix Neck Wildlife Trust, Edgartown, Martha's Vineyard. One day in July 1971, Soo took a group of those kids on an outing to a little, weed-choked pond high on the moraine in West Tisbury.

Everyone was splashing around having a good time. Soo stepped out on a chunk of granite at the south end of the tiny puddle and dip-netted up a fine sample of glorp. Everyone crowded around to examine the catch. They found lots of insect larvae, snails, and the usual pond-bottom assortment. They also found a tiny salamander. It was less than half an inch long, and just as mud-colored as could be. It had the big head, bushy gills, and tiny legs characteristic of larval salamanders.

But Soo knew this was different. The only salamander then known to survive on the Vineyard was the nearly ubiquitous woodland. Soo knew woodlands do not have a free-swimming gilled larval stage. It had to be new and different.

Anticipating placing one of those phone calls that brings me leaping to my truck and burning up the miles to Woods Hole and the ferry, Soo put the tiny creature in a tin can on the bank. She informed the assembled urchins of its remarkable value, and continued her lesson.

You know what happened. One of those blessed children kicked over the can. That child very nearly became the only *Homo sapiens* skin in the collection of the MCZ.

But Soo went back the next day. She scooped and strained and peered into the glorp. Finally, sweating and muddy, she went back to exactly the same rock, stood in exactly the same position, and scooped again. She got four. She phoned me; the truck chugged off; the ferry ran; and there were newts again from Martha's Vineyard.

Since that time I have hunted newts right there, and elsewhere, a dozen times on the Vineyard. Since then, William Alwardt found some red efts at Gay Head, and brought them to Gus Ben David, at Felix Neck, who saved them for me. But never, since then or before, have I ever caught a Martha's Vineyard newt—on Soo's chunk of granite or off of it.

Science loves the predictable and the repeatable. A series of steps that, carefully executed, always leads to the same result is the pinnacle of scientific value and achievement. Bearing that in mind, I submit to you a truly scientific method. You may elect to leave out some of the following steps, if you like, and try a short cut. I cannot promise you will fail, but I always have. I am a scientist, and I will stick with a proven procedure to the letter. If you want a Martha's Vineyard newt:

1. Ice down some beer and bring it.
2. Get Soo Whiting and her own dip net. (You can leave yours home; it's useless.)
3. Give Soo x-amount of cold beer and ask her to stand on that granite chunk at the south end of the pond.
4. Get her to dip you up some glorp.
5. Sort through the glorp and take out your newt(s).

That works. I have witnessed it time after time. I never saw any short cut that did.

We have those old, adult, normal newts from Seth's Pond. We have red efts from Gay Head. We have larvae from Soo's dip net. I took some of the larvae back to the lab and there they metamorphosed into little, yellow semi-efts, like the ones at Ashumet. What they do in or around their native pond, we do not know. Not even Soo has ever found an adult. (Tom Chase, a fine naturalist credited with many salamander coups, did get a normally metamorphosed adult in this pond in the summer of 1974. It is in the MCZ.) Dr. Healy (1975) has measured home ranges of efts. He finds that they occupy about 250 to 300 square meters in the course of any given year, and up to 700 square meters over a three to seven year life span. That is quite staggeringly different from the data for the spotted salamander, and probably reflects the fact that efts emerge on the surface at every rainy opportunity an actively hunt for food on wet nights.

I cannot leave the newt without saying a bit more about its taxonomy. Newts are members of the family Salamandridae, along with an assortment of Eurasian and North African species. In North America, there are the species and subspecies of *Notophthalmus*, like ours, and the Pacific coast forms of the genus *Taricha*. Now, our *Notophthalmus* used to be in the genus *Triturus*, like the European newts. Willy Wolterstorff removed them, and put them in the genus *Deimyctylus*. Sadly, they stayed there long enough to make the first edition of Roger Conant's famous *Field Guide*. Then, Hobart Smith (see his 1953 paper) discovered an older generic name: the awful *Notophthalamus*. So there they are. I think the whole thing was a little premature. Let's go back and be a bit more critical of Wolterstorff's notion in the first place. Are our eastern newts really worthy of a distinct genus? Recently, while reviewing a book on the European salamanders, I became impressed by the diversity of *Triturus* species, and even examined some specimens. I didn't do a really thorough job of it, but what I did see convinced me that our newts could happily fit right back into the genus *Triturus* again.

One last thing about newts: in my experience, they eat only what they can get completely into their mouths—small insects, mosquito larvae, and pieces of earthworm. If they can't get it all in (an entire worm, for instance), they spit it out. Otherwise, and if you can get around that, newts make fine pets in an aquarium or terrarium.

Salamanders, Order Urodela

Woodland Salamander

Dr. Allen E. Greer (1973) has proposed the name woodland salamander for *Plethodon cinereus*, long and often called the red-backed salamander or lead-backed salamander, depending on which of its two commonest color variants one happened to have at hand. No one is better qualified to propose adoption of woodland salamander than Al, for he has studied our populations exhaustively, and even made some sense out of them.

Indeed, we are blessed with another salamander species just as horribly complicated as the newt, but in a different way. What the newt does in stages of life history, the woodland salamander does in color phases, or *morphs*, that look strikingly different, and do so all their lives. There are a number of different morphs other than red-backed and lead-backed. Their abundance and percentages in the whole population vary both from season to season and from year to year. It is a mess.

Al Greer and I were graduate students together at Harvard. I left, and finished my doctorate at the University of Rhode Island, but Al stayed on long after he finished his doctorate. Al's wife, Phlyp, is a sculptor who can be induced, given good company, food, and drink, to go off in search of salamanders. In the Cape-Islands region it became a common sight to see Al and Phlyp, Numi and me, and usually Soo Whiting or another local enthusiast or two, rummaging through the woods, turning rocks and logs, and shouting, "red," "lead," "two reds and a lead," and so on into the night. Someone was keeping track of the count, and after we had scored two hundred or more, we would usually quit for a beer. Sometimes we would search for hours trying to find just twenty to count; twenty is about the minimum number for statistical significance.

The object of this game was to develop a map of morph frequencies. We assume that the different-looking sorts of woodland salamanders have some sort of adaptive significance. Even if the significance is not looks, per se, there are bound to be genetic and therefore bio-chemical differences between the morphs (it has been proven that they are genetic), and we assume these differences *matter* in some way to the salamanders; the world is not just chaos.

Well, if you knew where each morph occurred, and in what percentage of the population, and where woodland salamanders were common or rare, maybe you could see a pattern, or correlation to some factor like elevation, rainfall, soil type, or *something*. Many

Woodland salamander (*Plethodon cinereus*), adult male, about three inches: Truro, Cape Cod. This is the "lead-backed" color morph.

Woodland salamander (*Plethodon cinereus*), adult, sex undetermined, about three inches total length: Pasque, Elizabeth Islands. This is a "red-backed" individual in which dark pigment nearly obscures the color pattern. Specimens like this seem to occur in small, isolated populations, such as at Pasque and Coskata.

Woodland salamander (*Plethodon cinereus*), adult, sex undetermined, about three inches total length: Naushon, Elizabeth Islands. This is an unusual speckled red individual.

people have tackled this problem, but only Al, as far as I know, has ever come up with anything that fits, and even Al's fit isn't perfect.

Since woodland salamanders are by far the most abundant and easily observed of all our amphibians, we really owe it to ourselves to try to understand them. They are little fellows, just a couple of inches head-body length, and a maximum recorded length according to Conant (1958) of five inches total length, including tail. I never saw one that big. The females lay their eggs in proteinaceous capsules (non-cellular), that retard water loss, in a moist pocket under a rock or log. I have recorded from six to eleven (average eight) eggs per clutch, but have found only four clutches in the Cape-Islands area. When I have found clutches under logs, they have always been hung in a batch from the ceiling, so to speak. Under rocks I am not so sure. Some clutches seem unattached, but my turning the rock may have dislodged them. In my experience, the female salamander is almost always found coiled around her eggs.

Woodland salamanders seem to court and mate in both spring and fall, but I have never observed this. Those that are fertilized in the fall must hold the living sperm over winter (many species do this), for eggs are not laid until summer. All my egg records are for July.

Woodland salamander (*Plethodon cinereus*), the same Truro male: closeup of the head showing cirri and nasolabial groove.

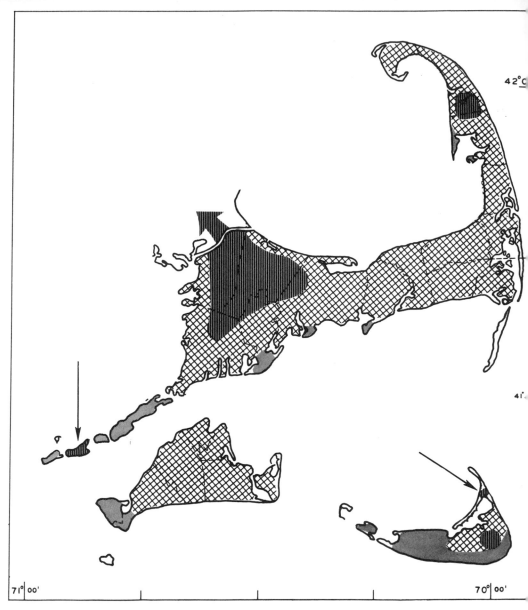

Distribution of woodland salamanders (*Plethodon cinereus*) showing relative abundance of the unstriped, solid, or "lead-back" color morph. Vertical bars: 15–30 percent unstriped; cross-hatching: 2–14 percent unstriped; and fine shading: less than 2 percent unstriped. Arrows indicate Nashawena and Coskata Woods.

The baby woodland salamanders go through their larval stage in the capsule, and so emerge as tiny, but metamorphosed, replicas of the adults. They are disproportionately big-headed and short-tailed. Often youngsters have rather bright bluish or silvery white dots on their sides or back, which can lead to much confusion in identification. To the north of us is the blue-spotted salamander (*Ambystoma laterale*) and to the west, in New York state, is the white-spotted, slimy salamander (*Plethodon glutinosus*). Blue-spots might well occur in the Cape-Islands region, and people who should know have reported seeing them to me. To make certain, look for a groove running from nostril to upper lip—the *nasolabial* groove. If it's there, it's not a blue-spot.

Anyway, woodland salamanders have their adult color pattern well before birth. Most are either striped or solid in color. Striped individuals have a broad band of light color—red, brown, yellow, orange, or whitish—beginning on the head and extending well down onto the tail. Since this stripe covers virtually the whole back, and since it is usually red or reddish brown, it accounts for the common name of red-backed salamander. The sides are slate grey, and the belly is salt-and-pepper, variegated greys.

Most unstriped individuals are similar, but lack the stripe, of course. These are just plain slaty grey, plumbeous, or lead-colored, and so called lead-backed salamanders. Some unstriped individuals are bright red all over, except for occasional and irregular blackish blotches on the sides of the tail. These all red fellows are common in some parts of Massachusetts, but none have yet been found on the Cape or Islands.

Some populations and individuals have irregular light coloration in blotches or suffusions on their sides and backs. Some like this, with yellow-orange suffusions or tiny red speckles, looked at first like lead-backs when we caught them on Naushon. We have found only two real lead-backs on that island.

Omitting Naushon oddities, all of our woodland salamanders so far have been either red-backed or lead-backed. Red-backs, in this region, are always commoner, though lead-backs may approach forty percent of some local populations. In upland areas of the bedrock New England mainland, lead-backs are virtually nonexistent. Al explains this as a result of their relatively poor ability to withstand low temperatures.

At a number of Cape-Islands localities, including Naushon, Warren's Landing woods on Nantucket, and Gay Head (all noted by Al in the 1973 paper), lead-backs are virtually nonexistent also. We have been able to add Cuttyhunk, Pasque, and Tuckernuck—but notably not Nashawena—to this list. All of these localities have wide exposures to the sea to their southwest. The prevailing summer winds are southwest, of course, and bring considerable salt spray inland. Is it possible that lead-backs are more apt to dry out than red-backs are? Or are they perhaps just more susceptible to salinity? Salinity certainly makes for dessication, because salt makes an osmotic imbalance on the outside of moist membranes, like salamander skin. The water diffuses out of the salamander to correct this imbalance; the salamander, in extreme cases, shrivels and dies. (This is why you should not handle pet salamanders, or even frogs and toads—your hands are salty. Taste and see.)

We have this view of the weakling lead-back, able to survive in a fairly high percentage of the population only in areas that do not get too cold or too dry and salty. This view fits with our known annual and seasonal fluctuations. In very dry years, as Al has noted, the percentage of lead-backs—even in populations that have plenty— drops off. Conversely, if you want to find a lead-back—one in several hundred—at Gay Head, go in the spring of a wet year. It sounds like we have a good explanation.

Nashawena is a fly in the ointment. On 26 July 1973, in the middle of an unusually wet summer, Numi, Nick, Peter Lynch, Rich, Bob, Bruce, the Richard Taylor family, and I all descended on Nashawena in what was probably the greatest herpetological inundation of all time. Not all of us counted salamanders, and those of us that did found only ten: eight red-backs and two leads. We hunted eastward through the oak woodlands from Middle Pond.

Since that percentage of leads (twenty) was too high, we came back on 29 July. This time Nick and I worked west of Middle Pond, explicitly to bring the total count to over twenty, the minimum Al feels he needs for statistical significance. We counted eight red-backs and four leads. One of the leads was a nesting female with a clutch of eight young, still in their capsules. All the young were red-backs. I preserved an adult of each color phase and the clutch of striped young.

Al prefers not to include larvae and hatchlings in the overall count, since natural selection has not had time to work its culling on these. Many might prove unfit, and fail to survive to adulthood, for hundreds of reasons other than color phase. If we just consider Nashawena's adult count, we have 22, with 16 striped and six solid leads. That is a distressingly high 27 percent. Even including the eight stripped larvae, it is still 20 percent. Nashawena won't be bent into fitting: anything over one or two percent is too high, we theorize, for a locality so exposed to the sea from the southwest. Perhaps some peculiarity of topography, soil, or vegetation (like the very abundant *Sphaghum* moss) accounts for Nashawena's departure from the prediction. I tentatively regard Nashawena as a puzzling exception to an otherwise perfectly good rule.

To understand the biological basis of woodland salamander variation, we must delve into the complex subject of genetics. The genetic material of all higher plants and animals is the chemical DNA (deoxyribose nucleic acid). It occurs in long strands in the nucleus of every cell of our bodies. When a cell divides to make two cells, the DNA replicates itself exactly. Each daughter cell gets a complete set of DNA strands exactly like the original cell's.

Most of the time, though, cells are not dividing. They are working to perform their specific functions for the good of the whole organism. In this working condition, DNA does not code for more DNA at all. Instead, it codes for messenger RNA (ribose nucleic acid). The structure, or sequence of components called nucleotides, of the DNA, dictates the structure of the messenger RNA. The messenger, once completed, leaves the cell nucleus, travels out into the main body of the cell, and performs some action specifically dictated by that structure—which was specifically dictated by the structure of the DNA.

We can call any length of the DNA strand that produces a specific messenger, that in turn performs (after various complex steps) a specific function, a gene. The general function of the messenger RNA is to produce proteinaceous chemicals called enzymes. So, one may say that one gene, made of DNA, results (via messenger RNA and those other complicated steps) in one enzyme.

Enzymes are biochemical catalysts; without them, no biochemical reaction can occur. Each specific enzyme, dictated by a specific structure of DNA, catalyzes a specific biochemical reaction. Blinking your eye requires a different set of enzymes than digesting a sandwich, two very complex processes. You have to have the correct, properly functioning lengths of DNA to produce all the correct enzymes needed for each process, or you won't be able to do it.

Well, we think woodland salamander color pattern is less complex. We think there are two genes at work, one for striped phase, the other for solid, or lead. We leave out, for the moment, all the complexities of stripe color, and all the other possible phases. Let's just stick to striped and solid. Almost all sexually reproducing organisms, like woodland salamanders, porpoises, and people (not to mention pine trees and wombats), have two genes for every possible characteristic. That is because we inherited a complete set of DNA strands from each of our two parents.

In effect, this means you have two chances to make the right enzyme in each case. If you inherit one bum gene that just doesn't work at all (a severe mutation), you may luck out and inherit a perfectly good one from your other parent. Since the good one works fine, you will never know you are carrying the bum one. A gene that doesn't work is called recessive. It is recessive in the relative sense that you will never know it is there if the other gene present does the work. The other gene, by working and hiding the existence of the bum one, dominates it. The notion of dominance, in genetics, has nothing to do with being good or better than the recessive. There are some perfectly horrendous genetic dominants in humans, like the one resulting in retinal blastoma. A genetic dominant is simply the one whose existence you can see in an organism where both it and a recessive are present.

Dr. Richard Highton, at the University of Maryland, has long studied all the woodland salamander species of the genus *Plethodon*. In 1959, he published a paper in which he presented evidence that the gene for striped (or usually red-backed) was dominant, and the gene for solid was recessive. If that were true, and nature religiously selected against the solids in the population, killing every one of them before it reached adulthood, more would still spring up in every generation. Some salamanders would have both genes for striped; let's call that RR. Some would have both genes for solid: rr. But lots would have one of each: Rr, the unrecognized carriers. When an Rr salamander mated with another Rr, about one quarter, on the average, of the offspring produced would be RR, another quarter would be rr, and about one half would be Rr ($Rr \times Rr$ gives RR, rr, Rr, and rR—the last two are the same thing).

If natural selection just slacked up a little, then, an rr might reach adulthood in a population normally made up of just RR and Rr salamanders. In an area where selection against rr was weaker (a warm, wet, unsalty area we have suggested), the population might approach one quarter rr. For the population to ever go above 25 percent, however, we must have either (a) a selection *in favor* of solids, or (b) a selection actively *against* stripes. There are plenty of areas where solids (lead-backs) do go over 25 percent.

Al says Dr. Highton announced in 1974, at the annual meetings of the American Society of Ichthyologists and Herpetologists, that in some populations it appears that gene r is dominant over gene R. That is, the Rr salamanders are solid lead-backs; only the RR salamanders are striped.

If this new twist is true, then we must discard the notion that gene R makes the correct, properly-functioning enzyme, and gene R is just one that doesn't function at all. Obviously, both genes must make an enzyme, and the fact that one appears to dominate the other has to be explained in a way other than the classical.

Let's accept the notion that each gene makes a working enzyme. Now RR has only one enzyme, rr has only the other. Rr has both enzymes—the lucky fellow. Now, as a corollary to that, we have to accept the notion that each enzyme does more than one thing. That is, the enzyme produced by the R gene does not simply contribute red, or a stripe, down the back; it *also* catalyzes a reaction somewhere in the sodium transport and balance system of the animal. Perhaps having gene R's enzyme permits tolerance of higher salt (sodium chloride) concentrations in the tissue fluids. If that were true, the salamanders with gene R would tolerate a greater salt concentration outside their bodies before an osmotic imbalance occurred and water began to diffuse out of them. Also, a higher salt concentration in their tissue fluids would tend to depress the temperature at which they would freeze. That would make sense.

How about gene r and its enzyme? An enzyme that performs two different functions, as we have postulated above, is called *pleiotropic*. The phenomenon is *pleiotropy*; the gene involved exhibits *pleiotropic effects*. Maybe gene r's enzyme isn't pleiotropic. Maybe it is just a bum for color pattern, and produces an enzyme beneficial to the salamander in certain habitats. That would explain why, in warmer, moister, unsalty regions the solid lead backs can break 25 percent: they are at no disadvantage and have some advantage we don't know about.

But that won't explain Dr. Highton's reversal of dominance and recessiveness, because an Rr salamander would still have a striped back.

Perhaps I'll have the answer for the second edition. . . .

Woodland salamanders live very well in terrariums. They eat small earthworms, insects, and vestigial-wing fruit flies, which are all available from supply houses and are perfect food for them. By raising them in captivity, you might discover all sorts of things about their genetics. You could easily set up experiments to determine temperature and salt tolerances. You could probably find out if one morph does have higher sodium concentrations in its tissue fluids.

Another problem with woodland salamanders that requires some attention is their taxonomy. Dr. Highton produced a revision of the entire genus (1962). I find it unsatisfying because Dr. Highton does not use the term *subspecies* in the same way most other taxonomists do. But the problems are too technical to go into here.

Four-toed Salamander

Although I grew up within the range of *Hemidactylium scutatum*, the four-toed salamander, I never saw one until the spring of my freshman year in University, March 1958, on the Cumberland Plateau of Tennessee. It was a cold, rainy night. My fellow herpetological enthusiast, John Alexander, and I were out hunting spotted salamanders in a sphagnum pond. John was then a student at the neighboring Academy. He later went on to Princeton, became a Rhodes Scholar, went to Oxford and Harvard, and now is a newspaper editor in North Carolina. Anyway, that night John found a four-toed salamander. *Hemidactylium* is a tiny (less than four-and-a-half inches) species, seemingly quite a nondescript brown at first glance. We were looking for big, bright fellows, and weren't much impressed by the find until we picked it up. Then there could be no mistake. The belly of the four-toed salamander is a bright, opaque, almost enamel-looking white; it has big ink-black speckles. Nothing else looks like that. It has four toes on all four feet; woodland, two-lined, and most other Plethodontidae have five toes on the hind feet. Also,

Atlantic white cedar and sphagnum moss make the optimum habitat of the four-toed salamander. But no one has found one here: Wellfleet, Cape Cod.

Four-toed salamander (*Hemidactylium scutatum*), adult, sex undetermined, about two-and-a-half inches total length: Naushon, Elizabeth Islands.

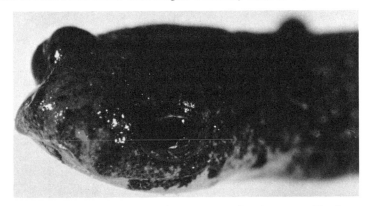

Four-toed salamander (*Hemidactylium scutatum*): the same Naushon specimen; a close-up of the head.

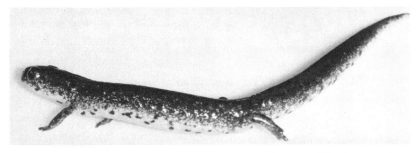

Four-toed salamander (*Hemidactylium scutatum*): the same Naushon specimen in lateral view, showing the spectacular black and white belly.

77

Hemidactylium has a striking constriction at the base of the tail. Here, the tail will readily break off if grabbed by a predator and give the salamander a second chance to escape. He can then grow another tail. Tails that break off purposefully in this manner are called *autotomous*. The place is an *autotomy* constriction.

John and I must have visited that sphagnum pond a hundred times over the next four years, but we never saw another four-toed salamander there. That is absolutely typical, since *Hemidactylium* is often a one time thing.

We did find a real population some miles away. There the sphagnum grew up on the trunks of the white cedars in the swamp. In April, under the sphagnum on these trunks, females could be found in numbers guarding clutches of eggs. There might be twenty-five or thirty eggs in one place, with two or three females. How many each laid I do not know. Like *Plethodon* the eggs are encapsulated and laid out of water. The larvae, however, hatch before they metamorphose, wriggle down through the sphagnum to the water, and swim about, breathing with gills, for a month or two before transforming into miniature adults.

After leaving Sewanee, Tennessee, I did not see another four-toed salamander until five years later. Then Mark Merrill turned one up at Rutland Brook, near Petersham, Massachusetts. All the four-toed salamanders I have ever seen since came from the Cape and Islands.

Tom Chase caught a lovely one in West Tisbury on Martha's Vineyard. Fortunately, Peter Rabinowitz was there, and knew what a rarity it was. It is now in the MCZ.

W. G. Lynn and J. N. Dent (1941) recorded two specimens from Woods Hole. I cannot find them in the MCZ, where most people would normally deposit them. The Woods Hole Oceanographic Institution apparently has not got them. I cannot find them in the collection of the Marine Biological Laboratories. Where are they?

Marshal T. Case, longtime Director of the Cape Cod Museum of Natural History in Brewster, now with the Connecticut Audubon Society, got a beautiful specimen in Harwich. He preserved it, but it has apparently been lost. Fortunately, his excellent Kodachromes of it have not been, and I could identify it to my complete satisfaction.

Just what is the problem? Why only one here and one there? Why can't we ever seem to find a population? There is plenty of lovely habitat: sphagnum ponds with, or without, white cedar, sunny or shady, with temporary water or permanent. They really ought to be more evident.

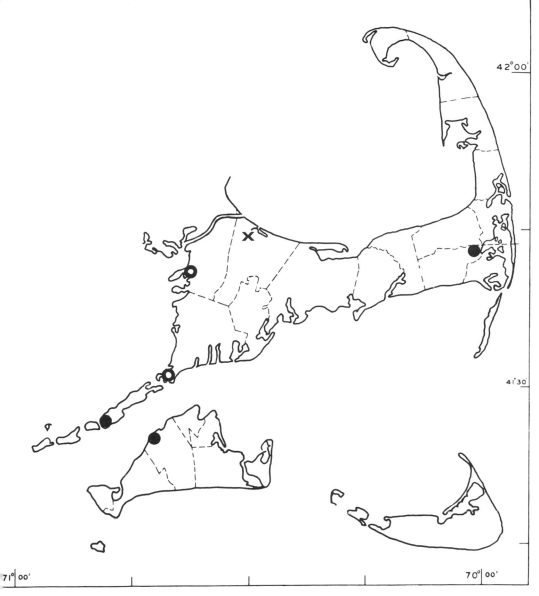

Localities for two rare salamanders. Dots are for the four-toed (*Hemidactylium scutatum*); the open circles are for the published records. X marks the spot for two-lined salamander (*Eurycea b. bislineata*); the two old Nantucket specimens have no precise locality data and are not mapped.

For years I mumbled about how ideal the habitats on Naushon were for this species. I crawled through the brush and excavated sphagnum by the hour. I just knew they had to be there. Well, Paul Elias and Sarah Robey found them.

It was midsummer 1972, and Paul and Sarah were staying on a

boat off the West End of Naushon. They had permission to go ashore for natural history purposes. They were rooting around in some sphagnum, and, suddenly, there was a four-toed salamander. They didn't have a bag or bottle to put it in, so Paul put it in his pocket. You know the rest. When they got back to the boat, it was no longer in the pocket. There were now two clear-cut choices: they could go back and get another one, which we all know was impossible since *Hemidactylium* is a one time thing, or they could try to keep the whole thing quiet. But they knew that some day I would find out. Being the more talkative of the two, Sarah argued for the first alternative; she begged Paul not to believe the repeatedly proven scientific fact that four-toed salamanders only come in *ones*. The scientists *might* be wrong; they don't always know *everything*. Finally he gave in, put down his marlin spike, and agreed to go back and look again the next day.

It was a real old-fashioned cookout. The sun broiled down on Paul and Sarah. The biting flies homed in from miles around. The greenbrier slashed and gouged them. They worked and worked. They must have turned out a hundred tons of sphagnum. But, of course, they had already caught the four-toed salamander and let it get away. As heat and blood loss slowly overcame them, they moved more feebly; able to turn less and less of the sodden mass of moss, hope gave way to despair and the anguished certainty of my recriminations. Paul slumped, pitched forward, his face plowing up the sphagnum carpet. Underneath it was a four-toed salamander: MCZ 86689.

"Shoo," said Paul, "no sweat. We go back get lotsa four-toed salamanders, anytime you want." So, back we went. This time it was the fifth of May 1973. Marty, Nick, Peter, the Taylors, Paul, and I— we all went. May can be lovely on the Islands, but this was not one of those days. The solid overcast had a lead lining. The wind whipped in sullen gusts, blasting salt spray and drizzle through our jackets and sweaters. We crossed the high ground, came out of the trees, and started down toward the sea. A sinuous tidal creek wound through the *Spartina* marshes and cut the barrier beach. Our course made a wide arc, skirting the salt marshes and flanking the beach. Then we started back across salt marsh. We traversed a zone of sedges, marking brackish water, and then, without a break in the watery terrain, entered cattails. Slogging through the dark water, the deep mud sucked down our soaking feet. There was a strand of sphagnum now, here and there. Then a clump. In a few more strides there was a great sphagnum mat.

Our feet were dead numb; our fingers dull blue. "May the gods grant we find them soon," said Paul, whereupon he caught three.

Paul went back in the summer of 1974, and says they are alive and well, doing fine. I'm damn glad they are, for I know of no other place to go and find one.

Two-lined Salamander

In November 1972 I was down in Pennsylvania hunting raccoons. Since one hunts them at night, I had spare time during the day, so I went to the Academy of Natural Sciences in Philadelphia to check for specimens of Cape and Islands reptiles and amphibians. I didn't have time to check all the species, but I was especially interested in tracking down two specimens noted by the late Dr. E. R. Dunn in his great monograph on the family Plethodontidae. Dunn said he examined two specimens of the two-lined salamander, *Eurycea bislineata*, from Nantucket.

I have hunted salamanders all over Nantucket, and examined hundreds of them. All I have ever found are woodlands—*Plethodon cinereus*. I have never even found a two-lined salamander anywhere in the Cape and Islands region, although I do find them abundantly as soon as I get on the solid bedrock foundation of the New England mainland. I have always fancied myself a good hunter of two-lined salamanders. I find them in springs and rocky brooks. I don't know of any such habitat on Nantucket.

But I found Dunn's specimens. They are ANSP 17282 and 17283. They are obviously old, and rather shriveled. Someone before me had snipped the lower jaws loose, so as to widely open the mouths, and reveal the *boletoid* tongues. Two-lined salamanders are among the relatively few species of their family that have such a member. The tongue is free from the floor of the mouth all along its mid- and forward-length (like ours), and forms a large, fleshy tip. It looks quite like a mushroom. The boletoid tongue may be flipped out of the mouth, and although I have never seen it done by a living

Two-lined salamander (*Eurycea b. bislineata*), adult, sex not determined, about three inches total length: Sandwich, Cape Cod.

salamander, it can be used like a toad's tongue to catch insect prey. In all other obvious aspects, these two specimens are typical *Eurycea bislineata bislineata*: the northeastern geographic race of their species.

An old slip of paper in the bottle reads:

Plethodon
erythronotus
Nantucket, [Something]
Mass.
Aug. 1886
R.C. Abbott

Plethodon "erythronotus" is a synonym of *Plethodon cinereus*. Someone before me seems to have assumed all salamanders on Nantucket to be this species and classified these two-lines as woodlands despite the gulf of distinction between them. A second slip of paper in the bottle reveals that Dr. Richard Highton, working on the genus *Plethodon,* had reidentified the specimens correctly, about half a century after Dunn.

The next line is more interesting, as I have indicated by brackets. It once said something else there. Today there are just some garbled pencil marks and what may be an end parentheses. I wish what it said there instead was:

> Found in the terrarium of little Sally MacGruder, over here on summer vacation from Worcester, Mass. She could not bear to leave her little pets, captured on Mount Wachusett, behind.

It *might* say, however:

> Harpooned at the Equator in the Sunda Sea on the thirty-fifth voyage of the barque *Reliable*, Elijah Coffin, Master.

Deep in my heart I believe it really says:

> Sweat, Sucker!

Well, there was still R.C. Abbott in August 1886. I checked Phillips and Phillips guide to manuscript collections of the Academy, but there is no mention of the fellow.

Many years ago, the basement of the Academy was flooded. Many of the herpetological specimens stored there were destroyed. Many more, with labels glued on the outsides of their jars, lost their data. I found no more clues at the Academy.

I wrote the Maria Mitchell Scientific Society of Nantucket and asked them to check both their records and those of the local historical society. Eileen McGrath did so and reports that no one by the name of Abbott figures in the early annals of Nantucket Natural History. I have drawn a blank. However, I will stick my neck out and state flatly that I do not believe those specimens

Two-lined salamander (*Eurycea b. bislineata*): the same Sandwich specimen; a close-up of the head.

originated on Nantucket, wherever Mr. Abbott may have lived when he sent them to the Academy.

Silas Wade, of Plymouth, Massachusetts, was taking a course in herpetology at the University of Rhode Island a few years back. I happened to visit the course, taught by my doctoral professor, Herndon G. Dowling. Silas told me then that he had found a two-lined salamander in Falmouth, Cape Cod. I went back to the exact spot—a log in a golf course about fifty feet from a small pond. Nothing.

There, until June 1974, rested the case for the inclusion of the two-lined salamander in this book.

Peter Lynch, then a student of mine, decided to do his spring term biology project on plant identification on Cape Cod. On a fateful day in June 1974, he and Nick Howell, a fellow student and superb field botanist, set out to add to Peter's knowledge. Both are avid and experienced herp collectors. I suggested, as long as they were going anyway, they should check a few possible, tantalizing verbal reports of elusive Cape Cod creatures. One report, from Bill Haas, then working in the herpetology department of the MCZ, was of marbled salamanders (*Ambystoma opacum*) in Sandwich.

Peter and Nick did not find a marbled salamander. Instead they got two beautiful two-lines under stones, in a little brook, up on the

Sandwich moraine. I went back in 1975 with Nick and seven other enthusiasts. We found lots of specimens, and recorded the brook's water at 52° F.

Two-lines are lovely little salamanders of a cafe-au-lait complexion down the middle, and with a wash of yellow or orange on the abdomen and under the tail. Their tails (unlike that of a red-back) are sharp-edged down the back. You can identify them by those field marks, plus their two, dark, dorso-lateral stripes, without checking for the boletoid tongue.

The secret of success in extending their known range in our area, I believe, is finding stony, small brooks that flow all year round. That is their optimum habitat.

In the Southeast, two-lined salamanders develop long projections from the upper lip called cirri. Each cirrus (as the singular is spelled) carries the nasolabial groove down from the nostril and out well beyond its normal termination on the lip (nasolabial means nose-lip). In the nasolabial groove are special lining cells with tiny hair-like projections, making up a tissue called *ciliated epithelium*. If you don't smoke, your bronchial tubes are lined with ciliated epithelium too. In both us and them, the cilia beat in a wave-like motion to transport particles and chemicals along the epithelium. In our case, up and out of the lungs; in their case, right into the nostrils.

Once inside the nostrils, the particles and chemicals can be sensed by the salamander's Jacobsen's Organ, which senses things like taste and smell. The vomeronasal nerve transports the information received to the salamander's modest brain.

It would seem to be an obvious advantage to have long cirri. The salamander could then "smell" or "taste" things better at a greater distance. Cirri are best developed in male two-lines during their breeding season in the Southeast. They are also very prominent on many individuals in the Northeast, like those at Rutland Brook Wildlife Sanctuary, in Petersham, Massachusetts. I would love to know why they are not so well developed elsewhere.

Two-lined salamanders do very well in a moist terrarium. They are active mostly at night, or in the dark underneath things like moss and stones. It might be easy enough, however, to observe their behavior by keeping them in a dark place, like a basement, under a red light. I feel sure they, like most other dark-adapted animals, cannot see red light. I can't promise fame and fortune, but someone might well come up with fascinating information about the lives of two-lined salamanders without ever leaving mundane old Massachusetts.

4

Frogs, Order Anura

===========

> . . . frogs are carried around by children of
> every race, without record.
>
> PHILIP J. DARLINGTON

ALL TOADS are frogs. I keep saying that over and over again. Nonetheless, one of the first questions most people ask me when they find out I am a herpetologist is, "What is the difference between frogs and toads?" Simple. It is the same as the difference between automobiles and chevys. One is a special subset of the other; toads are frogs that belong to the family Bufonidae. There are about a dozen families of frogs, in the Order Anura or Salientia, scientifically. Four of them occur in our area. If you call the Bufonidae "toads," and the Ranidae "frogs," what do you do with the rest? You can call them frogs, or toads, or neither, as you please. In this area the situation is fairly simple. The true frogs, family Ranidae, have rather smooth, shiny, wet-looking skin, fairly acute faces (viewed either from above or from the side), and disproportionately big, meaty, hind legs. The true toads, family Bufonidae, have variegated, warty, often dry-looking skin, blunt faces, and much smaller, almost scrawny-looking hind legs.

The treefrogs, or the tree toads, family Hylidae, look rather intermediate in head shape and skin condition, but separate out immediately on the basis of the enlarged toe disks—often likened to suction cups—that terminate each and every digit.

The spadefoot, family Pelobatidae, is our most distinctive species. It has several close relatives to the south and west in North America, and a few in Europe and such far-flung places as the Seychelles.

Frogs are frustrating to me. Our Cape and Islands forms are easy enough to identify and usually locate, but in my tropical travels I have been tormented by uncertainties and irritations that remain unresolved even today. The problem is that all frogs look alike. Well, no, the problem is really that no two frogs look the same. I well recall my first Guadeloupéen 'coon hunt, about fifteen years ago. I was up in the jungle rain forest of Guadeloupe's high mountains. My purpose was to get a raccoon, and I managed it. The problem was frogs. There seemed clearly to be two different sorts of frog voices. One was the normal, high-pitched whistle one hears all over the West Indies; the other was a peculiar sound such as can be made by tapping a thin glass goblet with a spoon. I had never heard such a voice before. I talked to a young man, M. Patrice Barlange, the son of the resident forest officer. Patrice assured me there were two different kinds of frogs. I was determined to come back the next night and follow him on a frog hunt. We carefully concentrated on the strange voice. We tried to zero in on its makers, and caught several dozen little frogs. No two looked alike. Some had a single stripe, some double, some two-toned—above and below—some solid-colored, and so on. We picked up a few of the ordinary sounding frogs too, to prove they occurred together. Next morning, with all my frogs pickled, I confidently expected to sort them into two piles. No way. No matter how I tried to divide them—size, shape, color— I always had a continuum from one extreme to the other. I gave up, and sent them off to Dr. Laurent, then the frog expert at Harvard.

Dr. Laurent did separate them into two piles. Most of them seemed to be the ordinary species, but three or four were very different. He sent them to Dr. John Lynch, then a graduate student at the University of Illinois. John separated them into the same two piles, and reached the same conclusion. He named the new species, only three or four specimens, *Eleutherodactylus barlagnei* for Patrice, who had caught most of the whole batch.

Other workers have reinvestigated the Guadeloupéen frogs and find the two species to be perfectly valid. I have never understood it. How did we manage to catch mostly the ordinary kind and so few of the new species; the exact opposite of what we thought we were doing? Well, frogs are the world's greatest ventriloquists. Those mean little beggars with the new voice knew we were coming, and Charlie McCarthied their unsuspecting cousins. I guess.

Anyway, best of luck to you if you take up tropical frogs. Our species, as I have said, are comparatively straightforward, but superb ventriloquists too—especially the little ones.

Green Frog

Rana clamitans is our commonest species. Most of our individuals are not especially green and perfectly fit the description and color picture of *Rana clamitans clamitans* provided in Conant's *Field Guide*. The trouble is that this form, called the bronze frog, is supposedly southern. Our subspecies, called *melanota*, is supposed to be different. I am totally unconvinced, and will call this species simply *Rana clamitans*, no subspecies.

Most individuals are brown, often bronze-colored, often mottled with darker slaty-grey-brown, and with green at least on the sides of the face. Some are green all over, though usually with darker and lighter mottling. Some individuals have a genetic mutation that wrecks their ability to make yellow; these come out blue whenever they would have been green. I have records of blue green frogs from Falmouth, Centerville, (in Barnstable), and Chappaquiddick.

Some green frogs are bright yellow. This is the result of a mutation wrecking the ability to make blue pigment. If they had been able to make blue pigment, they would have to come out green, of course.

Green frog (*Rana clamitans*), adult female, about two-and-a-half inches: West Tisbury, Martha's Vineyard.

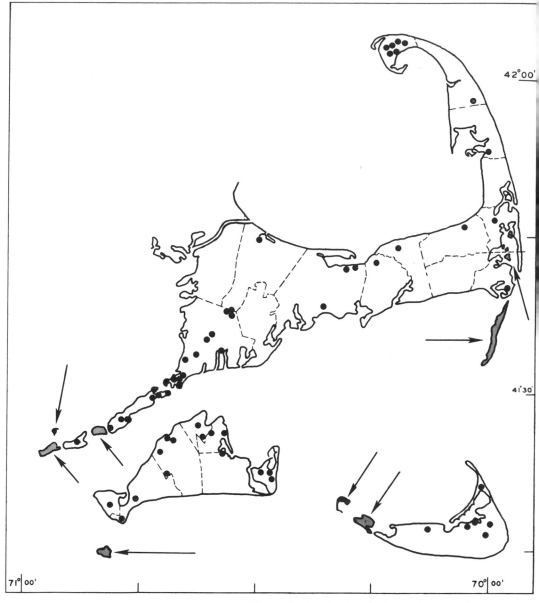

Distribution of the green frog (*Rana clamitans*): dots indicate where specimens have been examined. Arrows indicate places where the species apparently does not occur. Solid black (Penikese, Muskeget) are islands without apparently suitable habitat; shading indicates islands with seemingly suitable habitat where search has failed to discover specimens. I presume the species occurs *everywhere* else.

Yellow green frogs come from Brewster, and are rarer than the blue mutants.

Rana clamitans courts throughout the warmer months of the year, with egg-laying concentrated in May, June, and July. It tends to stay

88

pretty close to permanent water and is never as terrestrial as the pickerel or wood frog is. The species attains about four inches, head-body length—not nearly the size of a bullfrog. There are two obvious ridges, called dorso-lateral folds, one down each side of the back. Bullfrogs have no such ridges or folds.

The song of the green frog is the highly variable "plunk," "clung," or "jug-a-rum," well described as sounding like the twanging of "a loose banjo string," to quote Dr. Conant. The male, who does the "singing," has a *tympanum* (ear drum) larger than his eye and bright yellow pigment on chin and throat.

The reason green frogs call throughout their period of activity, instead of just at their breeding season, is quite simple. Green frogs stay at the ponds where they breed; they live there. Pickerel, leopard, and wood frogs move away and spread out over the land. Green frogs, thus, need a feeding territory. They are concentrated around the pond edges, and except on rainy nights and foggy days, do not travel far in search of food. If every male green frog spaces himself, by listening to his neighbors, far enough away from the next individual calling to allow a sufficient foraging area to support two frogs, all will work out perfectly. The females are about equal in numbers to the males, so a two frog space insures survival of the population. Such a behavior pattern requires no mentation on the part of the frogs. Individuals who fail to establish territories big enough to support two adults will simply show a much higher failure rate at both surviving and reproducing. The ones with such a stereotyped, genetically in-herited behavior pattern will be the successful parents of the next generation. That is basic natural selection: survival of the fittest.

Professor Albert Hazen Wright and his wife Anna Allen Wright coauthored the classic *Handbook of Frogs and Toads*. They were residents of Ithaca, New York, and I have assumed that their data on tadpoles applies to our region. I don't go in for tadpoles much, because if the adult frogs are a pain, just imagine how hard the tadpoles are to identify. Anyway, the Wrights say green frog tad-poles over-winter just once before metamorphosis. In the spring or summer after their hatching they change to froglets at a tailed tad-pole length of about an inch or inch-and-a-half. The tadpoles have a fairly blunt tail tip with large dark spots or mottling in the fins, both above and below. Bullfrog tadpoles are much larger. Pickerel and leopard frog tadpoles have a tapering, very pointed tail.

The green frog is a staple in the diet of many familiar creatures: raccoons, otters, skunks, various snakes, herons and egrets, and, perhaps most frequently on Cape Cod, bullfrogs.

89

Pickerel Frog

This species, *Rana palustris*, is a boldly patterned, pretty creature. It is well-known for its ability to produce noxious skin secretions poisonous to other frogs and many potential predators. If you put a pickerel frog in the same container with frogs of other species, you will probably kill them. The resulting bacterial bloom will probably kill the pickerel frog too. I do not know what the toxin secreted by the pickerel frog is. It can be very irritating to humans if, for example, you rub your eyes after handling a specimen. This is true for many other species as well, including toads, treefrogs, and newts, that are not noticeably poisonous to their fellow amphibia.

People usually call pickerel frogs leopard frogs, which they most emphatically are not. It is very easy to separate the two species. Pickerel frogs have bright yellow or orange on the undersides of their thighs and on the abdomen. Leopard frogs are not distinctively colored in these parts, which are pale green or whitish, like the rest of the ventral surfaces. In addition, pickerel frogs have big, giraffe-like spots with little ground color between them. Leopard frogs have smaller, rounded or oval, scattered spots. Pickerel frogs are patterned in warm browns and ochres. So are some leopard frogs, but most of these go in for bright greens and blues, at least on the head.

Pickerel frog (*Rana palustris*), adult male, about two inches: Gay Head, Martha's Vineyard.

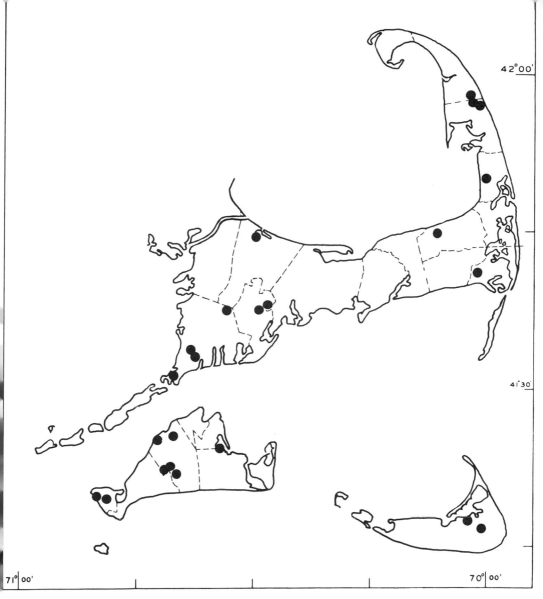

Black dots are localities at which I have recorded pickerel frogs (*Rana palustris*). I am so ignorant of the habitat requirements of this species, and so little able to make generalizations about where it lives, that attempting to speculate a general range is impossible.

I recorded a pickerel frog at Ashumet Holly Reservation, Falmouth, on 11 June 1969 that was bright yellow all over the entire ventral surface: chin, forearms, everything. This individual was the yellowest I ever saw. I have seen specimens in which the yellow was so orange it looked more like salmon red.

Dr. Conant, in his *Field Guide*, gives the record length for a pickerel frog as 3⅛ inches, which is about 80 mm. I know I've seen them a good deal bigger than that, but I rarely collect specimens, and then only for locality records. I have never actually collected a bigger pickerel frog, so that is a good project for someone who wants a bit of fame (no fortune, I'm afraid).

All of my breeding records are in May. All of my metamorphosing records are in August. Wright and Wright, in the *Handbook*, basically agree, giving breeding dates as 23 April to 15 May and metamorphosis simply as August. A detailed look at my data may prove useful.

I have them breeding during the first ten days of May from various Cape Cod localities: Sandwich, Chatham, and Eastham. On Nantucket, I recorded some breeding on 24 May, but real activity peaking on 27 May. Of course, the seasons are prolonged on Nantucket. The winter never gets as wintry, but the spring progresses towards summer more slowly.

I have tadpoles in process of metamorphosis in Falmouth on 6 August, and fully metamorphosed at Truro and on the Vineyard by the middle of the month. Wright and Wright say tadpole life is seventy to eighty days; my data indicate it may be shorter. It is amazing to me that the tadpoles can grow to such great size—three inches—in so short a time, but I am no authority on tadpoles. I even failed to record the sizes of the ones I found metamorphosing, but I think I would have, out of sheer amazement, if they had been as big as Wright and Wright say.

The distribution of this species in our area is a mystery to me. *Rana palustris* is abundant on the main part of Nantucket, but I cannot find it at Coskata. It is locally abundant on the Vineyard, especially in West Tisbury. I have never found it on the Elizabeth Islands, despite repeated searches simultaneous with loud calling and active breeding on Cape Cod. On the Cape itself the species is widespread and locally abundant right up to Truro. North of the Pamet River I simply cannot find it. Numi and I checked over two hundred frogs one rainy August night, in Provincetown, when pickerel frogs *should* have been all over the place. Nothing but greens.

I cannot find this species on any island smaller than Nantucket, or on lands made entirely or largely of drift sand. It seems to be confined to the big moraines and outwash plains. I do not believe the controlling factor can possibly be salinity because some of the ponds it breeds in most abundantly on Nantucket are occasionally breached by northeasters and inundated by the sea.

Is this a species where ground temperature becomes the limiting factor? I know that the smaller and lower the land area the less stable the ground temperature. Which extreme gets them—the warm of summer or the chill of winter? Or is there another explanation entirely? Or am I just a bad frog hunter serving up weird ideas to account for faulty observations?

Leopard Frog

It is with genuine reluctance that I include this creature, *Rana pipiens*. I am convinced there are no native leopard frogs anywhere in the Cape-Islands region. Yet, every year thousands are imported from the Connecticut Valley, Vermont, Minnesota, North Carolina, and other exotic spots. I know of one pond in Falmouth into which hundreds of eggs or tadpoles have been dumped year after year for decades. And would you believe the people who do this call themselves biologists!

These frogs are imported for classroom demonstrations. Usually, breeding condition adults are shipped. The females are manually stripped for their eggs; the males "pithed," which destroys the brain.

Leopard frog (*Rana pipiens*), adult female, about three inches: laboratory specimen, courtesy Department of Biology, Clark University, Worcester, Mass. This exotic species has been repeatedly introduced to the Cape and Islands, but apparently does not long survive in the wild.

The testes are removed from the males and *macerated*—smashed up, literally—in water. Then eggs and sperm are mixed so the students can watch embryological development. Sick.

Of course, when the stalwart educators are finished showing development to the kiddies, they take out all the little tadpoles (or eggs) and dump them in the nearest local pond. Any adults they didn't use up they probably dump too. Even sicker.

Just what in hell is wrong with our *native* frogs? Why not go out on a nice, healthy field trip to the nearest local pond with a good frog population, have them collect *native* developing frog eggs, and strain their brains over identifying the developmental stages and even the different species? Why not try solving some of the *real, important,* local biological problems begging for answers, rather than just repeating moribund experiments whose results were made clear in total detail a hundred years ago?

I do not know of any extant *Rana pipiens* population in our region. Of course, it took twenty tries before starlings were successfully established here from Europe, but with persistence and luck they managed to do it. So, I cannot possibly be surprised by a locally caught leopard frog. There are some, in fact.

In the collections of the American Museum, in New York, there are four big adults from Cuttyhunk and a tadpole from Woods Hole. I cannot verify the identification of the tadpole; I only looked at him through the side of the jar. The Cuttyhunk adults look like typical Minnesota specimens to me. I believe a local school teacher, even back when they were collected in 1915, was responsible for their appearance on the island.

It is important to know the differences between pickerel and leopard frogs (discussed under the former, native species), so that identifications can be made. If we are going to have leopard frogs living here, we must try to find out all we can about them. In habits, it is said that this frog is quite similar to the pickerel frog. It comes to water to breed, of course, but like *Rana palustris* it tends to wander when out of its breeding season, and might turn up anywhere.

Until I am aware of surviving populations, I cannot map the range of this introduced species.

The taxonomy of leopard frogs is in an unholy state of chaos. There are so many described and named subspecies, sibling species, genetic morphs, and so on, that Wright and Wright donated forty pages to this complex alone. That was back in 1949. Since then, new forms, new opinions, and new taxonomic arrangements have erupted like a volcano. It does seem likely that there is a native leopard frog in the uplands of New England; if so, its correct name is probably *Rana pipiens pipiens*: the northern leopard frog.

Wood Frog

This beautiful little species, *Rana sylvatica*, is a true harbinger of spring. The duck-like, quacking call of the nuptial males may be heard as early as late March. Most seem to breed in early April, and I have no record of their breeding on Cape Cod after the end of April. More than any other species, this one depends on temporary ponds.

As the name implies, wood frogs are creatures of moist, shady forest. Here they lead the rather terrestrial existence of typical toads, and come to water only to court, mate, and lay eggs. For some reason, probably predation by fish, they seem only to establish populations around temporary waters: ponds, puddles, and swamps that dry up in late summer. Obviously, fish cannot survive in such places, and the larvae of wood frogs, spadefoots, spring peepers, spotted salamanders, and myriad invertebrate animals metamorphose soon enough to utilize these safe habitats. But the temporary pond is despised by man.

People just cannot bear to see a pond dry up. It somehow affronts their sense of how things should be. To solve the problem, people bring in a back hoe or a bulldozer and dig the pond out deeper, so it will hold water all year round. Then all they need to do is introduce some goldfish and mallard ducks, and everything is made right. Nature has been improved upon. Of course, a hundred species have been extirpated in the process.

Another popular approach is to just fill the temporary pond in completely. That works just as well.

Of course, he who leaves a temporary pond alone asks for some troubles directly resulting from the same thing that makes it a haven for the wood frog and his associates—no fish. Fish not only eat wood-frog eggs; they eat mosquito larvae. Temporary ponds are good mosquito breeders. I will still defend them, however, not only because I do not much mind mosquitos, but because so many creatures of the temporary pond eat them. Spadefoot and spotted salamander larvae are voracious hunters of such plump, soft-bodied prey. Many of the invertebrate larvae of temporary ponds are heavy carnivores and fine mosquito eaters, too.

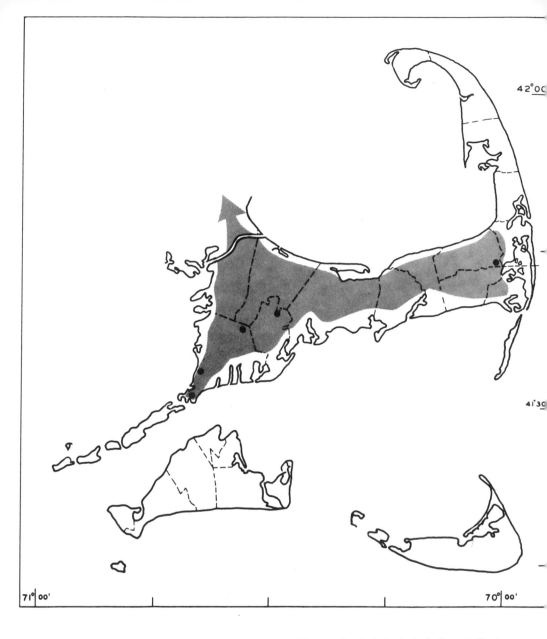

A speculative range for the wood frog (*Rana sylvatica*) is shaded. Dots indicate localities from which specimens have been examined. With small effort, it should be easy to render this map obsolete.

So, stay the bulldozers and the fill. Hold off on that kerosene to oil the swamp. Let temporary ponds have their place. A whole community of creatures depends on them and can survive nowhere else. The wood frog is just one of the most charming.

96

Wood frog (*Rana sylvatica*), adult female, about two inches: Harwich, Cape Cod.

Wright and Wright describe the tadpole as olive with a very high dorsal tail fin. It metamorphoses at a length of about two inches, and the adult frogs grow to about three inches head-body length.

Wood frogs are the color of red-cedar shingles. They may be as grey as the oldest, weathered red-cedar on Cape Cod, or as rich and red as newly cut heartwood. The upper lip is boldly whitish. The area from the ear forward, along the side of the head, to the eye—and often beyond it to the tip of the snout—is smoky black. This gives the wood frog a masked appearance.

The wood frog is a truly boreal species, occurring from Alaska and Labrador southward to Maryland, and in the uplands all the way to Georgia. Southern wood frogs have longer legs than northern ones. The heel reaches or passes the nose tip if the leg is straightened out alongside the body. It seems that as one looks farther and farther north, the heel fails by more and more to reach the snout. Subspecies have been based on this characteristic, and it seems simple enough to define them: *Rana sylvatica sylvatica*, with leg to or beyond the nose tip; and *R. s. cantabridgensis* (named for Cambridge, Massachusetts, where it does *not* occur) with heel failing to reach nose tip. However, if we are just arbitrarily dividing a gradual cline, if it is just a continuum of variation from Georgia to the Bering Sea, then claiming there are two different sorts is most misleading. Most authors seem to reject the notion that there are two different sorts of wood frogs, a short-legged and a long-legged. I will go along, for the time being; no subspecies.

Bullfrog

When Numi was just a little girl she acquired a bullfrog. She did not really want a bullfrog, and her mother certainly did not want her to have it. But unavoidable circumstances prevailed. It was, initially at least, the fault of Numi's erudite, literary, and lovely mother, for she had taken Numi to Walden Pond. There Numi encountered two little boys who had caught, and were jubilantly torturing, a bullfrog. They hauled it around by one leg or the other and attempted to insert various objects where Nature had planned only exits. Numi was incensed. In the manner that little girls handily prevail over little boys in vocal contests, she presuaded them to let the bullfrog go. But, she insisted, they had to let it go just where they had caught it. They were vague. Bullfrogs, Numi knew, are animals of a highly territorial nature with strict home ranges. This was an adult male, the most territorial of the species. If they would not take it home, and could not tell Numi where, *exactly*, its home was, there was no alternative. Displaced, it had to have a new home. That was Cambridge.

Numi's bullfrog lived well over a year in its new home, and finally

Bullfrog (*Rana catesbeiana*), adult male, about five inches: Falmouth, Cape Cod.

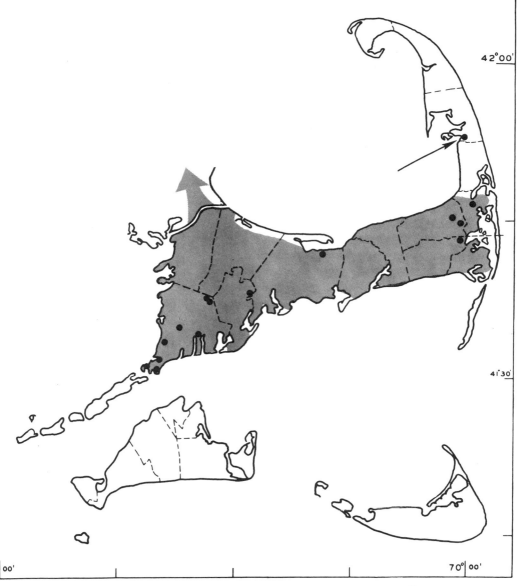

A speculative range for the bullfrog (*Rana catesbeiana*) is shaded. Dots indicate where specimens have been examined. The arrow points out the Wellfleet population, which I believe was introduced. There are old specimens from Nantucket without a precise locality; I believe these represent an unsuccessful introduction.

succumbed to causes unknown while Numi was off in Baja California. If Numi had stayed at home, the bullfrog would probably still be alive today. We inadvertently traded the life of a bullfrog for a new biologist. Anyway, in the months it lived in Cambridge we learned a great deal about that bullfrog.

99

Numi set him up in a big aquarium with wall-to-wall, indoor-outdoor washable carpet. This is important, because bullfrogs cannot live long in water alone. She provided him with a copper trough big enough to submerge completely. That is important too, for copper inhibits bacterial growth which so often kills captive frogs. She fed him mice. Of course, bullfrogs will eat any sort of animal small enough to swallow; feeding one is merely a matter of providing enough. Numi's frog ate a mouse every week or two, and could go for a month without looking really emaciated.

Kept at about 75°F, near a radiator, this fellow stayed boldly bright green with olive mottling and a yellow throat. He ate heartily, and would sing his sonorous "browww-umm" song to the accompaniment of baroque music. We used to try all sorts of sneaky maneuvers to actually see him singing; Numi once managed, but almost invariably he would stop as soon as we could see him, which we firmly believe was the same thing as he seeing us.

At cooler temperatures he would turn quite dull, muddy brown and submerge in his water until just his eyes and snout were visible. To us, he clearly seemed uncomfortable and phlegmatic.

Bullfrogs can be readily and abundantly observed in the wild at such places as Grassy Pond, Ashumet Holly Reservation, Falmouth. They begin calling in May or June, though egg masses are usually most conspicuous in July—great, floating jelly-masses dotted with buckshot-sized, black eggs. The tadpoles take several years to reach the age of metamorphosis. They grow to four inches or more in total length. The adult females get much larger than males; lengths of head and body up to eight inches. Mark Merrill and I once caught a dozen to feed a field trip (the forelegs and back meats are just as good as the justly-famed hindlegs). They totalled over sixteen pounds.

Bullfrogs call for the same territorial reasons as green frogs, but within a shorter season. Not only are they not so well adapted to cool weather, but they seem to care less about young individuals encroaching on their lands. Young bullfrogs are a favorite food of old bullfrogs.

Numerous attempts have been made to establish bullfrogs outside their natural range, for example on Nantucket and the Vineyard. Most of these transplants have fortunately failed, but the Wellfleet Bay Sanctuary introduction took. Here bullfrogs are greatly increasing in population size, and rendering the native green frogs scarcer and scarcer each year. We can only wonder how long it would have taken bullfrogs to expand their range naturally northward along the Outer Cape.

Frogs, Order Anura

Rana catesbeiana commemorates Mark Catesby, the young English naturalist who lived and travelled in Virginia, the Carolinas, the Bahamas, and Jamaica in the early decades of the eighteenth century. Except for his ponderous *Natural History*, printed in England about 1730, we know virtually nothing about Mark Catesby. He appeared from, and disappeared into, oblivion—leaving our most magnificent frog to bear his name.

Spadefoot

Neither a true frog nor a true toad, *Scaphiopus holbrooki*, the spadefoot, belongs to a peculiar, primitive amphibian family. I recorded one of the most dramatic of my herpetological adventures with the Nantucket spacefoot back in 1970:

The shriveled, wizened little body was huddled in a deep pocket in the sand, beneath old planks and debris, a good eight feet below the adjacent ground surface. Worn knees and elbows, ragged scar tissue, and a damaged and healed right eye attested to a long, hard life. How many decades had he lived there? Would this long, dry winter have been his last, or did we find him just in time? How many brothers, sisters and cousins of his still live on Nantucket? When was the last time they ever bred here? How did his weird primitive species ever get to Nantucket to begin with?

I wrapped his body, little bigger than a prune, in wet paper towels and put him in a plastic bag in my pocket. There was life in him. His tissues would soak up the moisture. Things would be easier for him from now on. It was about eleven o'clock in the morning, the seventh of March. The Palfrey Street School Solar Eclipse Expedition still had much to do this morning. As head of the Science Department,

Spadefoot (*Scaphiopus holbrooki*), adult, sex undetermined, about two inches: Eastham, Cape Cod.

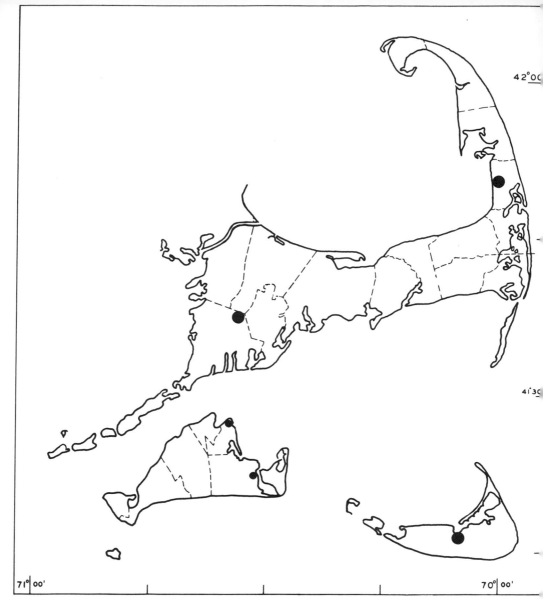

Localities for the spadefoot (*Scaphiopus holbrooki*): big dots are for living specimens or recently preserved individuals examined by me. The small dots (Martha's Vineyard) are breeding localities vouched for by Charles B. Cook, Jr.,
of West Tisbury, and backed by other observers, as active *before* 1950. The
species may still occur literally anywhere.

driver of the vehicle, holder of reservations, etc., I had responsibilities
elsewhere just then. I will never forget the clear, cloudless sky that
turned a star-studded deep purple, the 360 degree "sunset," and the
brilliant white corona of the total eclipse—the last visible from New

England in the twentieth century—but with that little creature safe in my pocket, I'd have been a happy man even if it had rained all day.

Our headquarters were the home of Danny and Hannah Haynes, and my association with them has always been enjoyable and fruitful, especially in the area of natural history. So, when Danny told me of a friend of his, Henry Huyser, who said he had toads in his basement, I was anxious to follow up the lead. Ross Harris, our expedition photographer, had huge lenses, cases of wondrous optical equipment, and pages of tables and calculations spread all over the Haynes' house. He was hard at work, so Larry Rottmann, a fellow faculty member, and Eric Hermann, a previous student, and I set off to investigate the Huyser's basement.

The basement was neatly ordered and concrete-floored. It didn't look like the sort of place to hunt toads. I noticed a small nook, however, that was unfloored and full of concrete blocks and discarded lumber. This, I thought, would be the place to look. We shuffled objects around and groped in the gloom. Without fanfare, Larry said, "Is this it?" and pointed to the dark lump. My fingers closed on it and retrieved it to my face. I let out a whoop of joy when I realized what I held; a Nantucket spadefoot.

Years ago, Reginald Reed found a spadefoot on Nantucket, and quite properly took it to the Maria Mitchell Association. Sadly, it was lost, said to have been accidentally fed to a snapping turtle, and thus counted as nothing more than a hearsay record. Now, here was the proof: another spadefoot. When I looked at him an hour or so after capture he had nearly doubled in size. His desiccated body rapidly absorbed moisture. He blinked his good eye, and looked content enough. He was going to be just fine.

Mrs. Huyser told me they had installed a new pump system in the basement that didn't flood periodically like the old one. This was the new system's first winter, and very likely would have been the spadefoot's last.

The spadefoots are a strictly North American group, widespread to the south of New England. They belong to a peculiar family, the *Pelobatidae*, whose skeletons show affinities to the fossil ancestors of both frogs and toads. The living species of spadefoots are not closely related to either of those groups, however. The eastern spadefoot reaches the northern limit of its range in coastal, southern New England. It is probably abundant on Cape Cod. I say probably because all spadefoots are almost wholly fossorial, which means they live by burrowing deep underground. It is rare to ever see a spadefoot on the surface except when they breed—and that can be very rare indeed. The last time I have personally recorded breeding spadefoots in Massachusetts was in April 1966, on Cape Cod. There were bushels of them then, but our Nantucketer is the very first one I've seen since. It takes prolonged, extremely heavy rains to bring up the spadefoot. Then in a matter of a night or two they make up for lost time in an orgy of raucous squawks and frantic courtship. Their eggs hatch almost immediately, and their tadpole stage is a brief matter of days. Then they disappear again, sometimes for many years.

There were well-documented breeding colonies known from Martha's Vineyard, but no living specimen has been seen there since the great insecticide spraying campaigns of the late 1940s and '50s. No record exists, to my knowledge, of spadefoots ever breeding on Nantucket. The very existence of the spadefoot on this island poses a zoogeographical puzzle. In a nutshell, here is the spadefoot dilemma:

During the Ice Age, so much water was held in the form of ice that the sea's level was much lower than it is today. As the ice melted, retreating and leaving behind the lands of the Cape and Islands, the sea level correspondingly rose. As the climate warmed, Nantucket would have been the first island to become isolated by salt water; then the Vineyard, and last the other islands like Chappaquiddick, Muskeget, Tuckernuck, and the Elizabeth Islands.

Thus, the zoogeographer would predict that animals best adapted to take cold weather—the situation close to the face of the retreating ice—would spread across dry land to Nantucket before the rising sea level isolated it. Following this line of thought, we would expect to find only cold-adapted species on Nantucket and both warm- and cold-adapted species on Cape Cod. Martha's Vineyard and the smaller islands might rank intermediate in species mix. The warm country species just didn't get up here in time to walk to Nantucket, and the spadefoot is a warm country animal indeed.

Well, couldn't they cross water? The answer is yes. Many species, especially reptiles and mammals, do. Sometimes they swim on purpose. Sometimes they are washed out to sea in storms on floating vegetation, and by rare luck made a fortuitous landfall. But amphibians, like frogs, toads, salamanders, and sapdefoots, have a skin that offers little protection against dehydration. Exposed to sea water, the phenomenon of osmosis inexorably draws their body fluids out through their skins, and death quickly follows. Just how long a spadefoot can take exposure to salt water no one knows. Perhaps a combination of a short trip, long enough ago for sea level to have been somewhat lower, and the toughness of these little beasts is the answer to the dilemma. In any case, spadefoots got to Nantucket. I can only hope that the next heavy rains will surprise us and show them to be numerous there.

I am especially grateful to Danny Haynes, the Henry Huysers, and of course Larry Rottmann for, herpetologically speaking, eclipsing the total eclipse of the sun.

Since then I have encountered another great breeding congress of spadefoots at Eastham, on the rainy night of 18 June 1970. Marshal Case found them in the same area in July 1968. I also found a single individual in the pump pit at Ashumet Holly Reservation. Anyone finding a spadefoot, or especially a breeding congress, should carefully take notes on it, and try to get photographs. If there are lots of them, please preserve a voucher specimen.

Mr. Fowler's Toad

Samuel Page Fowler, 1800–1888, was a resident of Danvers, Massachusetts, all his life, and a tanner by trade. By avocation he was a naturalist. Like most nineteenth century naturalists, his primary interests were horticulture and birds. Mr. Fowler contributed several papers on these subjects—most notably an excellent report on insects injurious to cultivated plants, and how to minimize their damage. Samuel Fowler was one of the twelve organizers of the Essex County Natural History Society, founded in 1834, and served as its curator from 1846 to 1848, when it merged with the Essex Historical Society to form Essex Institute. He continued as curator of that until 1856. Despite all that, however, it seems likely that Mr. Fowler would have drifted into obscurity but for one fact. One of our most abundant, widespread, and conspicuous creatures bears his name: *Bufo woodhousei fowleri*, Fowler's toad.

Just how it happened seems mysteriously lost. True, Samuel Fowler did take an interest in frogs and toads. It is noted in the *American Naturalist* that he contributed to our knowledge of the spring peeper (a tiny treefrog) by reporting the habits of one found in November 1872. Certainly no one in the earlier part of the nineteenth century realized that there were two kinds of toads; all were summarily dismissed in the annals of natural history as common toads, *Bufo americanus*. Was it Samuel Fowler who first noticed that one kind trills long on the first warm nights of early spring, while the other bleats loudly and late? By the time Fowler's toad begins

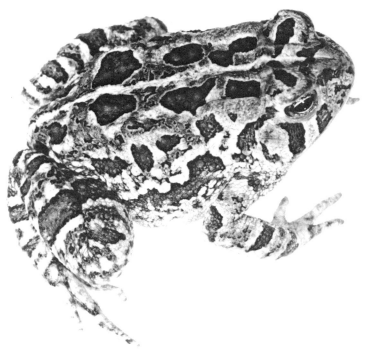

Fowler's toad (*Bufo woodhousei fowleri*), adult female, about 2 inches: Gay Head, Martha's Vineyard.

its bleating and breeding, the common toads have usually long since stopped and disappeared into the woods. Even if you have them both together, it is much harder to tell them apart by looking than by listening.

It was Mary H. Hinckley of Milton who, in 1882, initially and officially christened *Bufo w. fowleri*. But it was an accident. Miss Hinckley was an authority on the *Batrachia Salientia* (or frogs and toads, if you like), and had published a treatise on the anatomy of tadpoles and their diet. She noted the tadpoles of *B. w. fowleri*, but attributed the authorship of the name to Mr. F. W. Putnam. Now, Frederick Ward Putnam was one of New England's prominent scientists. He was Permanent Secretary to the American Association for the Advancement of Science, Curator of the Peabody Museum, and Harvard's first professor of American Anthropology and Archeology. He was also Samuel Fowler's cousin. Nowhere, however, in all of Mr. Putnam's published works, from the caves of Kentucky to the whales of Boston Harbor, do we find an official naming of Fowler's toad.

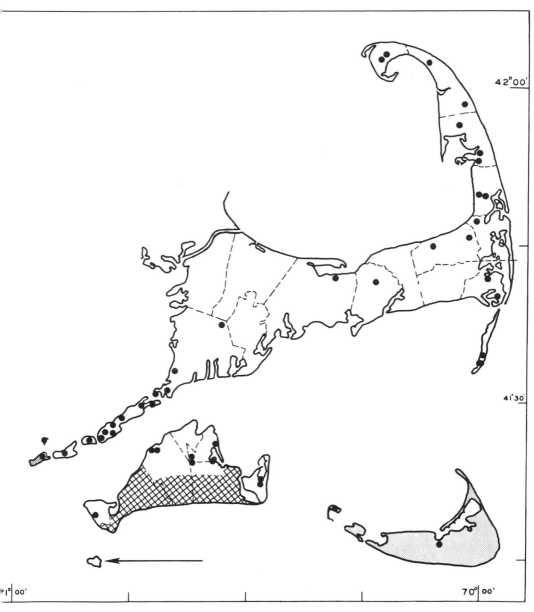

Fowler's toad (*Bufo woodhousei fowleri*) once occurred virtually everywhere. Dots indicate specific localities represented by anything from ancient museum specimens to huge living choruses of thousands of breeders. Shading indicates the islands where the species was apparently totally extirpated by insecticide spraying between 1940 and 1960. Hatching indicates the portion of Martha's Vineyard that still seems to lack living toads, despite their survival and recovery elsewhere. The arrow points to No Mans Land, where the species may never have occurred.

Anyway, by the time Miss Hinckley got through describing the differences—from voice and habits to the tadpole's upper lip—there was no doubt about it; Mr. Fowler's toad was here to stay.

Back before 1620 the two species of toads probably had the world pretty well divided up and sorted out between them. *Bufo americanus* took the wet, deciduous woodlands and uplands, while *Bufo w. fowleri* occupied the dry scrub, sand dunes, and open country. That is still about the way they like to do it, but with the coming of Europeans the face of North America was radically changed, and with it the toads. The forest was felled, and supplanted by open fields and pasture. Fowler's toad spread farther and farther into areas once solely the habitat of the common toad. Habitat disruption, and the presence of Fowler's toads where none had been before, led to hybridization: late breeding common toads took incoming Fowler's toads as mates, and the hybrids flourished at many of the new, man-made open areas. The hybrid toads, unlike most mules, were not sterile. When ecological modifications destroy the natural barriers that once kept two closely related species from interbreeding, several things can happen; hybrids may be produced that are so totally unfit, deformed, or sterile that they fail to reproduce themselves and thus cannot perpetuate.

At the opposite extreme, the hybrids may be so well adapted to the new conditions that they out-breed either parental stock and the phenomenon known as "introgression" occurs. If this happens, a blend is achieved, and the two parental kinds were probably not fully distinct species to begin with, but more likely just variant forms of the same species. Sometimes ecological disruption leads to the complete takeover of the area by one of the species; they are too similar in needs to share the habitat, and competition favors one of them. In the case of our two toads there seems to have been a period of flux followed by stabilization. Some areas were taken over by Fowler's toads, but common toads still managed to hold on in many of the new habitats. Introgression never got very far, and the hybrids seemed ill adapted to most habitats as generations passed. Today, both species occur together over most of eastern North America, and hybrids are getting very hard to find.

Despite the fact that the range of Fowler's toads has probably expanded, it is still not as widespread as is the common toad. Common toads occur throughout New England, and northward into Canada; Fowler's toad occurs only as far north as southern New Hampshire, and has not been actually recorded from either Vermont

American toad (*Bufo a. americanus*), adult male, about three inches: Mashpee, Cape Cod.

or Maine. Quite possibly Fowler's toad occurs in both these states, but has just never been noticed.

Well, if you don't hear them calling, how can you tell them apart? Frequently, even in this modified world, the habitat is a strong clue. You won't see *americanus* on the Provincelands, and will hardly find *fowleri* in Harvard Forest. There are plenty of toads, though, at both places. Better than habitat, in suburbia, is the handy (though not too precise) "toad score" method. If your toad has no big warts on his lower hind legs, just wrinkly skin, give him four points. If he has lots of big warts there, give him a zero. Scores of one, two, and three should each be given for intermediate conditions. If your toad has a plain white belly, give him a four; if he's got one black spot on his chest, give him a three; for black peppering on the chest, a two, and so on. Dark spotting all over chest and tummy gets a zero. Your toad will have big oval, spongy-looking skin glands (paratoids) on the back of his neck; one on each side. Also, he'll have bony ridges—cranial crests—on the back of his head behind the eyes. If the glands broadly border on the ridges, give him a four. If the glands don't touch the ridges at all, give him a zero. You can estimate in between. Last on the "toad score" is the best identification mark of all. Fowler's toads tend to have big dark areas on their backs that contain small warts. Common toads have small dark spots with big warts. So, count the total number of warts contained in the largest dark area or spot, and add that to your toad's score; it may be six or more for a Fowler's toad.

Add it all up. If your toad scores under eight, he's *Bufo americanus;* if he scores over twelve, he's *Bufo w. fowleri.* If he's between the two, he's probably a hybrid. If you find a few hybrids in an area with otherwise identifiable toads, that's not remarkable; but if you find a lot of them, please let me know!

The aerial spraying of insecticides, especially DDT, during the late 1940s and continuing well into the 1960s, decimated all toad populations and actually exterminated this species on many islands. There are fine preserved specimens from Nantucket, Cuttyhunk, Penikese, and Muskeget. J. Clinton Andrews recalls Fowler's toads as exceedingly abundant all over Nantucket before World War II. They are utterly extinct there today. Wilfred Tilton tell the same story for Cuttyhunk, the only one of the Elizabeths that was saturated by fogging. Once the native toads were dead, Mr. Tilton says, he reintroduced toads from the mainland. Sadly, he did not check his species and brought in American toads, *Bufo americanus,* instead of the originally native species. Toads may still live on Penikese, but I cannot find them. I have not been there during the breeding season, when they would be most conspicuous. Since no one lived on Penikese during the great DDT era, we do not know whether some fun-loving pilot soaked this little islet down or not. I suspect one or two did, and the toads are gone.

Muskeget, strangest of our islands, tells the saddest tale of all. Two fine series of preserved toads, quite different from normal *B. w. fowleri,* exist: one batch each in the MCZ and the American Museum. In these specimens the dark spots are run together, often to the extent of making bold, broad, longitudinal stripes—with thirty or more warts in the dark areas. The cranial crests are hypertrophied into wide, massive, bony ridges. Muskeget—with its unique sand vole, unique population of horse-heads (grey seals), and bizarre plant associations—may once have supported a remarkable and similarly unique race of toads. They are gone forever.

The program of aerial insecticide spraying was conducted on a town-by-town basis. Each town contracted for the fogging separately. On Cape Cod and the Vineyard, some towns were not spraying during any given year, so toads had a chance to reproduce successfully at least occasionally. In the Elizabeth Islands, the Trustees would not permit aerial spraying, and thus Naushon, Pasque, and Nashawena were spared. Nantucket took hell. Being all one town, it was all sprayed, relentlessly. Tuckernuck and Muskeget, also part of the town, lie to the west. People reasoned that their marshes would supply wind-blown mosquitoes to the rest of Nantucket. The planes were called in on them, too.

The spraying has not stopped. Even today, every reported case of equine encephalitis brings a new outburst of public sentiment to send up the planes with their deadly loads. Today it is malathion, one of the most horrendously effective amphibian poisons ever developed. And why? Because people are just too damn cheap, lazy, and ignorant to get their horses vaccinated.

It is a supreme irony; a testimony to the mindlessness of man, that we exterminated perhaps our finest natural insect predators—toads—while trying to kill off their prey.

American Toad

I have discussed the differences between this species, *Bufo americanus americanus* (it has subspecies in Canada and west of the Mississippi), and *B. w. fowleri* under Fowler's toad. American toads grow larger, breed later, and are confined pretty much to well-forested morainal land. This species is fairly common in Falmouth and Mashpee, and occurs as far east, at least, as Dennis. Randy Thacher, of West Dennis, brought a lovely albino specimen into the Cape Cod Museum of Natural History, Brewster, in September 1974. I was there and admired its diagnostic big warts, especially on the calves of the hindlegs, its lack of paratoid contact with the cranial crests, and its irritated chirp when handled. Don Schall took lovely color photos of it. It was not a true albino simply because its eyes were dark and normally pigmented. We had no heart for killing it, and Randy assured us he would take it right back and put it under the same board where he had found it.

Similar albino Fowler's toads have occasionally been found on Cape Cod—always with pigmented eyes—but this was the first such *Bufo americanus* I had ever seen.

Hybrids between this species and *Bufo w. fowleri* occasionally occurs in Falmouth. I recorded two out of several hundred toads examined there during the summer of 1970. In midsummer, heavy rains often start both species of toads to unseasonal calling. Any actual mating that occured at this time might be pretty indiscriminate, and tend to perpetuate hybrid individuals in areas of disturbed habitat where ecological segregation of the species is weak.

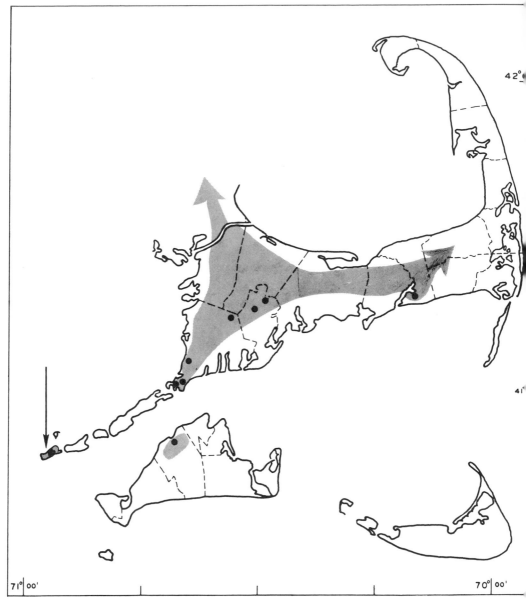

Known localities for the American toad (*Bufo americanus*) are indicated with dots. Shading suggests where habitat and terrain seem suitable. This species has probably merely been overlooked farther east. The arrow indicates Cuttyhunk, where this species was introduced from Concord and Westborough, Massachusetts.

On the Vineyard, this species is today known only from the high moraine in West Tisbury. It no doubt once had a larger range, before insecticides, and will probably expand again as reforestation increases, and if spraying is really stopped.

The exotic population of *Bufo americanus* on Cuttyhunk derives from stock introduced there by Wilfred Tilton, and friends, after the native *Bufo w. fowleri* was exterminated by spraying. Wilfred says he got them from Concord and Westborough, Massachusetts.

Grey Treefrog

This beautiful, though rather comical, species, *Hyla versicolor*, is rather scarce over most of the Cape, but exceedingly abundant on unsprayed Naushon and its annectent little islets to the east.

Grey treefrogs breed in May, announcing their amorous intent with a charming, low, short, and very musical trill. The males are apt to start calling in late afternoon from high up in a tree, and then climb down, closer and closer to a chosen marsh or pond, as twilight gives way to night. The tadpoles grow to well over an inch, and sport striking rose-pink or wine-red tail fins. At metamorphosis, in August, baby grey treefrogs are a tasteless shade of bright yellow-green. Soon they develop the pastel shades of mossy green and lichenate grey characteristics of the adults. The undersides of the thighs, calves, and often the abdomen, are brilliant yellow.

Grey treefrogs are amazingly salt-tolerant. On Naushon, they breed right at the edges of saltmarsh, even among the *Spartina* at its brackish interface with the cattails. I believe this species had a far more extensive range prior to insecticide spraying than is evident today. It may well have originally been present on Nantucket and the Vineyard, for salt-tolerance combines with its moderate tolerance for cool climates to make its absence from these islands seem strange.

Treefrogs are apt to call on any damp or rainy night of spring or summer from some aboreal perch. This trilling is claimed to be their "rain call," and to forecast precipitation. It has always rained after I heard one give this call, but I won't put money on how soon after.

Look for grey treefrogs on windows at night, when indoor lights are on. These wonderful insect predators are fond of policing window panes—which they climb with ease—to do you the favor of eating up the bugs.

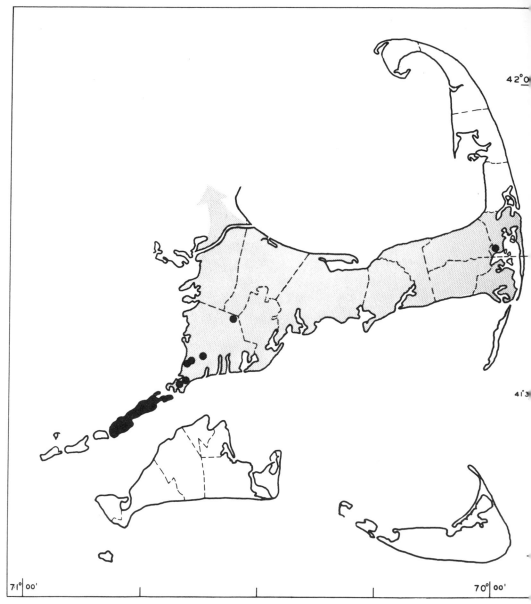

Range of the grey treefrog (*Hyla versicolor*). Dots indicate specific recorded localities. Naushon and its eastern annectant islets are blackened; here this species is unusually abundant and ubiquitous. Shading indicates a postulated Cape distribution, based on habitat and topography. My decision to stop at the Orleans line is purely arbitrary; I can hardly imagine the species really stops here.

Grey treefrog (*Hyla versicolor*), adult male, about one-and-one-half inches: Falmouth, Cape Cod.

Spring Peeper or Pinkletink

The name pinkletink is the delightful favorite of the inhabitants of Martha's Vineyard for *Hyla crucifer crucifer*, the little cinnamon treefrog and famed harbinger of spring. Peepers are among the most abundant of all vertebrate animals from the valley of the St. Lawrence to the Gulf of Mexico. There is a different subspecies in southern Georgia and northern Florida.

Peepers begin their breeding activities in early March, as a rule, but can be heard at least giving their "rain call" during any month of the year. The sheer volume of a peeper chorus on a warm spring evening is amazing.

Where do all the peepers go? Along with "how can owls live without drinking water?" and "how do green turtles find Aves Island?" this is, for me, one of the great unsolved biological puzzles. I have carefully estimated numbers of *calling* peepers all over the Cape and Islands. My figures indicate there are often more than a thousand per marshland acre. Of course, the calling ones are just the males. Females are bigger—up to an inch-and-a-half, versus less than an inch on the average. Perhaps they are more succulent to snakes, raccoons, fish, other frogs, birds, and all the other things that eat them. Let's say there are only half as many females as males. That makes a total population of at least 1500 concentrated at one acre of breeding marsh. From aerial photos, automobile recon-

Beetlebungs, or tupelos, indicate fresh water close to the surface: Naushon, Elizabeth Islands.

naissance, and topographic maps, I estimate about thirty percent of Cape Cod's approximately 350 square miles is breeding ponds and marshes. That amounts to more than 100 square miles. Now, there are 640 acres in every square mile, as near as matters. That's $100 \times 640 \times 1500 = 96,000,000$. That is the same thing as ninety-six million, for those of you, like me, who don't think well in terms of large numbers. It is awfully close to a hundred million. Now where do all those peepers go?

Numi and I were examining frogs in the Provincelands one rainy August night. Right off, about the second frog we came to (and there were hundreds) was a peeper. "See," Numi said, "there's no problem. Peepers are right out here with all the rest of the frogs, just as you should expect." We never saw another one.

Sometimes I have found peepers away from their breeding grounds. I once found a half dozen in tangles of Nantucket greenbriar. I once found one in tall grass. One popped in the window of my truck near the Hidden Forest as I drove along one afternoon (I stopped and searched for more—none). I have recorded a dozen or more hopping around in wet woods, like the State Forest on Martha's Vineyard, over the past eight years. None of that gets close to an explanation. There is no way to extrapolate a hundred million little frogs from that scanty data.

I have heard a lot of facile, specious explanations for where they go (and how owls live, and how turtles find Aves), but none that would ever stand up to a little cogent criticism. I challenge *anyone* to go out in the field with me at any time other than breeding season and show me those peepers.

Native American holly grows beside a tiny, salt-sprayed pond, the breeding place of myriad grey treefrogs: Naushon, Elizabeth Islands.

Peeper or pinkletink (*Hyla c. crucifer*), adult male, less than one inch: Naushon, Elizabeth Islands.

Let's do a little more arithmetic. Let's presume that all 96 million spread out evenly all over Cape Cod's 350 square miles. That means 274,286 (to the nearest whole frog) per square mile. I'll settle for 275 thousand. Now, there are still 640 acres in each square mile, so there must be about 430 of the little beggars out there on every average acre.

Of course, they aren't evenly distributed. There must be optional areas where they live, and quite a few acres (like all the paved part of Route 6 and the bottom of Wequaquet Lake) where they do not live. All right, if you think you know where peepers go, pick your absolute favorite, best-of-all-possible acres, and let's go. If you can show me four peepers on it—less than one hundredth—less than one lousy percent of all the ones that must be somewhere—I will be snowed.

Come on all you canny, old New England naturalists, all you sharp young students, all you nature lovers, hikers, and campers: put your minds to it. They are little, brown to pinkish, disk-toed froggies. They look like they ought to climb, but I never heard of anyone who found one very far up in a tree (maybe fifteen feet?). Get out there. Observe. Maybe my figures are off by a factor of a hundred or so. Refute me if you can. Even so, *where do all the peepers go?*

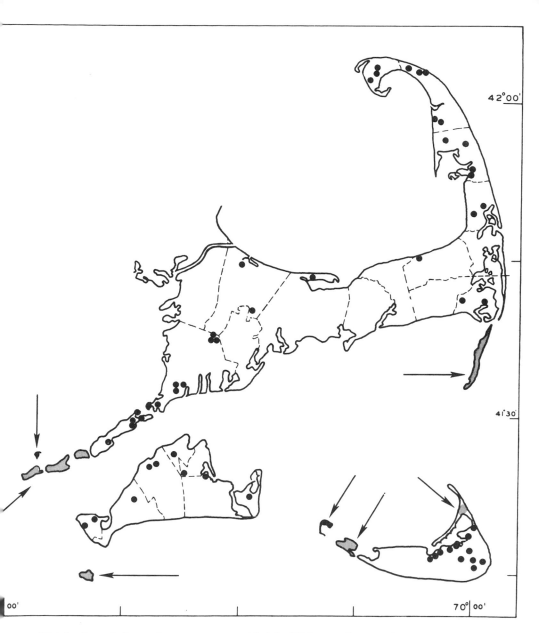

Distribution of the spring peeper or pinkletink (*Hyla crucifer crucifer*): dots indicate recorded specimens or breeding choruses. Arrows point to islands where the species apparently does not occur. Solid black islands (Penikese and Muskeget) apparently lack suitable habitat; shading indicates places with seemingly suitable habitat, but where search has failed to reveal specimens. I believe the species occurs *everywhere* else.

5

Turtles, Order Testudinata

> *The great feeling inspired by these creatures was that of age: dateless indefinite endurance. And in fact that any other creature can live and breathe as long as the tortoise of the Encantadas, I will not readily believe. Not to hint of their known capacity of sustaining life, while going without food for an entire year, consider that impregnable armor of their living mail. What other bodily being possesses such a citadel wherein to resist the assaults of Time?*
>
> HERMAN MELVILLE

TURTLES are the strangest living vertebrate animals. As often happens in evolution, they combine some extraordinarily primitive features of the "living fossil" with some specializations so outstanding that no other lineage has ever evolved them. Turtles are the sole survivors of the earliest reptilian subclass, called the *Anapsida* because they have no temporal arches on their skulls (your cheekbone is a classic temporal arch). The rest of the anapsids flourished 250 to 300 million years ago, and there is nothing like them left alive.

Not even turtles are much like the rest of the anapsids, and no fossil forms have ever been found that help much in tracing their lineage. Unique in all nature, the turtles have evolved a skeletal arrangement that results in their limb girdles lying *inside* of their ribs. To understand how strange this really is consider yourself or anyone else. Locate your shoulder blades on your back and note how they move when you move your arms. A turtle's shoulder blades move too, but you can't feel them do it. Imagine that, like the turtle, your shoulder blades were *underneath* your ribs. Of course, your pelvic girdle (hip bones) is separated entirely from your ribs, but not the turtle's. A turtle has ribs all the way to its tail, and its hip bones are *underneath* them, too.

This bizarre arrangement of the girdles and ribs makes for the widespread and obvious feature of turtles: the shell. Not all turtles have true shells and not all turtle shells are similar in structure, but at least all turtles do have some sort of relatively rigid protective covering on their backs, extending *over* their mobile limb girdles. The shell consists of dermal bones in the main, and the ribs (made of unrelated cartilaginous bone) do not play much of a role in it. Thus, a fossil anapsid with a shell of great expanded ribs (called *Eunotosaurus*) is often classified as some sort of link to the turtles but really is not related at all. All links between turtles and other animals remain missing.

We may speculate that once a couple of hundred million years ago, two perfectly normal, healthy anapsids mated in their normal, happy time. Then, in the early stages of her eggs' development, the mother anapsid was inundated with ghastly radiation from an incredible cosmic event. Sickened and dying from radioactive poisoning, she nevertheless laid her eggs and died. In due course the eggs hatched, but they were not normal, healthy little anapsid babies at all; they were hideous, deformed little mutants—short, squat, beaked, and toothless. In their misbegotten embryology, their ribs had arched upward and grown out over their limb girdles. And so these pathetic little monsters waddled away from their eggshells with their awkward, clumsy gait, to the mortification of their normal, healthy anapsid relatives. They wandered on and, in their time, mated and laid their own eggs. Their rheumy eyes blinked sadly at the passing of every last one of their relatives. They never conquered the earth, but they never suffered extinction either. It would be hundreds of millions of years before they encountered the earth-conqueror who called them turtles, but perhaps they would still be around after his passing too.

As a history of the origin of turtles, all of that is as wildly unlikely as I can conjure, but it is fun to fill gaps in facts with implausible fictions. As for the future, perhaps my story is not so unlikely.

Experiments and actual field data have shown some turtles to be extraordinarily resistant to chemical pollutants, chemical mutagens, and even radiation poisoning. Here in New England, snapping turtles are so impervious to man-made horrors that they even survive, and attain great size, in the Charles River. But man has been death's knell to many other turtles, especially the larger tortoises of oceanic islands. Here in New England, habitat destruction, automobiles, pet-seeking children, and malicious adults have decimated the box turtles and wood turtles. Far from our shores the population explosion that has generated the vast, relentless world of human misery and starvation in the tropics has brought the mighty sea turtles to the brink of extinction.

Turtles have another peculiar feature much noted by the ancients, but rarely thought of, even by biologists, today. That is, their elbows bend the *wrong* way. The next time you see a turtle, look at its arm, or front leg. Then try bending your arm that way. The name tortoise is said to be derived from the word "tortue," which commemorates this fact: apparently making people's arms bend the way a turtle's do was once considered a useful substitute for today's lie detectors or plea bargaining.

There is much disagreement over how to classify turtles. To begin with, some people call their order Testudinata, as I have, and others Chelonia, which is confusing because *Chelonia*—when italicized— is the proper generic name of a group of sea turtles; our green turtle (of soup fame) is an example.

Once settled on the ordinal name, we may note that most of the world's turtles fall into two groups according to how they pull their heads into their shells. You may never have thought much about a turtle pulling in its head, but it certainly is a major issue to the turtle. A number of scientists, in fact and fiction, have been fascinated by the process. (You might read Kurt Vonnegut's *Cat's Cradle* for perspective.)

Some turtles pull their heads in sideways in an S-shaped pattern in the horizontal plane. This way the head ends up over by one front leg, and the neck makes a big U-turn over by the other one. I spent a lot of time looking at a Matamata (a peculiar South American side-neck) trying to decide if he was right- or left-necked. I mean, did he usually store his head over by his right foot or his left? He could apparently do either with equal ease, and could whip his neck from one position to the other so fast I worried that his tiny eyes might fly out. To do this, he has to have a modified vertebra at the U-turn like a ball bearing. Well, anyway, there aren't any native side-necked turtles in New England.

Most of our turtles pull their necks completely out of sight into their shells. They do this by bending their S shape in the *vertical* plane. A ball-and-socket joint between the first thoracic (rib-bearing) vertebra, anchored into the shell, and the last neck vertebra combines with another ball-and-socket where the neck makes its hairpin turn. (Hairpin because the turn is in the vertical, not horizontal, of course.) The head stays in the middle, between the front legs, but the neck has to fold up into the body. Since most turtles have pretty long necks (more than fifty percent of their body length!), this costs them a lot of space inside the shell. It must be hard for them both to take a deep breath and to pull their necks in on a full stomach. Some, like the box turtle, can pull in the head, neck, and four legs, and then, with hinges at the sides of the shell and one across the bottom, close up completely. Only a skinny box turtle can do it, though.

The sea turtles of the family Chelonidae fit with the other hidden-necked turtles, even if they cannot really pull their heads in. They still manage some back-and-forth movement of the head and neck, and their vertebrae are much like those of their freshwater and land-dwelling relatives.

The leatherback, the greatest reptile, is weird in so many ways that its neck comes as slight surprise. A leatherback can hardly move its head or neck at all—sideways or back-and-forth. To move its head, the leatherback merely sculls with its flippers: hard astern right, forward left, and its head turns right. So does the whole leatherback. This gets leatherbacks into a lot of trouble with lobster pots, about which I shall say more below.

If we classify turtles in two groups, the side-necks or Pleurodeira, and the hidden-necks or Cryptodeira, we really ought to leave out the leatherback. Dr. Archie Carr, in his *Handbook of Turtles*, did just that. He put the leatherback in its own suborder, called Athecae, which means "without shell."

Not only does the leatherback not fit either the side- or hidden-neck arrangement, it also does not have a shell like other turtles. All other turtles have their ribs, however short, fused to the big, broad dermal bones of the shell. The leatherback's ribs are quite free of the overlying shell, and the shell itself is made of thousands of tiny little bony ossicles fitted together like a mosaic. I think the leatherback deserves status separate from regular turtles.

Our Cape and Islands turtles come in five different families. The leatherback, of course, has the Dermochelidae all to itself (the Pacific leatherback may be different from the Atlantic, and thus be the only other member; someone should consider the question). The name literally translates as "skin turtle family." The other sea turtles, as noted, belong to the Cheloniidae, which might as well be translated as "turtle family"—it means no more. The basking, freshwater turtles, spotted, wood, and box turtles, and the saltwater diamondback terrapin all belong to the Emydidae. Since *emys*, like *chelos* or *chelys*, just means turtle, their family name is equally unexciting.

The snapping turtle and its Dixie relative, the alligator snapper, are the sole representatives of their own family, the Chelydridae. Those turtle-namers were an imaginative bunch!

Last of all, the inconspicuous little musk turtle belongs to a group with a dandy name: Kinosternidae. *Kinos* refers to movement, as in kinetic energy or kinetic joints, the *stern* part refers to the breast bones, or sternum. This family is named, then, for the hinged or kinetic plastron, or bottom shell (breast bones). You might have thought the name more appropriate for a box turtle, but—too bad— it's an emydid. The poor musk turtle has a tiny little bottom shell, which, though soft and flexible, cannot really hinge or move voluntarily. It got into the kinosternid family because its very close relative, the mud turtle of points south, does have a big, hinged plastron. Our musk turtle, in fact, is probably not honestly even different at the generic level from the mud turtle, because in the southeast there are lots of varieties of mud and musk turtles, some of which quite effectively bridge the apparent anatomical gap: small, partly hinged bottom shells.

There is one more truly unique feature of turtles—a combination of behavior and physiology. Although older than any other ordinal group of birds, mammals, reptiles, or amphibians, the turtles have outclassed them all in handling the problem of cold weather. Other reptiles and amphibians must hibernate during cold weather; they go down below the frost line and remain in a dormant state of semi-animation. Most turtles, some mammals, and at least one bird species do that too. But some birds migrate away from cold weather. So do some turtles—the only migratory reptiles alive today. Most mammals and some birds ignore the winter, and just try to get along as best they can: so do some turtles. And last of all, most mammals, most birds, and even some snakes (pythons) generate and conserve body heat. Thus warm blooded, they stave off the chill: so, by damn, does the leatherback.

Turtles are the only vertebrates I know of above fishes that have evolved so many ways to get around cold weather.

Turtles, Order Testudinata

Snapping Turtle

"Yes, the Chelydra serpentina. A ferocious foe. Where did you meet it?"
"Meet it?"
"Encounter it."
"At a literary cocktail party by a lake."

* * *

"I'm asking about life. What is life?"
"I guess what comes before death. Please put its heart in a small amount of salted water and be kind enough to send us a note reporting how long the heart beats. Our records indicate ten hours."
"Then it isn't dead."
There was a pause. "In our sense."
"What is our sense. . . . Is it alive or is it dead? That's all I want to know, please."

* * *

"I've caught two turtles. What would you like to do with them?"
"Kill them. Make soup."
"You're sure?"
"The first of anything is hard. . . ."

* * *

I bumped my head against the pilings of the West Chop pier, threw my arms around a post, and remembered all three of us, and the conversation that took place four days after the turtle died when I said to Hammett, "You understood each other. He was a survivor and so are you. But what about me? . . ."
"I don't know. . . ."
Holding to the piling, I was having a conversation with a man who had been dead five years about a turtle who had been dead twenty-six.
LILLIAN HELLMAN, *Pentimento*

I know of no creature that clings to life with greater tenacity than the snapping turtle. For no other species is the question "What is *life?*" more cogent. There are two sorts of answers: theological, as Miss Hellman's man at the zoo (quoted above) suggested, and biological. Theology is the business of providing relatively simple, passably plausible, but incorrect answers to questions that have very complex, almost incomprehensible answers. Getting the complex answers is the business of a small group of largely underpaid, overworked persons called scientists.

Snapping turtle (*Chelydra serpentina*), young male, about six inches carapace length: Nantucket. This species attains weights of over sixty pounds in the wild and more than eighty pounds in captivity.

Which sort of answer you want is purely a matter of personal taste. Over the centuries, the overwhelming majority of people have been delighted to accept the theological answers. So delighted, in fact, that they are more than willing to battle each other to wholesale death over which theological answer is righter or rightest. Most people *love* theological answers and *despise* scientific ones.

It is necessary to point out that the biological answer does exist— in excruciating detail. Scientists really are getting at what life is; they

are finding out. They know so well that Drs. Kornberg and Goulian, years ago, were able to make a perfectly alive, functioning, reproducing virus *de novo* from chemicals off the shelf. One hears little about this today because all the fellows who prefer theology simply agreed to redefine "life" with the viruses defined out. One of the most vocal of these fellows is Dr. Barry Commoner, of ecological fame. About one half of the things Dr. Commoner says are true and need to be said. His fellow scientists, like me, wonder if the other half—all the egregiously wrong things he says—make listening to him worth it. He certainly is wrong about viruses; they are alive.

The difference between making the virus *de novo* from chemicals off the shelf and making a kangaroo is, to me, a difference merely of *degree*, not kind. One needs no different or new theories or procedures to make the kangaroo; all one needs is about twenty billion times as much time and money. It's sort of like saying, "I don't believe Hiroshima proves that atomic bombs are bad for people. That was just one incident. You can't generalize from the first few primitive experiments. Now, you do me twenty billion (would you settle for a thousand?) Hiroshimas and I'll really be impressed. Then I will put you and your atomic bomb in my new textbook."

A virus is just the simplest of all living things. A kangaroo is basically different from a virus in that it is staggeringly more complicated. All right, there is part of the answer: *life* can be thought of in degrees. Complexity equals being more alive. Viruses are hardly alive at all, but you and I and the kangaroo seem very much alive.

Life is not a thing; it is a process. It is a process made up of a vast number of interconnected subprocesses, each of which can be separated out, studied, repeated experimentally, and if you are good enough, set up artificially so that, when combined in a manner just like the original, they work. That is exactly what Kornberg and Goulian did.

Life is a matter of physical chemistry. The chemistry is atoms and molecules. The atoms are the same old ordinary, mundane ones we are totally accustomed to hearing about: mostly hydrogen, a lot of carbon, some oxygen and nitrogen, and a scattering of others like sodium, potassium, phosphorous, and chlorine. These atoms bond to make life's molecules just exactly the way they do to make table salt, water, polyethylene, or gasoline. The difference between life's molecules and water and gasoline is that *millions* of atoms are involved in each molecule basic to life's processes, while only three or twenty-six are needed to make water or gasoline, respectively.

The physics of life's processes is the actual shape—curves, bends, distances—of the critical portions of the giant molecules. Their shapes will determine the literal mechanics of their function. Scientists could make nucleic acids—the most basic of life's molecules—years ago: they had the chemistry all right. But those nucleic acids did not work, at least not well enough to give rise to a complete series of subprocesses resulting in an overall life process. That was the genius (and incredible, time-consuming drudgery) of Kornberg and Goulian. They took apart an actual virus and learned its actual structure; then they made a precise mimic of it which worked.

All right, now back to Miss Hellman's turtle, so alive—in a sort of implacable, primitive sense—that enough of his subprocesses did keep going well enough to make a recognizable, overall life process long after he was essentially decapitated and all hope of continuing life was gone. That is the real question, after all: how does a decapitated turtle walk down the stairs and out across the garden?

First, the common statement, "Death was instantaneous," is never true. What is meant by it is this: loss of consciousness, including all caring, feelings of desire, and knowledge of or ability to choose between alternatives, disappeared in a very short time (fraction of a second, perhaps) as part of an overall breakdown of life processes that eventually lead to the total cessation of life throughout the organism. No one—no thing—dies totally, instantly. There is always a grey period during which the subprocesses are slowing down and stopping, before the whole process stops for good. We are all aware of this. We all know the grizzly stories of the decapitated victim carrying

Snapping turtle (*Chelydra serpentina*), adult female, about ten inches shell length: Chappaquiddick. Note the *pointed* nape tubercules; they are not supposed to be that way.

on as though alive for seconds or even minutes after the head is in the basket. We all know that an apparently drowned, dead person may still have a heartbeat, or still be within the grey zone where stimulation of a heartbeat is possible. Many times such people recover fully and go right on living just as before, despite the fact that a medical doctor would have considered them dead.

If the theological answer were right, if life were a thing instead of a process of physical chemistry, there would be no rational way to account for these empirical observations.

But, you say, the real point is that there is some sort of incredible difference between a man, who dies in seconds or minutes, and the turtle, taking hours or days. There is indeed, and the difference results from two readily measurable characteristics of all living things: metabolic rate and nucleic acid complexity.

The first is the simpler. Metabolic rate is the rate at which the whole organism consumes oxygen, and therefore nutrients. Of course, tissues in different parts of the organism have very different rates of consumption. Brain tissue is made of very demanding cells; bone cells like osteoblasts can get along quite a while on very little. So, the different parts—tissues and organs—of an individual die at different rates. But we can measure the total metabolic rate of the whole organism and that will serve our purpose very well. If a human continues to show some life signs in some tissues and organs up to, let's say, six minutes after decapitation, and a human has a metabolic rate, let's say, one hundred times higher than a snapping turtle, where are we? By simple arithmetic we can expect the turtle to still have some tissues or organs that show some life signs after about ten hours—just like Miss Hellman's man at the zoo said. There is no more mysticism to that than there is to saying a car that gets twenty miles to a gallon will go twice as far, at a given speed, as a car that gets ten.

In my travels I often encounter reptiles, like turtles and snakes, mortally injured on the highway. If I want color photographs, for example, of one picked up at night, and I want the photos to be of a live specimen, I pack it into the iced-down beer cooler. That plummets its metabolic rate, and the animal's life process is spectacularly extended. Sometimes, of course, by slowing the metabolic rate, and thus slowing total death, I give certain healing processes time to work. In a few cases I have had a reptile no one could possibly believe would live recover completely.

The second aspect, nucleic acid complexity, is more difficult. Basically the nucleic acids are the huge molecules that run and regulate all the little subprocesses of life. You and I and turtles use a nucleic acid called DNA (deoxyribose nucleic acid). Our chromosomes are made of it, and every cell of our bodies has the same sorts of chromosomes—barring some accident occurring during our lifetimes. Most of us have forty-six chromosomes per cell. I don't know how many a snapping turtle has, but certainly a lot less. We can measure the chromosomes, count them, and calculate how much DNA we actually have. It is really how much *per cell* that matters.

If you have a great deal of DNA, as we do, you pay the price: your subprocesses, controlled by the DNA, are going to be more complicated. If more complicated, disruption is more devastating and much easier to accomplish. Animals with complex nucleic acid systems die more rapidly than those with simpler systems; nothing mystical about that either.

The most complex nucleic acid systems and highest metabolic rates occur together in some sorts of mammals and birds. Hummingbirds, warblers, mice, and artiodactyls (even-toed ungulates like cows, pigs, sheep, and goats) are fine examples. Humans are slightly less complex and often much lower in metabolic rate. We die more slowly than mice and cows.

So, Miss Hellman, your decapitated turtle, which walked down the stairs to the garden, was still alive in our sense. He was in that grey zone between receipt of a mortal injury and total cessation of the life process. Next time, try dropping your snapper in boiling water. Heat denatures those huge molecules, nucleic acids, and the life process ceases relatively quickly. Also, the turtle will be much easier to skin, often the most laborious part of preparing snapper soup. Good eating to you. I have never objected to anyone killing snapping turtles for food, but don't kill them simply because you imagine them to be dangerous predators.

Snappers are a persecuted and maligned species in this area. They are a genuinely important part of our natural ecosystem; their role in the maintenance of a healthy waterfowl population is often misunderstood. Snappers become active waterfowl predators between mid-April and May. Healthy, well-adapted, *native* duck species—like woodies and black ducks—should have their broods well along by this time of year. The young are canny, fast swimmers, and almost impossible for a snapper to catch. In other words, sickly or ill-adapted mothers—raising their broods too late—lose their young, as they deserve to. Sickly, ill-adapted young birds in otherwise healthy broods similarly become turtle food, as they deserve to. Turtle predation is thus beneficial to our native species. Non-native species, like feral mute swans, feral geese (we have no native breeding geese in this area), and mallards with their white, "pekin," farmyard counterparts, are the species most heavily preyed upon by snappers. While many people enjoy having these interlopers breeding in Massachusetts, we must acknowledge their adverse role in competing with the native species. Furthermore, their residence here in the summer depletes food stocks much needed by the migrant species who will come in from the north in the autumn. Included here are the genuinely wild Canada geese, who nest where they are supposed to, in Canada.

Killing snapping turtles because they eat ducks and geese is therefore ill-informed and detrimental. Such killing can only be justified by the belief that Europeans arrived here only just in time to save our waterfowl from extinction at the jaws of their native predators. This utterly fallacious reasoning, current at the turn of the century, brought on the wholesale slaughter of our hawks, owls, coyotes, cougars, and other native predators. Why does it persist with respect to snapping turtles when we are so comparatively enlightened about the other species?

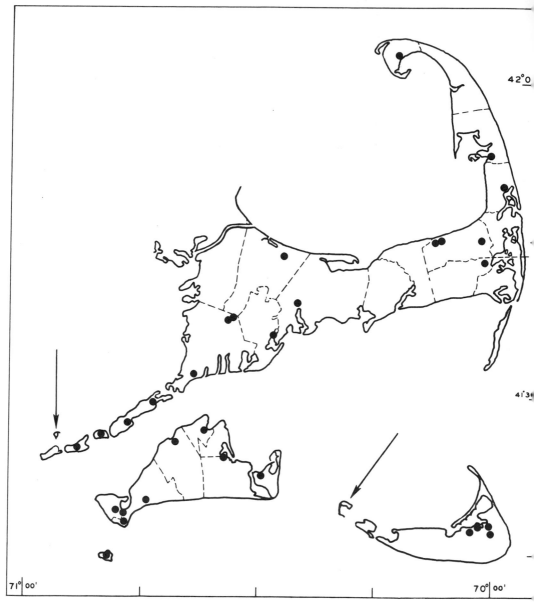

42°0̲

41°3̲

71° 00'

70° 00'

Records for the snapping turtle (*Chelydra serpentina*) indicated by dots. I believe this species occurs virtually everywhere. Arrows indicate Penikese and Muskeget, where suitable habitat is in short supply. The lack of records for Monomoy, Cuttyhunk, and Tuckernuck testifies to shoddy work, lassitude, and apathy.

Snappers are the natural prey of skunks and raccoons, who eat their eggs, and bass, who eat the young.

In his *Field Guide*, Dr. Conant recognizes two subspecies: *Chely-*

dra serpentina serpentina all over most of the eastern and central portions of the country, and *C. s. osceola* on the Florida peninsula. The distinguishing features are the location of the bumps within the carapace scutes relative to the borders, and pointed neck tubercles. Dr. Peter Pritchard, Florida Audubon Society, points out that *osceola* also has more flared ribs. Drs. Ernst and Barbour, in their 1973 *Turtles of the United States*, accord *osceola* rank as full and distinct species. There is no evidence to support that. The best advice I can obtain keeps the two as geographic races, with ours in New England being *Chelydra serpentina serpentina*.

Robert Taylor (no relation to Richard) took a fine series of Kodachromes of a mating pair of snappers in Eastham in May 1965. May seems to be the usual month for mating. I have a dozen or so egg-laying records for eastern Massachusetts. Only two—one each from Naushon and Nantucket—are within the Cape and Islands region. Both are in the first week of June. My outside dates go from late May to late June. The Naushon female laid eighteen eggs; I did not count the Nantucket clutch. My other data vary from twelve to twenty-eight, with an average of twenty-four eggs laid.

Many people, especially on Martha's Vineyard, call snappers loggerheads. This is a most unfortunate misnomer because there is a real loggerhead: the sea turtle, *Caretta caretta*. It belongs to a totally separate family.

I must clear up a couple of other occasional misconceptions about snappers. Like all other turtles, they bury their eggs and do not sit on them—or even guard their nests. The hatchlings do not find their way to water by chance. On the contrary, they hatch with a strong positive *geotropism*: a sense of gravity. They proceed downhill as fast as their little legs can waddle them. Their positive geotropy is a genetically inherited characteristic, solidly codified in that very real, non-mystical DNA.

Snappers weighing in excess of eighty pounds have been recorded, but the Plymouth County specimen photographed by Theodore Steinway is the largest wild-caught specimen known to me. Any specimen much over thirty pounds is unusual today.

While most snappers are dark and somber, some (especially on Martha's Vineyard) are a pale *cafe-au-lait*—almost platinum blonde.

Snappers are most common in fresh and brackish ponds, creeks, and marshes. They often do go into genuine sea water, however, and I would not be surprised—and certainly grateful—to see a specimen from the most remote and unlikely locality.

Musk Turtle

I don't know anything about musk turtles, except that they *are* there.

Every once in a great while I stub my toe on one while wading around in some pond or marsh; I pick it up; I say (usually to myself), "yes, it *is* a musk turtle." I measure it, record its sex, and plop it back in the marsh. I could never bring myself to pickle a musk turtle, so photographs will have to do.

At first glance a musk turtle looks like an over-sized ripe olive pit, such as you often find in ashtrays after cocktail parties. They have that matted, fuzzy look because a nondescript brownish alga grows on them. Dr. Roger Conant has given *Sternothaerus odoratus*, our musk turtle, the official common name of stinkpot. (Official common names aren't much use; you tell someone in Mississippi that you just caught a rough earth snake and he will think you are nuts.)

Anyway, I am so utterly ignorant of my neighbor the musk turtle that I cannot even smell him. To me, he smells just like the rest of the pond bottom of which he is such an integral part.

Musk turtles, like 'possums, open their mouths as soon as you pick them up. Their jaws are sharp and powerful, so a musk turtle bite (it is said by the experts) can be painful and even bloody. I regard being bitten by a musk turtle as a little like drowning in a tea cup, or going to the moon: possible, but easily avoided.

Musk turtles have fairly bold, light lines (often bright yellow) along the sides of their heads: two on each side. One stripe runs just above the eye and may serve to make its position less obvious; the second runs along the mandible and might serve to distract a potential predator from the first. Some predators, like egrets and herons, are famous eye-stabbers. Our native egrets and herons could certainly swallow young musk turtles, and these are the most boldly marked. Musk turtles rarely grow to more than four inches in total shell length.

I had a pet musk turtle in Pennsylvania when I was a kid. I learned a few things about it, aside from the fact that it would eat salamanders, fish, dead birds, mice, and so on. Unable to float (as most pond turtles can) and just barely able to swim, my pet musk turtle nearly drowned of exhaustion swimming again and again to the surface of a full aquarium to gasp for air. After putting it in a deep ten-gallon tank, I had gone off and left my new pet for several hours. When I came back, it had apparently drowned. It was utterly limp and devoid of any life-response. I hung it up by the hind feet.

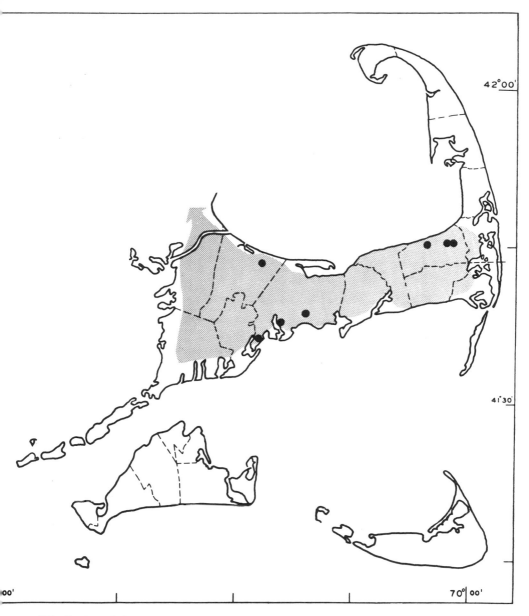

Distribution of the musk turtle (*Sternothaerus odoratus*). Dots indicate localities at which specimens—often several—have been examined. A sort of smallest tenable range is shaded, based to some extent on habitat (the species seems very salt tolerant), but also on the fact that I have waded around in an awful lot of ponds and marshes, notably at Woods Hole, Chatham, and Provincetown, and not come up with a specimen.

Its head and neck, half its length, dangled straight down and water dribbled out of its lungs. I surely hoped the local ASPCA representative wouldn't drop in to look over my stock.

135

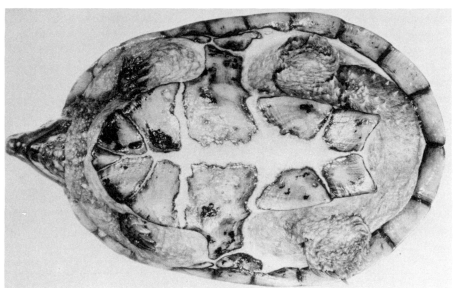

Musk turtle (*Sternotherus odoratus*), adult female, about three-and-a-half inches carapace length: Brewster, Cape Cod.

After a couple of hours, the turtle came around, and seemed no worse for wear. I was afraid that long oxygen deprivation had wrecked its brain, but I was glad to note that it fully recovered all its canny acumen and scintillating wit.

Dr. Babcock (1919) quotes Raymond Ditmars, the great herpetologist late of the New York Zoological Society, extolling the superb swimming abilities of musk turtles. Ditmars found they could swim better than pond turtles and could live weeks in deep water. Perhaps mine was just inferior.

I can't remember how many years I had that musk turtle. I *did* decide to keep it in a shallow tank, with the water just deep enough to cover its shell. When I went off to University I took it back to exactly where I had caught it, and plopped it back in the marsh.

I have the vague notion that the natural range of our musk turtle extends only onto basal, upper Cape Cod. I do not believe it occurs naturally on any of the Islands, or even north of old Jeremiah's Gutter. Betty Andersen, however, found a three-inch female musk turtle in the bathtub at the day camp at Wellfleet Bay Wildlife Sanctuary. We asked all around, but never found out who put it in the bathtub. For all I know, it came from Pennsylvania.

Some authorities claim that musk turtles do not bask in the sun, but I have watched them doing it; I know musk turtles bask.

I have scant reproductive data on our musk turtles. A Barnstable female laid four hard, glossy, thick-shelled eggs that, when I saw them at the end of July, measured 25 to 27 mm. in length, by 13 to 15 mm. in diameter.

The Basking Turtles, Genera *Malaclemys* and *Chrysemys*

> *One of our universities recently made a survey of the reading habits of the American public; it decided that forty-eight percent of all Americans read, during a year, no book at all. I picture to myself that reader—non-reader, rather; one man out of every two—and I reflect with shame: "Our poems are too hard for him." But so, too, are* Treasure Island, Peter Rabbit, *pornographic novels—any book whatsoever.*
>
> RANDALL JARRELL

After more than a third of a century of living on this planet, most of it spent speaking English, I have decided that the time has come: I have no alternative but to invent a new word. My qualifications for word invention are superb, and, to further authorize my status, my years of exposure to other herpetologists have finally brought necessity to a festering head.

The word I have to, and do hereby, invent is *ignorence*. Ignorence is not the same thing as *ignorance*. Ignorance is the condition of lacking knowledge; we may pity the ignorant. Ignorence, to the contrary, is to ignore what one knows damn well is obviously true and factual. One may not pity the ignorent. They deserve some other, less compassionate, fate.

Many—perhaps not most—but many, and some of the most influential, herpetologists are among the most *ignorent* people on earth. In several cases, I would be surprised if they would admit the earth is round. Of course, in all fairness, they are nothing compared to ornithologists. There are superb anatomical works on various bird groups that are utterly ignored by ornithologists, who, out of perverted preference, go right on using defunct, untenable, thoroughly disproven, and archaic taxonomic arrangements for birds today.

The most painful case I know of (relax, poor herpetologists) is the so-called giant panda. D. Dwight Davis (1964) published a 339-page monograph just before he died, detailing the anatomy of the black and white bear in crystal clarity. He proved beyond any hope of rational refutation that: (a) the giant panda is *not* related to the true, or "lesser," panda; (b) the giant panda is *not* a member of the raccoon family; and (c) the giant panda is a bear—just like any four-year-old could plainly see. So, what did such influential "authorities" as Morris and Morris (1965) and R. F. Ewer (1973) do? Nothing. They published the black and white bear right back into the raccoon family beside its friend, the "lesser" panda.

The Provincelands: a herpetologist's view of good turtle habitat.

Well, back to pond turtles: Dr. Sam McDowell worked over the genera of pond turtles and their close relatives and published his results in the Proceedings of the Zoological Society of London (1964), no obscure publication. Dr. McDowell's credentials are above reproach: he has all the requisite degrees and titles. This was no case of a graduate student printing his opinions in *Home Pets Magazine*. Still, in the four 1971 issues of *Copeia*, the proudest journal of herpetology, I found a dozen references to the defunct genus *"Pseudemys"* and (even worse) to the dubious genus *"Graptemys"* (a synonym of *Malaclemys*, the diamondback terrapin's genus).

Now, just what is going on? Have all these authors simply not checked the literature? That would be excusable: no one could possibly check it all. References are bound to escape any of us. But no; when questioned, these fellows mostly admit they knew about McDowell's work. They just ignore it. That is very interesting. They did not attempt to refute it, consider. That would be a legitimate, scientific response. Not these fellows: *they just ignore it*.

Because they did so, and continued using the defunct names, they made the question *appear* controversial. Actually, there has been very little controversy. True, some fellows have found blood chemical differences between saltwater diamondbacks and freshwater map turtles and sawbacks, but what did they expect? Blood chemical dis-

139

tinctions are not valid generic characteristics in any case; at best, they clue impotrant physiological differences (salt *versus* fresh?), and can, when similar, be used as an indication of close relationship. They are far more plastic than anatomical characteristics, and in no way superior as indicators of relationship.

Genera must be founded on major features of comparative anatomy. A genus is a group of closely related species *immediately and definitively distinct* from any other such group. Ideally, if education prevailed, any educated biologist should be able to pick up just about any species of animal (or plant, for that matter) and tell you what genus it belongs to. Genera are the basic, obvious, different sorts of living things. Species can be devilishly difficult to identify, but not genera.

Genera like *"Pseudemys"* and *"Graptemys"* are simply invalid, defunct, and untenable. People who use them should be corrected— by you or me if in speech, by their editors if in print. Anyone wishing to use them should be required to publish a refutation of McDowell's work, or a compendium of new evidence. The excuse that these names are controversial is just not good enough. They are not: they are sunk.

The three species I treat here are—or would be were they common enough—our most conspicuous turtles, because they love to bask in the sun. Red-bellies and paints (sun turtles) haul out on logs, and even rocks (although rock is severely abrasive to their shells), and enjoy in-sun temperatures up to 100°F. Diamondbacks less commonly bask in such open sites, preferring the peaty edges of little creeks winding through the *Spartina* marshes. All are beautiful, desirable members of our fauna.

DIAMONDBACK TERRAPIN

The diamondback, *Malaclemys terrapin*, delight of epicures and staple of the marsh hunter, reaches the northern limit of its natural range in the grassy reaches of Wellfleet Bay, Cape Cod. When I published my original paper on our native diamondbacks, in June 1969, it was already too late to prevent one of the great biological travesties of our region. One James G. Hoff, a member of the biological faculty at Southeastern Massachusetts University, North Dartmouth, proudly reported in 1972 that he had introduced 100 diamondbacks from southern New Jersey into the Slocum River estuary of Buzzards Bay, back in 1968.

While these exotic individuals will probably not adversely affect the genetics of the native Cape populations, at least in the near

Diamondback terrapin (*Malaclemys t. terrapin*), adult female, about eight inches carapace length: Barnstable, Cape Cod.

future, the result for Buzzards Bay could be most deleterious. If the southern individuals mated during the 1968 summer (they were introduced in April) with native turtles, or did so during subsequent years (at least some had survived until 1971), maladapted offspring would probably result; natural patterns of genetic variation would be seriously disturbed.

Why on earth did Hoff do it? Hoff's thesis is that his introduction could in no way "endanger a 'native' population of terrapins," because diamondbacks were *not native* in Massachusetts to begin with. He looked over the early literature of the nineteenth century and found no records of the species. Of course, that proves nothing. The huge, gaudy, sun-basking, red-bellied turtle lives in the ponds of the town of Plymouth. Plymouth was settled in 1620, but the red-bellied turtle was not reported in scientific literature for nearly 300 years. The turtle is surely native: its remains are common in pre-European midden remains, as reported by Dr. Joseph Waters (see, for example, Ritchie, 1969). Muhlenberg's bog turtle was not officially recorded in Massachusetts until the last decade; it is a small and perhaps inconspicuous form, but it has been extremely popular in the pet trade. It managed to escape our notice for a similar 300 years. Or how about the great leatherback? There were, of course, a few records for the species from our waters, but no one ever dreamed, apparently, that they were perfectly native, migratory, *warm-blooded* animals until just a few years ago. This book is largely a chronicle of how little was known, and how much remains unknown, about our native species of reptiles and amphibians. One thing I will guarantee, however: diamondback terrapins are native to Massachusetts.

Next, Hoff figures the supposedly newly arrived Massachusetts terrapins were extirpated by the resturant trade. Well, our native populations *were* severely decimated. Colonel E. S. Clark, who grew up on the Cape, recalls that when he was a boy, about 1910, literally thousands of terrapins were barreled and shipped out of Pleasant Bay to Boston and New York. But when the prey gets rare enough, the predator can no longer make a living hunting it. So, rarer, the diamondback survived. Since I wrote in 1969, diamondbacks have clearly become more abundant in areas where they have always been known, like Barnstable Harbor, and are even becoming conspicuous in Pleasant Bay again, where I could then find none at all. Diamondbacks are coming back, slowly, in the normal manner of turtles—but surely, and of their own accord.

Finally, founded on the firm balloon juice of unnatural occurrence to begin with, and extinction after that, Hoff reasons that reintro-

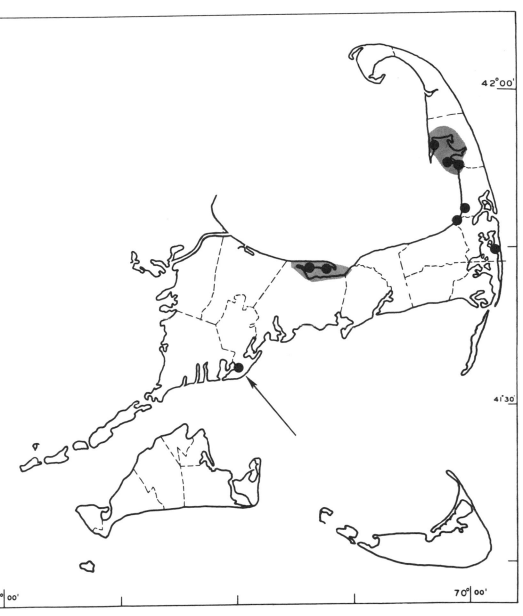

Locality records for the diamondback terrapin (*Malaclemys t. terrapin*). Dots represent one to three specimens. Within the shaded areas of Barnstable Harbor and Wellfleet Bay the species is more common; here a dot may represent six or more individuals. An arrow indicates the lone Mashpee specimen: my only first-hand record for the south shore, despite all the assurances I have heard that the species is widespread there.

143

ducing the species from New Jersey adds "a valuable asset to the estuarine fauna of Massachusetts." In other words, might Hoff be predicted to propose reintroduction of the European starling or the Japanese beetle, should these interlopers be wiped out here?

Our native diamondbacks apparently lay two clutches of eggs—probably less than ten per clutch—each year. At least, there are two hatchings. Baby turtles, little bigger than a quarter, can be found hustling down the dunes toward the saltmarshes in July, presumably from May layings, and again in October. The October hatchlings must come from eggs laid in July or August. There is some evidence suggesting the late hatching may, during cool years, overwinter in the nest; hoards of the little turtles would then erupt the following April or May.

Terrapins grow rapidly during their first few years and reach maturity at five or six. Females grow much larger than males and are apt to be paler and more richly patterned: ash greys and buff tones, marked with dark grey or brown. Males, and some females, turn very dark with age and lose most of their pattern; the Mashpee specimen, photographed by James E. Cardoza of the Commonwealth's Division of Fisheries and Game, is typical of this condition. In carapace length, males approach six inches and females nine. In the market trade, which reached its apex before World War II, the standard system of diamondback measurement was along the *plastron*, the shorter bottom shell. Nevertheless, Dr. Babcock quotes references to specimens up to nine inches in plastron length. Finding such a brute today would be difficult indeed.

This is our only reptilian species for which Cape Cod is the absolute northern limit of the range. There is an old Nantucket literature record, noted by J. A. Allen (*Proceedings of the Boston Society of Natural History*, volume 13, page 260). J. Clinton Andrews, who has worked Nantucket's marshes and bays through most of this century, is sure the species does not occur there and never heard from his predecessors that it ever did. I suspect the Nantucket specimen was transported to the island as a food item, perhaps on its way from Cape Cod to New York.

During the early decades of this century, the diamondback was so esteemed as food that no champagne dinner was complete without it. Truly a gourmet's delight, these succulent creatures commanded a wholesale price of up to a dollar apiece and could cost ten times that much when actually served. Such an enthusiastic reception was not without its disadvantages, and decades ago laws were enacted to save the diamondback from extinction. Today the species occurs in good numbers from Long Island Sound southward.

Although the records are not so complete, it does appear that diamondbacks are rather continuously distributed along the coast as far as the northern shores of Buzzards Bay. Then, for some reason, things seem to get tough, and the species reaches its bitter end on Cape Cod. What happens at the end of a species' range? Do individuals just get more scarce until they peter out completely? What factors actually limit the diamondback? Does the climate become too severe? Does its food supply fail? Is the habitat suddenly different? All these are questions of special interest to environmental biologists and ecologists. These are questions of broader scope than just the diamondback terrapin, or some other single species; man, too, reaches limits beyond which he does not or can not go. The answers to the question why are rarely simple.

The delicious diamondback is a creature of quiet salt water. Shallow bays, salt marshes, and estuaries are its favored habitats; it rarely takes on the surf and swells of the ocean. The jaws are heavily

Barnstable, Cape Cod: here the great *Spartina* marshes provide a habitat for the diamondback terrapin.

armored and broadly expanded into a vice well-suited to crushing the shells of mollusks—clams, mussels, snails, etc.—that these turtles eat. The hind feet are huge, with a vast webbing that must come in very handy to these highly aquatic creatures. Rather inexplicably, there are a series of bumps, or knobs, down the middle of the carapace (back shell): one on every large plate.

Although my distribution map for this species is far more reasonably complete than it was in 1969, there are still puzzling—and frustrating—blank spots. Several people have reported diamondbacks in the Falmouth marshes. One even made the newspapers. The *Falmouth Enterprise* (2 July 1974, page six) reports a specimen taken to the aquarium in Woods Hole. Well, I don't doubt it, really, but no photograph exists, and the turtle was, quite properly, released. Everyone who saw it may be quite certain it was a diamondback, but all I can deliver is the Scotch verdict: not proven. I have the same problem with reports from Sandwich and Bourne below the Canal: plenty of people cheerily assuring me the turtles are there, but nothing I can come to grips with to prove it. A lot of people are sure there are monsters in Loch Ness, too; there probably *are*, but I am not going to publish on them.

Perhaps remarkably, the species is fairly common in Wellfleet Bay —the northernmost known extent of its range.

There are records for the coast of Cape Cod Bay between Barnstable and Wellfleet, but they are very few. Generally, this stretch of coast is not particularly habitable for the species. Salt marsh exists in two small patches between Dennis and Brewster, and in three patches in Orleans and Eastham. The largest are the Rock Harbor Marsh area and Great Salt Marsh at Eastham.

Why has the diamondback never colonized the Islands? I am rather certain that they never have, for I have hunted them long and hard there. People who have spent their lives peering into the waters around the Elizabeth Islands, the Vineyard, and Nantucket —people who know the local turtles and describe them accurately— seem never to have seen or heard of the diamondback terrapin.

Just what factors are limiting for the diamondback? Climate, at least in a general sense, cannot be it: terrapins are as common at Wellfleet as they are in Buzzards Bay. The range of the species stops with a large population; they do not gradually peter out. Food —clams, mussels, and snails—hardly limits the species: they are abundant far to the north and all around the Cape. Good habitats, in many areas, seem to go begging: they apparently support no terrapins.

What are the answers? Here is a large, obvious species with a very specialized diet and very restricted habitat, yet neither diet nor habitat seem to limit its range. Perhaps it is not quite large or obvious enough, and has been long overlooked in places where it does live. Perhaps this summer will bring new information, and a glimmering of the answers.

For the sake of taxonomic completeness, I point out that there are several different subspecies of terrapins to the south of us. Ours is the first-named, the *nominate* form: *Malaclemys terrapin terrapin.*

PAINTED TURTLE

It was one of those fabulously clear, cold, mid-January days in 1964 when a Massachusetts painted turtle—*Chrysemys picta*—first intruded into my life. I was then a teaching assistant in Professor George Clarke's ecology course at Harvard, and the class was on a midwinter field trip to Beaver Pond in Lincoln. I was dutifully sweeping the snow off the ice with a big pushbroom; the students were all gathered around, rigging plankton nets and bottom samplers for our assay of the pond's life. Then, just below the crystal-clear ice, a painted turtle swam by.

Now, I have been a herpetologist all my life, and painted turtles are about the most abundant, obvious sort of reptile occurring in the northeastern United States. I thought I knew all about painted turtles. Painted turtles, I thought, like most other reptiles, hibernate in the winter. They don't hibernate by swimming nonchalantly around, either. Well, the secret is that where I grew up knowing painted turtles, in the South Jersey Pine Barrens, you couldn't go out and walk around on the ice very well. It wasn't strong enough most of the time. In Massachusetts, though, I found I could learn what turtles were doing in the winter. Most of our species do hibernate; some, the great sea turtles like the loggerhead, ridley, and leatherback, migrate south to escape winter. So far as I know, the painted turtle is the only one to be up and around all year round.

To understand how this works, one must look at the temperature regime of a typical kettle hole, the favorite habitat of the painted turtle. In winter, the air temperature usually averages under freezing; hence that good, solid ice. The water just below the ice, however, never gets below freezing, 32° F. The ground, below about eighteen to twenty-four inches, is not much affected by the changes in air temperature. It stays the same temperature all year round: here, about 45–48° F. For a few feet below the ice, ground temperature tends to warm the pond water up from 32° F.

147

Painted turtle (*Chrysemys p. picta*), adult female, about five inches carapace
length: Nantucket.

Water is very peculiar stuff. Unlike practically everything else, water gets less dense when it turns to a solid. Thus, ice is lighter than water, and it floats in water. This unique property of water is what makes life on earth possible. Strangely, fresh water reaches its maximum density—and thus weight—at between 39° and 40° F. (4° C.). This water, just below 40° F., settles to the bottom of all ponds. So, a pond's winter water-temperature profile is a sort of sandwich: cold water (32° F.) lies just under the ice; cool water (39° F.) settles in the deep holes; relatively warm water (up to 48° F.), heated constantly by the ambient ground temperature, lies between. Dr. Carl Ernst (1972) found that painted turtles become active just above 48° F. (8° C.). And there they are, swimming around all winter long.

I must point out that I was not the first person to observe midwinter activity in painted turtles. Dr. Roger Conant recorded the same phenomena many years ago; I just had not checked the literature. Perhaps, though, I have added a bit of explanation.

Our painted turtles are remarkable in ways other than midwinter activity. Their genetics are off-beat, and who their relatives are is unclear. The problem derives from the peculiar appearance of Nantucket painted turtles: they often have dark mottling or figures on their plastrons (bottom shells). So do midwestern painted turtles. Dr. Joseph Waters (1964) first noted this fact and presented an ingenious theory to explain it. Midwestern, or midland, painted turtles are well adapted to the cooler temperatures of the uplands west of here to the Great Lakes region. Eastern painted turtles are well adapted to the warm coastal plain of the Atlantic coast south of here. When the last great Ice Age was over and the glaciers began their retreat, midland turtles were able to invade and colonize the newly exposed land areas. As the climate warmed, eastern turtles moved northward. By the time a great influx of eastern genes from the south reached this area, sea levels had risen to the extent that Nantucket was an island, and thus midland influence remained strong there: painted turtles rarely cross salt water.

Well, that sounded good, but then along came the Poughs (1968). They examined painted turtles from all over eastern Massachusetts, and other places too. They considered all sorts of other characteristics that are different in midland and eastern forms—not just plastron markings. One obvious feature was the alignment of scutes on the shell. In painted turtles, the top shell has a row down the middle— vertebral scutes—and a set along each side—costals. There are little ones all around the edges too, called marginals. Eastern turtles have the forward edges of their second set of scutes—both costals and the vertebral—lined up. Midland specimens do not; the forward edges of the scutes are staggered and the costals are well behind the vertebral. The amount of alignment can be measured and statistical information generated.

Using such measurable characteristics, the Poughs showed that our painted turtles in eastern Massachusetts are a highly varied lot. They vary from locality to locality, but basically any population is just about as intermediate between midland and eastern types as any other.

That destroyed the clear simplicity of Dr. Waters' argument. However, it is still true that Island turtles have a far higher incidence of plastral markings. If this is not because they are more similar to midland turtles, then what is the explanation? After examining about four hundred Cape-Islands turtles, and lots from other places too, I began to generate some statistics of my own.

I found that about 20 percent of Island turtles had dark plastral figures of the Midland type. About 15 percent had pink middorsal stripes, like Gulf Coast specimens. About 10 percent had strange, dark plastral markings unlike those on any other painted turtles I could find. And last of all, 5 percent had bright red, irregular spotting on their plastrons—also unlike any others I have ever seen. Thus, a total of 50 percent of Island painted turtles have some sort of peculiar pattern.

Now, it is well known that inbreeding tends to exaggerate the frequency of unusual characteristics, and that small, isolated populations are an ideal stage for intensive inbreeding to take place. I suggest that this explains the peculiar aberrations in color pattern on the Islands: whatever genetic possibilities existed in the original colonizers have been intensified in frequency. Strange combinations, which natural selection would weed out in the more complex ecosystem of the mainland, tend to pop up. Evolution can proceed much more rapidly in a small, inbred population than in a large, well-dispersed one. Advantageous characteristics, suited especially to the precise features of an island's environment, are able to sweep the population rapidly.

All of this brings up a major ecological and conservation issue: do not transport live, wild animals and release them in new habitats. All wild species vary from one locale to another. The differences may be obvious, like the markings on painted turtles, or seemingly trivial changes in invisible body chemistry. However, the differences are real and to the animals, at least, important. You do not do an animal a

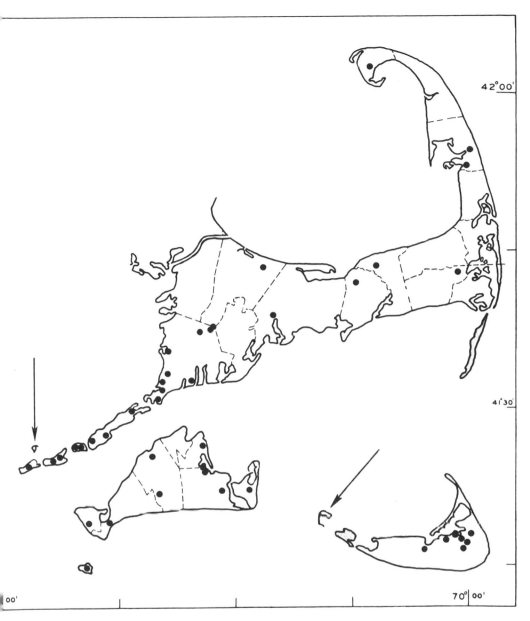

Distribution of the painted turtle (*Chrysemys picta*). Dots indicate where specimens (often 100 or more) have been examined. Arrows indicate Penikese and
Muskeget, where I do not believe the species occurs. Hatching (shading) indicates islands (Monomoy and Tuckernuck) where suitable habitat seems available,
but where the species has not been found. I assume painted turtles occur *everywhere* else.

favor by releasing it far from home. Probably the population into which it is released is done a real disservice. Release wild animals exactly where they came from, or give them to a museum or zoo. Or don't catch them in the first place.

Painted turtles play a major role in the balance of our freshwater ecology. Dr. James Oliver (1955) shows that adults eat about 65 percent pond weeds and other vegetable matter; they consume about 20 percent insects. In young turtles the percentage of insects is even higher, and they are a very important predator on mosquito larvae.

In a massively documented work on the painted turtle, H. M. Wilbur (1975) presented evidence that females (at least) remain actively reproducing and fertile for over thirty years. He figured a generation time of ten or twelve years (ours is about twenty). His evidence indicates that females lay *two* clutches of eggs each summer, but only about a week apart. My only clutch data are for a nest of six found (being laid) by Ray Dunfey on Naushon, 9 June 1972. These measured from 30 to 34 mm. in length (average 32), and from 17 to 20 mm. in width (average 18.5), when I measured them on 13 June. Hatchling paints are common enough from mid-July (my earliest date is actually 17 July) on, and there is no evidence of a double hatch as in the diamondback terrapin.

Painted turtles are confirmed sunbathers. As soon as the ice is off the ponds, every clear, sunny day will see dozens of them up on every log and stump above water. Often they bask in piles, and it is difficult to see how the bottom turtles derive much benefit. The reason for this basking is the reason painted turtles tend to dwindle and die, over months, in captivity: they need ultraviolet light. Ultraviolet light does not go through glass; the turtles must actually be out in the sun. Of course, they have to be able to get away from the sun, or they literally might cook on a hot day. Without ultraviolet, turtles cannot metabolize calcium. Young ones cannot form healthy shells and bones; these become soft or rubbery, and eventually the baby turtles die. Adults do not show the symptoms so obviously and may live for years. Their health degenerates too, however, and it is cruel to keep them without ultraviolet. This fact applies with equal force to the red-eared turtle (*Chrysemys scripta*) so often sold as a hatchling in the pet trade, and to most other pond turtles.

In addition to death in captivity, automobiles are a major source of death to our native turtles. Whenever a road is put through a wetland, or at the edge of a wetland and an upland, turtle slaughter results. Each spring, the female painted turtle leaves her watery home and seeks high ground on which to lay her half dozen or so eggs. A road bed is high and dry; often it is exactly between the mother turtle and where she has always laid her eggs. If not killed trying to cross, she may commit involuntary suicide actually trying to lay her eggs along the roadside.

There are a lot of us around who think we would all be better off to have more turtles and fewer highways.

RED-BELLIED TURTLE

The red-bellied turtle, *Chrysemys rubriventris*, is a somber, largely vegetarian, freshwater species of large size: up to twelve or even fourteen pounds. It is known to occur today in several lakes and ponds, especially Hoyt's, Gunners Exchange, Island, and Crooked Ponds, Plymouth County, and on Naushon Island, Dukes County. There are probably less than two hundred individuals living in the state. The nearest other locality for the species is the Pine Barrens of New Jersey.

Knowledge that red-bellied turtles occur in Massachusetts is quite recent. They were discovered in Plymouth, at Gunners Exchange, early in this century. Dr. H. L. Babcock (1937) described the Plymouth turtle as a new subspecies, *Chrysemys rubriventris bangsi*, in honor of Outram Bangs, a local (and widely traveled) naturalist active around the turn of the century.

Dr. Roger Conant (1951) felt the subspecies *"bangsi"* not worthy of separate recognition from the red-bellied turtles of New Jersey and points south. However, Dr. Terry Graham (Department of Biology, Worcester State College) studied Massachusetts red-bellies for several years; he belt *"bangsi"* worthy of reconsideration as a subspecies (1969). Final word awaits a statistical review of the characteristics.

Dr. Joseph Waters, in his considerable work on vertebrate remains in Indian middens, extended the recent range of red-bellies northward to the Ipswich River, Essex County (1962), noted the museum specimen (MCZ 46965) from Naushon, and identified considerable red-bellied material from Martha's Vineyard (1966). This body of evidence indicates the red-belly was widespread in eastern Massachusetts from more than four thousand years ago until a thousand years ago. The Plymouth and Naushon populations are relics.

The red-bellied turtle is remarkably shy and cautious. Apparently always regarded by man as a culinary treat, red-bellies are virtually unapproachable. Here, at the northern extreme of their range, their

Red-bellied turtle (*Chrysemys rubriventris*), adult male, about one foot shell length: Plymouth, Mass.

Red-bellied turtle (*Chrysemys rubriventis*), sex undetermined, about eight-and-a-half inches carapace length: Naushon, Elizabeth Islands.

well-being depends on the amount of time they can spend basking in the sun. Human activity keeps them under water and may lead to serious metabolic deficiencies, weight loss, and eventual death. These big turtles make almost irresistible targets for people with .22 rifles, especially as most people call all big turtles "snappers" and believe they are benefitting the world by killing them. Terry Graham has found two shot to death by .22's in recent years.

In his studies Terry has captured, marked, and released thirty-five adult red-bellies in Plymouth County. He estimates the population at not more than a hundred. I have identified three or four Naushon specimens, but two were dead. I have only a vague notion that there might be from twenty to fifty on the island.

Red-bellies lay their eggs in May and June, on high ground near their home ponds. I have no clutch size data, but the closely related painted turtle, *Chrysemys picta*, a much smaller species, lays three to eight eggs. I estimate eight to ten as normal clutch size. Hatching is probably in July. Young red-bellies are quite colorful, as the name implies. They darken dorsally with age, and the red of the belly may fade to pinkish or dull orange. Conant's *Field Guide* provides excellent pictures. Dr. Babcock's major work, *The Turtles of New England* (1919), is now available in a Dover reprint facsimile edition; the color plates and account are excellent.

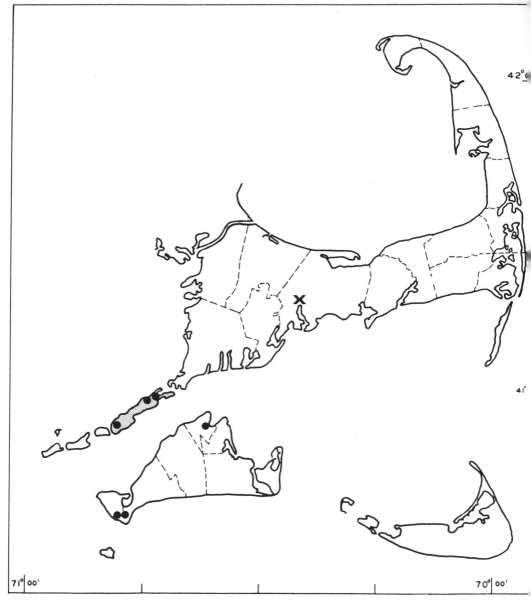

Records for two rare turtles. Dots indicate localities for the red-bellied turtle (*Chrysemys rubriventris*). Shading, on Naushon, is the area in which the species still survives; the Vineyard records are all of bones from Indian middens. X marks the spot for the only wild-caught wood turtle (*Clemmys insculpta*) known to me; I suspect it was introduced.

The most colorful individual I ever saw, and the only one as bright and bold as Conant's female shown in the *Field Guide*, was a big, old female observed in Mary's Lake, Naushon, on 23 June 1968. That was my first trip to Naushon, and I have never been rewarded with so excellent a view since. In fact, except for the MCZ specimen the only other Naushon specimen agreed on by all observers present was a smashed shell found in the jeep track of the north shore by Paul Elias, John Alexander, and me on 19 September 1971. Paul and I observed a turtle that I thought was a red-belly in a little pond just west of Tarpaulin Cove on 6 May 1973. We were about fifty feet from the turtle, and it was about half submerged; the head and neck were high, and most of the carapace was visible. I thought it too large and too dark to be a painted turtle; I like to believe I could have seen the yellow on the head of a paint, if it had been one. We were as plainly in the turtle's view as he was in ours, but he did not move in the several minutes during which I tried (in vain) to badger Paul into admitting it was a red-belly. Paul slowly shed his clothes, hurtled over the intervening rocks, shrubs, and logs, and flung headlong into the pond. The turtle disappeared while Paul was still airborne. We had no seine net to drag the pond, so his escape was clean.

Paul has always maintained that it was probably just a painted turtle, and he saw it closer up than I did. I never saw Paul run after a painted turtle before.

One spring morning in 1974, I went with Terry Graham, Al and Phlyp Geer (of woodland salamander fame), and several others to spy on Plymouth red-bellies in an area we hope will be set aside for conservation. It was one of the most spectacular animal watch trips I have ever been on. We snuck along a heavily wooded ridge high over a cove on a large lake. There were several huge old pine logs lying on the cove's surface. On one log was a massive black red-belly. Its belly was canted up towards us and reflected brilliant coral and rose on the pond's dark surface. As we watched, a second, then a third example of these grand creatures emerged to bask. They were so much bigger than any other New England basking turtle, and their red bellies so vivid, that they made an awe-inspiring sight.

Housing and resort development are rapidly moving in around the Plymouth County ponds and lakes; motor boats roar; rifles pop. Even on Naushon, I know several people who used to shoot every big turtle they saw; there is nothing to prevent resumption of this habit.

Is our native red-belly a different form from those farther south? Can it survive long enough for us to find out? Separated by hundreds of miles from its nearest relatives, our tiny, remnant populations have persisted three-quarters of the way through this century of extinction. No species could be easier to save: just grant them isolation and peace. It is easy and dramatically rewarding to view them without disturbing them. Will it even be possible in the future?

Box Turtle

Pity the poor box turtle, genetic hodge-podge of the subspecies of *Terrapene carolina,* victim of human fondness, the greatest destroyer of life on earth beside outright slaughter and habitat destruction. Have I said an unkind word about people who transport and release wild animals? Those who introduce exotic genes into natural populations? Those who disrupt natural ecosystems with individuals and numbers never intended or adapted to live there? I will say a few more.

When I was a little boy, I adored box turtles as much as—or more than—any kid alive today. My long-suffering mother drove me down to Mississippi (from Philadelphia) with my crates of pets burgeoning from our little Austin: a few prize bantams, a couple of snakes, a fine old yellow dog, and a dozen box turtles. I kept my box turtles well penned up and kept accurate notes and data on them. When I went off to college, I released some of them *exactly where I had caught them,* but most I donated to the Philadelphia Zoo, or pickled and put in museums. That is where I differed from most turtle lovers. They too reach the day when they no longer want, or can keep, their turtles. Most of them just let their turtles go.

They let them go wherever they happen to be, or decide—in their all too human minds—that it would be "good for" the turtle. If they brought a three-toed box turtle from Louisiana, and they are now on Martha's Vineyard, that is all right with them: they let it go.

What happens? Well, there is a vast literature on all sorts of vertebrate animals, from fish and frogs to wolves and men, that proves they *try* to go home. They may have very primitive, sun-compass orientation systems that merely set them on a course that would bring them back to a given shoreline if they had been displaced straight out into the water by, for example, a flood; that is about the best small frogs can do. Or they may have an incredible set of stimulus receptors—visual, auditory, gravitational, magnetic, and more—that far exceed anything human beings can even invent, let alone transport. Homing pigeons remain a mystery today. Turtles, at least the terrestrial ones, are somewhere in between. A box turtle can and will start off in the general compass direction of home; so will a raccoon, a squirrel, a wolf, or a ground hog. These animals are quite easily confused. Their compass bearing depends on how much sky they could see as you displaced them, how long the trip was, and how devious the route. *But they will do the best they can.*

Box turtle (*Terrapene c. carolina*), adult female, about six inches carapace length: Oak Bluffs, Martha's Vineyard.

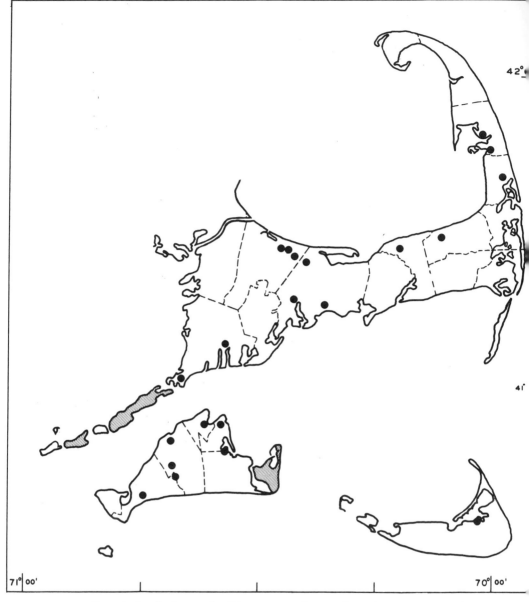

Records for the box turtle (*Terrapene carolina*) indicated by dots. The real range of native populations is probably lost forever amid the welter of local extirpations and exotic introductions. Shading indicates those islands (Naushon, Nashawena, and Chappaquiddick) from which I have responsible verbal reports, but no hard evidence—specimens or photographs.

Remember that, all you soft-hearted, gushy types who think you are being kind. Remember, the animal is not going to just sit there. He is going to *try* to get home: right through every town, right across every highway, perhaps hopelessly headed in the wrong direction, but he will still *try*. Box turtles will not usually attempt large bodies of water, so if you released your turtle on the Vineyard, he will never make it home. He will come to the edge and stop.

Now you have *successfully* introduced your animal. Successful introductions are those that, still alive, have not made it home. Now it is no longer the life of an individual animal at stake. Now you have jeopardized the whole population. Aside from the instinct to go home, your turtle also has the instincts to eat, drink, and make love. If it is spring, summer, or fall, the introduced specimen will, if it gets a chance, mate. Box turtle females store sperm alive for over a year, so a single mating can be very productive. A female will lay up to a dozen eggs each spring, usually in June. A single mating can thus result in more than twenty little turtles, even if the male turtle dies immediately after encountering the female.

Of course, if your turtle comes from Havre de Grace, Maryland, or Shreveport, Louisiana—or East Overshoe—he is hardly going to be well adapted to the new environment. He may die fairly soon, or he may take a few years running down, becoming weaker, sicker, more emaciated, and beset by diseases and problems totally unlike those at home. Evidence is that introductions almost invariably die. It took twenty tries to establish the starling.

The offspring of the introduced parent each inherit one half of his genes, so they will be half as badly off in the new environment as the parent was. Certainly, as nature takes her inevitable course, the maladapted gene bearers die out. In a few generations natural selection will right the wrongs of introduction. But in the meantime the natural population has been severely reduced, and perhaps forever altered in characteristics from what it originally was.

Introduction is, *at best*, a slow way to torture individual animals to death. That is when it fails. At worst, it is a fabulous mechanism for disrupting whole populations and ecosystems. That is when it succeeds. You would think people would have got the point after the English sparrow, the Japanese beetle, and the starling. Please get the point with respect to box turtles. The populations of Cape Cod and the Islands are dwindling rapidly. Habitat destruction and automobiles account for some of this, but none of it on the Elizabeth Islands, for example. Simple transport and release, with concomitant genetic deterioration of the population, is the major factor.

I have two records for Florida box turtles (*Terrapene carolina bauri*), three for three-toed box turtles (*T.c. triunguis*), and one for the ornate box turtle (*Terrapene ornata*)—not even a member of the same species. Ornate box turtles are native to the Southwest. They *will* mate with regular box turtles, given no choice, and can produce fertile offspring. Our native box turtle was *Terrapene carolina carolina*. Even that subspecies is extremely geographically variable; southern specimens can be quite unlike our native stocks.

Those of you who have been responsible for transporting all these exotic box turtles to our Cape and Islands know who you are. You better hope I never find out.

The best paper I have read on box turtles is a Master's thesis written at the University of Tennessee by R. A. Dolbeer (1969). He cites all the relevant literature: Allard, Cagle, Cahn, Carpenter, Carr, Ewing, Gould, Klimstra and Newsome, Nichols, Stickel, E. C. Williams, and others. Check that out if you really want details.

Dolbeer found that in natural populations there are about seven to nine individuals per acre, and that box turtles, not aggressive territorial defenders, *are* very much homebodies. They tend to wander about 150 feet way from home every day, and return to the same place each night. They may be active in warm weather during any month of the year, although they do hibernate in seasonally cold weather—usually four to six inches below the surface in stump holes.

Box turtles are fond of fruit, some leafy vegetables, and flesh of all sorts. They love worms, slugs, grubs, and all kinds of detrimental insects. Despite the imbecile on Nantucket mentioned in my 1969 paper, who tried to exterminate box turtles there "because they eat flowers," box turtles are really very good for the garden.

The original range of native box turtles in our area can probably never be reconstructed. I have never seen a specimen from the Elizabeths, but am assured they have or did occur on most of those islands. Whether they were native or introduced no one knows. I do know one fellow who caught one on Nashawena and transported it to Cuttyhunk where he released it. No one has reported seeing a box turtle on Cuttyhunk in at least five years. Oh well, what can I do?

Wood Turtle

I do not believe the wood turtle is a Cape Cod native. I have only seen one wild-caught specimen of *Clemmys insculpta* from the Cape: a beautiful young adult female in the living collection of the turtle-loving Thew family of Marston's Mills, Barnstable. She is the one Marty photographed for this book.

Wood turtle (*Clemmys insculpta*), adult female, about six inches carapace length: Barnstable, Cape Cod.

I have seen several other wood turtles on Cape Cod, but all were captives brought there from somewhere else. One that spent the summer at Wellfleet had been imported from Maine. Sadly, its original captor could not remember just where in Maine, except that it was crossing the highway. From Wellfleet it moved to Cambridge where it waxed fat and happy for another year, only to be killed by a dog eventually. It finally came to rest at the MCZ, for Maine specimens of wood turtles are very rare, and valuable even without a precise locality.

The problem with wood turtles is that people just can't leave them alone. They must pick them up and carry them off. Once made captive, the wood turtle has only two possible fates: death—whether soon or after many years—genetic, biological death no matter, or release—whether intentional or by escape. It goes without saying that virtually *no* wood turtle has ever been released or escaped where it actually came from. If it goes back to nature at all, it usually does so quite a distance from its original home range and territory: the place it was genetically adapted and behaviorally habituated to live. Well, I have damned the public enough for transporting and releasing box turtles. Wood turtles are just one more pathetic case in point.

Wood turtles are the biggest member of the genus *Clemmys*, which includes the spotted turtle and dimunitive Muhlenberg's, or bog, turtle. Wood turtles are dark grey-brown or olive above, usually with a shower of tiny, punctuated streaks: little yellowish Kohouteks —look closely or you will miss them. The plastron is boldly yellow and black. The skin of neck and limbs, at least on the undersurfaces, is pink to orange, rich and bright. The eyes are flecked with gold.

Wood turtles were, I believe, originally upland creatures. They seem best adapted to hilly, forested country with cascading streams. Many individuals take to stream life more or less permanently and grow lovely green moss. Most wood turtles seem to live a pretty much terrestrial existence quite like box turtles.

The sculptured look—and the name *insculpta*—comes from the fact that each annular scute, the layer of horn or fingernail-like covering on each plate of the bony shell, remains attached to its replacement below. This same phenomenon occurs in box turtles and, to a lesser extent, in spotted turtles. With age the laminated stack of scutes builds up. The wood turtle's are remarkably thick, steep-edged, and durable; an old wood turtle looks quite like a contoured, cardboard, landscape model of hilly country.

Wood turtles are omnivorous and fond of fruits, vegetables, and even some foliage. They need animal protein and seek out cutworms, beetle grubs, and worms with zealous vigor.

Turtles, Order Testudinata

I have never lived in an area where wood turtles were of regular occurrence. Dr. Babcock (1919) states that they nest from 10 to 25 June and presents evidence of courtship and mating throughout the warmer months of the year. It is said that wood turtles of both sexes can whistle.

Spotted Turtle

> It occurs in ponds and streams with muddy bottoms. I have frequently taken it in salt marshes. It not uncommonly travels about on land at considerable distances from water.
>
> HAROLD L. BABCOCK

This pretty, polka-dotted little species was regarded by Dr. Babcock as second only to the painted turtle in general abundance. I know very little about spotted turtles, but I do know they are far less common today than they were even a decade ago. While still of regular occurrence throughout most of Cape Cod and on Martha's Vineyard, the species is not really common—compared to the painted turtle—except on the Elizabeth Islands and Nantucket. In all the dozens of turtles rounded up by the day campers at Wellfleet Bay Wildlife Sanctuary, and examined by me over the years, there has never yet been a spotted turtle. I believe that this species, *Clemmys guttata*, like the other members of its genus (wood and bog turtles) has undergone a real decline, and man is to blame.

Habitat destruction, by filling and draining the marshes, has combined with the automobile to eliminate spotted turtles. They lay only a few—two to four—eggs and tend to wander far from the safety of ponds and streams, especially in summer. Thus, they are prone to a heavy death toll crossing roads and have a low rate of replacement: only about half as many young are produced by spotted as by painted turtles. Although quite omnivorous, and genuinely fond of insects, worms, and other meaty morsels, spotted turtles have a passion for cranberries. Their habitat puts them in areas of cranberry farming, and the horrible super pesticides—from DDT to aldrin and dieldrin —used by growers on the bogs may well have poisoned spotted turtles far more effectively than other species.

Males are easily distinguished from females by their long, stout tails and concave plastrons. At hatching, the carapace is dull brown and the yellow pigment is confined to a central blotch on each scute. With age, the shell blackens and the bright yellow spots appear.

Spotted turtle (*Clemmys guttata*), adult male, about four-and-a-half inches
carapace length: Naushon, Elizabeth Islands.

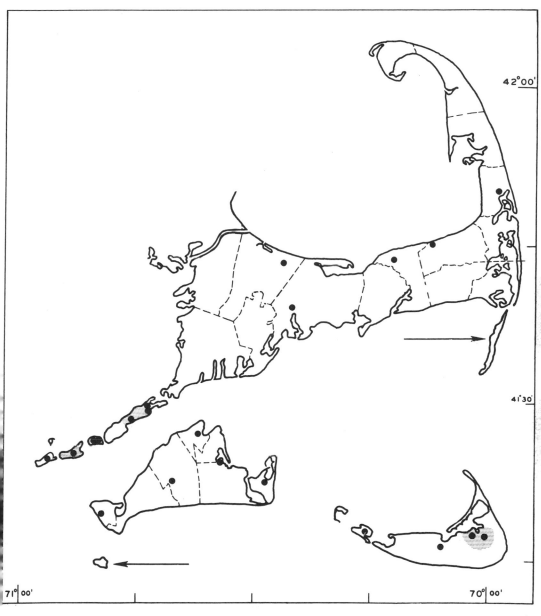

Distribution and relative abundance of the spotted turtle (*Clemmys guttata*):
dots indicate where specimens have been examined. Shading indicates areas
where the species seems unusually abundant; I estimate at least 40 per square
kilometer, or about 100 per square mile, in these areas. Arrows indicate No
Mans Land and Monomoy where suitable habitat seems to occur, but the
species has not yet been recorded.

Usually, each old lamina of the horny outer covering of the shell is sloughed off. So, unlike wood and box turtles, it is usually difficult to count growth stages—about equivalent to years—and thus age the specimen. There is considerable orange or yellow blotching on the heads and necks of most specimens, and poorly spotted ones can be confused with *Clemmys muhlenbergi*, Muhlenberg's bog turtle. The latter species is rare and endangered; it is known only from the western part of Massachusetts, and southwestern Connecticut, in New England.

Dr. Babcock notes that spotties lay their eggs in June, like the painted turtle; I have never observed this. I have often found them in the little temporary ponds where I hunt spotted salamanders in March, April, and May. When thus encountered, at night, they are usually sitting still on the bottom, well drawn into their shells. Frequently I find just two, a male and a female, in each pond. There is something peculiar about finding these black, bright-yellow spotted turtles and the similarly black, yellow-spotted salamanders together at the same time and place.

No subspecies of this form are recognized. I have examined them from Maine to the Carolinas and they all look quite like Cape and Islands individuals to me.

Perhaps, with the awareness that they are suffering a real decline in numbers, people will stop taking them into captivity, where they usually die, and give them a "brake" on the roads. Then, if marshland destruction can be halted, and pesticides effectively banned, spotted turtles may make a comeback.

The Sea Turtles, Family *Cheloniidae*

> *Their crowning curse is their drudging impulse to straightforwardness in a belittered world.*
> HERMAN MELVILLE

Most New Englanders encountering a sea turtle in our waters are amazed. They generally regard these creatures as rare and tropical, never thinking of them as natural, native, important members of our ecosystem. There are four genera of the true sea turtle family, Cheloniidae, and every one of them has a member that occurs in Cape Cod and other Massachusetts waters. Three of them occur regularly; two of them are abundant. There is also the greatest reptile, the leatherback, but that is another story.

If freshwater and saltmarsh turtles are an unsurprising common-place to us, why should marine turtles be different? First of all, the pond and marsh habitats heat up in the summer months to temperatures warm enough for normal reptiles without the ability to internally regulate their body temperatures: 80° to 90° F. Second, the pond and marsh turtles can walk on land, and so can clamber out of the water and bask in the summer sun. In the sun temperatures go way over 100° F., which is actually too hot, so no turtle basks in it for long.

Even in summer, however, the sea does not go much over 70° F. south of the Cape and stays pretty much in the 50° to 60° F. range to the north, in the Gulf of Maine. That is warm enough for turtle activity, but only marginally. The sea turtles have gone so totally aquatic that they have evolved flippers and rudders, fore and aft, and are almost helpless on land; like a true seal, they are able only to drag themselves torturously and slowly on their bellies for a few feet. Sea turtles *do* bask on the surface, carapace exposed to the hot sun, but they *never* come out of the water to bask. Only the females ever leave the water, and then usually in the secrecy of night, to lay their eggs.

With the coming of winter our pond and marsh turtles can hibernate, if they want to, but hibernation is impossible at sea. Instead, the sea turtles turn back southward and migrate to the tropics. Each year a few get caught—it gets too cold too quickly in a suddenly strengthened current, or they wait, enjoying the boreal feasts of our rich waters too long. Each year November, December, and even January see dead or dying stragglers washed ashore. These few are the ones most people see, and they belie the numbers who made it south safely.

You can go out right now and see all four of our native sea turtles —three of them well represented by Cape and Islands specimens— alive and well. Sea turtles (as opposed to leatherbacks) do very well in captivity, and our various public and commercial institutions that exhibit living marine life almost always have a fine selection: the New England Aquarium in Boston; the Atlantic Aquarium in Hull; the Northeast Fisheries Center at Wood Hole (Woods Hole Aquarium); Sealand of Cape Cod in Brewster; the Aquarium of Cape Cod in Yarmouth; and the Provincetown Marine Aquarium.

There is one distressing feature often associated with these excellent live exhibits: the sea turtles are often misidentified. Indeed, the identification of sea turtles seems to be exceedingly difficult for most people; they become hopelessly confused, and often begin to believe they are seeing hybrids or bizarre aberrations from the norm.

Do not feel badly if you have trouble telling sea turtles apart. Even natives of the tropics who hunt them for food and shell have trouble and call many of them hybrids too.

There are not any hybrid sea turtles, at least not between the four major generic sorts. They are members of different genera, after all, separated by great anatomical gulfs. Most of the major differences are internal (features of the skull, for instance), but the obvious, external differences are major, too. You just have to know what to look for.

Marty, his daughter Carol, Numi, and I went off to photograph all our native sea turtles one fine August day in 1974. The staffs of the various aquaria were kindly and cooperative; they let us make nuisances of ourselves in the interests of science and education. We photographed all the kinds, took exact data on all the ones we photographed, and observed (and recorded the data for) literally dozens of others. When we set out, Marty, Carol, and Numi could not tell one kind of sea turtle from the next. Marty even questioned bothering to photograph them; he wanted to know if there were any differences between them that *people* could really see. Wouldn't just *a* picture of *a* sea turtle do the job? No, no, I said, please come with me and I will show you; you will know the sea turtles by the end of this expedition. Thirty-six hours later, as we drove home, all three of them knew they could identify sea turtles. No sweat, every time. Marty, from the backseat, pointed out a grand truth:

Sea Turtles, Like Glacial Maxima, Go in *Alphabetical Order*.

If you can remember the names, and remember the alphabet (that is where I have trouble), you've got it.

How about the great ice ages? Can you do it? There were four and they came in alphabetical order. Ah yes, there's the Gunz, and the Mindel, the Riss, and the Wurm.

How about sea turtles? There are four basic generic types, and they come in alphabetical order of scaliness: the Green, and the Hawksbill, the Loggerhead, and the Ridley. (I do not normally capitalize common names of animals, like dog, cat, and ridley; I did here only for emphasis.)

All right, in alphabetical order of scaliness: from the least scaly to the most scaly. First off, be sure your turtle *has* scales, or scutes, at all. Are there separate scales on the head and flippers? Is the shell divided into scutes? If not, it isn't a true sea turtle. The leatherback has *no scales or scutes at all*.

Once you are sure the turtle you are looking at has scales on head and flippers, and scutes on its shell (scutes are just shell scales), you need to know what to look for next.

Turtles, Order Testudinata

All turtles with shell scutes have a row of little *marginals* around the outside; forget them. All have a row of big *vertebrals* down the middle of the back; forget them too. Now look along the side of the carapace between the marginals and the vertebrals: there are the *costals*, the side-of-the-back scutes. Pay attention. Are there just four great big ones from front to back? Or is there a sneaky little extra one—smaller than all the rest—tucked right up there on his shoulder? Be sure: *not* a marginal; but an extra, small, *shoulder scute*.

If he has a shoulder scute, he is too scaly to be either a green or a hawksbill. He must be a loggerhead or ridley. If he doesn't have a shoulder scute, we will proceed to tell the least scaly of the shoulder-scuteless turtles—the green—from the more scaly hawksbill. Look at the top of his head, from his eyes forward to his snout: here are also scales, or head plates. Is there just *one* pair—two scales, one on each side? If so, he's not very scaly, so he's a green. Or are there *two pairs*—four scales, two on each side? If so, he's the scalier hawksbill. The hawksbill is also scalier-looking all over. His carapace (and even plastron) scutes are enlarged posteriorly and extend out over their next neighbors. One says that his scales are *imbricate*, overlapping, like the shingles on a roof. Some greens have this a little bit, too, but never to the extent of a hawksbill. After your first few, you won't need to count head plates: greens and hawksbills do not look similar in general.

Green turtle (*Chelonia mydas*): close-up of the head of a young female, about eighteen inches carapace length: Falmouth, Cape Cod. Note the *two* big scutes on the front of the head.

But if he's *got* that shoulder scute, what next? This is a little bit harder: look at the *bridge*, on the side of his belly, between the carapace and plastron (between the flippers, front and hind). Here the turtle is basically all whitish, and the lines between the scutes are harder to see. Are there just *three* big bridge scutes? There may be a cluster of little ones at each end of the bridge; don't worry over those. Just count the big ones: three is the least scaly of the shoulder-scute-bearing turtles, the loggerhead. If there are *four or five*, he's a ridley.

Like the green and the hawksbill, the loggerhead and ridley do not look much alike in general. Loggerheads are basically brown (Numi says "like a wet paper bag"); they often have rich tones of red or even maroon. Ridleys are grey; concrete-colored.

So, the trick of sea turtle identification is that *shoulder scute*. Once you are sure the turtle either *has* it or *has not* got it, the rest is easy.

Put in summary form:

Green: no shoulder scute; only one pair of plates on top of snout, carapace scutes not broadly imbricate.
Hawksbill: no shoulder scute; two pairs of plates on top of snout; carapace scutes broadly imbricate, like shingles.
Loggerhead: shoulder scute present; only three big bridge scutes; brown.
Ridley: shoulder scute present; four or more big bridge scutes; grey.

And remember now: it's the Gunz and the Mindel, the Riss, and the Wurm. They're all glaciations that I made you learn. . . .

GREEN TURTLE

Chelonia mydas, the green, is perhaps the most economically important of all reptiles. It is the victim of green turtle soup, the favorite of the late Sir Winston Churchill. They are named for the green color of the fatty *calipee*, the internal material for which they are primarily butchered, and which is rendered to make a greenish soup. Some individuals may be greenish on the outside too (especially if algae are growing on them, as they do on any sea turtle), but most are variegated and mottled in tones of grey and brown. The meat is good eating too, and steaks of this turtle are highly esteemed.

Dr. Archie Carr of the University of Florida is the world's foremost authority on sea turtles, family Cheloniidae. His delightful books about them are classics of popular natural history. In *So Excellente a Fishe*, he chronicles the decline of the green turtle from widespread abundance to the pitiful remnant surviving today. While it is doubtful that any greens ever nested along our coasts north of Florida, the species was once abundant, and nested as well, at Bermuda. It nested virtually throughout the tropical Atlantic, wherever suitable beaches were found.

On the nesting beaches greens, like other sea turtles, are most vulnerable to predation by man. The females must drag themselves ashore to lay their eggs—often hundreds—above the high tide line. Unless prevented by laws and law enforcement, men await them there. They turn them on their backs: these turtles cannot right themselves again as our land, pond, and marsh turtles can. There they are butchered for calipee, meat, and eggs; if they have already managed to lay their eggs, men find them by probing the sand with a stick, and dig them up. No species can long withstand such exploitation.

Today, there are laws almost everywhere protecting greens from death on the beaches, but such laws are hard to enforce in remote areas of the overpopulated tropics, in the dead of night. It is still legal to harpoon greens on their feeding grounds—shallow, submarine banks that support rich pastures of turtle grass. As adults, greens feed largely on turtle grass and stay pretty much in the tropics. No one knows what the young ones do, but we do know that they are primarily carnivorous and feed on fish and other marine life. They travel widely and frequently come to our waters. I have never seen an old adult from New England, but youngsters, up to two or three years old and usually less than forty pounds, are often caught here in pound nets and weirs, or on long lines. An old adult may go over five feet in shell length and weigh over 800 pounds.

One of the great enigmas of biology is the magical ability of many species to "home." Pigeons are famous for it, of course, and Marty, before he took to photography on a large scale, did his doctoral research on them. It is now known that pigeons can use landmarks, sun positions, and even magnetism to find their way. But green turtles cannot fly; they cannot possibly see landmarks from the surface of the open ocean. Yet, greens return at least every two or three years to their place of hatching to mate and lay their eggs. That may not be difficult if *any* Caribbean shore will do for a Caribbean turtle; she can swim just roughly west and be sure to hit land. But greens nest in large numbers on Ascension Island, in mid-Atlantic, on Aves, in mid-Caribbean, and previously on Bermuda. They do not remain around these islands; they do migrate elsewhere to feed. Tagging proves they do return. How can they possibly do it? No human being could without complex mechanical instruments.

This is the least common of our regularly occurring sea turtles, but one of the most frequently exhibited in aquaria. This is because many are now reared in captivity. We may hope that the efforts of Dr. Carr and his associates will pay off, and green turtles will become abundant again. Man need never lose this once-great resource if he learns to manage it wisely and zealously.

Green turtle (*Chelonia mydas*), young female, about eighteen inches carapace length: Chatham, Cape Cod.

HAWKSBILL

Eretmochelys imbricata, with the imbricate scutes, is the prettiest of the sea turtles. It was widely slaughtered for its calico-colored "tortoise shell" prior to the development of plastics. What will happen as plastics disappear, as their mother petroleum is exhausted? Hawksbills, definitely rare and endangered, are still widely killed for meat and eggs.

I believe this species comes only rarely to New England waters, living out its entire life largely in the tropics. Dr. Babcock cites references to its occurrence in Buzzard's Bay earlier in this century, but I strongly question the identifications involved. The hawksbill,

Hawksbill (*Eretmochelys imbricata*), close-up of the head of the Culebra specimen. Note the *four* big scutes on the front of the head.

as the name implies, has a massive beak, but so do ridleys. No specimens seem to exist to prove those older literature records, and I believe they were based on the regularly occurring ridley.

There is one authentic hawksbill from Cape Code in the MCZ. It was picked up by Dan Meany, of the Massachusetts Herpetological Society, and he donated it to the Museum. The turtle was dead and rotten, so he just saved the shell, but that is enough to identify it beyond any doubt. I think it was a straggler that died of the chill and washed ashore; it is small, only about ten inches in shell length.

Hawksbills are all rather small, attaining shell lengths (measured straight-line) of about three feet and apparently not exceeding 300 pounds. They seem to remain quite carnivorous throughout life.

The hawksbill Marty photographed for us was caught by a native fisherman known as Big Pedro, with a cast net, at Culebra, an island east of Puerto Rico. It was shipped up to John Dinga, now curator at the Atlantic Aquarium in Hull. John had lived for years on Culebra and believes that the island still supports nesting hawksbills.

Perhaps laws can be enforced to protect the hawksbill, and it may begin to regain its numbers. Perhaps then it will prove to be more regular in New England, and we may be able to show a native specimen one day. I hope so.

OPPOSITE PAGE: Hawksbill (*Eretmochelys imbricata*), young female, about ten inches carapace length: Culebra, West Indies. This specimen is in the living exhibit collection of the Atlantic Aquarium, Hull, Massachusetts.

LOGGERHEAD

Caretta caretta, the true loggerhead sea turtle, largest and common-est of our Cheloniidae, is not to be confused with the snapping turtle, so often called loggerhead by New Englanders (especially on Martha's Vineyard). This species is said to attain a length of more than 80 inches, shell length, and weights of up to 900 pounds. Most of ours are less than 300 pounds and rarely longer than three feet. I have records with data for 21 Cape-Islands region loggerheads, and have examined a dozen or more others whose data has been lost over the years. This carnivorous species does very well in aquaria.

Sightings in my records extend from Georges Bank, in the north-east, to Long Beach, Gay Head, Martha's Vineyard, and Coatue peninsula, Nantucket. The Nantucket specimen, a young female of about eleven inches, was washed up dead on the beach in the winter of 1971. J. Clinton Andrews found her on 8 January; she is in the collection of the Nantucket Research Station (University of Massa-chusetts) at Quaise Point. The latest living winter record is for "Marge," a 200-plus-pound female who came ashore at the Marconi Station in Wellfleet on 1 December 1973. (There are 1974 records as late as 15 December: Curt Horton, Sealand.) She was rushed to Sealand, in Brewster. Her body temperature was only a half degree

Loggerhead (*Caretta caretta*), female, about two feet in carapace length: Georges Bank, east of Provincetown, Cape Cod.

above 0° C.—about 34° F. Curt Horton and the Sealand staff had her eating six pounds of fish by the next day.

In a previous publication I suggested that the loggerhead is probably our most dangerous reptile. I'm sorry I said that, really, at least without modifying it to *potentially* dangerous. A big loggerhead could, I admit, pretty well chunk a man up into little pieces, but all the ones I have handled (and that's quite a few) were very docile and never tried to bite at all. Respect the jaws of the loggerhead, but do not fear him. I rarely go swimming at all, but when I do, I like to do it among loggerheads.

This species nests abundantly along our coasts as far north as Virginia. In the days of Audubon and Bachman, it nested in New Jersey; it has done so again, just a few years back. My good friend Dr. Roger Conant, then Director of the Philadelphia Zoo, was party to digging up a clutch at Ocean City; Dr. Carr was party to accepting the eggs when shipped to Florida. I was incensed. What earthly purpose could be served by sending our only recent New Jersey loggerheads to Florida, where there are thousands? I called the Ocean City police to see if they had deemed it necessary for the little turtles' sakes. No, they said, they thought the eggs were perfectly safe right where they were. No domestic carnivore, like a dog, has been allowed to set foot on Ocean City's beaches for years. No wild carnivore, like a raccoon or skunk, has been seen in the city limits recently either. That mother turtle could hardly have picked a safer place.

Dr. Conant defended the act. *People* are abundant on Ocean City's beaches. They might well use the emerging hatchlings for games of catch or ping pong. Well, the police said they were more than willing to keep an eye on the area. Sea turtles, no matter when they actually hatch from the eggs, usually wait to erupt from their nests until the middle of the night. This way they avoid predatory sea birds, crepuscular raccoons, and resort sea-bathers.

Please folks, next time let's give Nature a chance. I fondly hope to see a great loggerhead haul out a warm June night to nest right here in Massachusetts.

RIDLEY

Lepidochelys, the genus of the ridleys, means "scaly turtle." There are two species: the grey or Gulf ridley, *Lepidochelys kempi*; and the olive ridley, *L. olivacea*. The one we have here is *L. kempi*; it nests in the western Gulf of Mexico and migrates (once by the thousands) to our waters. The olive ridley nests on the coasts of South America, Africa, and all over the Pacific (it is sometimes called the Pacific ridley, but is certainly Atlantic too). It is possible that an olive ridley *might* stray into our waters, so let us extend our alphabetical identification scheme to include that possibility. Ah yes, the farther down the alphabet the scalier the turtle. Now grey, Gulf, and *kempi* all come well before olive and *olivacea*, so the olive ridley must be even scalier than the grey one. Sure enough, grey ridleys have a shoulder scute and *four* additional costals. Olive ridleys have the shoulder scute, of course, and *five or more* additional costals.

Isn't Nature wonderful! You see there *is* a Grand Design. Who could doubt the existence of God, great alphabetizer of turtles?

Anyone interested in good entertainment, natural history, and the pursuit of knowledge should read *The Windward Road* by Archie Carr. For decades scientists sought the answer to the riddle of the ridley, and none more diligently than Dr. Carr. It was well known that a small (to thirty inches, shell length), grey sea turtle occurred abundantly along our Atlantic and Gulf coasts. Young ones had even been found in the British Isles. No one knew where they nested, and Dr. Carr could not find out. It had to be somewhere in the Caribbean-Gulf basin. The trade winds blow onshore there from the north and east; the windward road is long; the ridleys kept their secret.

The natives had a simple explanation. The ridley was a bastard turtle—a hybrid between loggerhead and hawksbill or green. It could not lay eggs, any more than mules have colts. That could not and did not satisfy Dr. Carr: *Lepidochelys kempi* is very much its own turtle anatomically. Well, helpful people suggested, perhaps it is a live-bearing species, producing its young at sea? About as likely as an "egg-laying dog," mused Dr. Carr.

Finally, Dr. Henry Hildebrand (1962), well known to ornithologists for his pioneering work in Texas and Mexico on the effects of insecticides on nesting sea birds, revealed the secret: the *arribada* of the ridleys.

Along a short stretch of Gulf coast, from southern Texas to Tamaulipas, the ridleys *do* come ashore and nest. At the central area, Aldama, Tamaulipas, they came ashore up to 40,000 strong, all at once, in broad daylight, on stormy, windy days. No other phenomenon like it is known.

The strategy was perfect for avoiding their natural predators, the raccoons, coatis, coyotes, and skunks. All of those tend to be twilight or evening creatures. The strategy was a debacle for avoiding man. The ridleys were slaughtered by the tens of thousands for meat, eggs, oil, and leather. The blowing sand that hid their tracks and scent from the wily coyote did not hide them from humans.

The Mexican government quickly passed legislation to protect the *arribada,* and even posted guards. But it has proved nearly hopeless to save the Mexican turtle populations from starving, impoverished humanity. Hope for the species rests with the relative few that nest along Padre Island National Seashore in Texas. Here protection seems to be working. A remnant of the incredible spectacle of the *arribada* may remain.

I have sixteen records for ridleys in the Cape-Islands region, but

Ridley (*Lepidochelys kempi*), young female, about eighteen inches carapace length: Dennis, Cape Cod. This specimen is in the living exhibit collection of Sealand, Brewster, Cape Cod.

some have very imprecise data. Five are from Cape Cod Bay, with solid localities in Dennis and Barnstable waters. Three are from Buzzards Bay, from Quisset Harbor to Pope's Island (the latter over on the mainland side). A Vineyard Sound specimen is from Nonamesset, Naushon. A Nantucket Sound specimen is from Monomoy. The remainder are just "Massachusetts Bay," synonymous with the western Gulf of Maine.

Ridleys are quite carnivorous and the most belligerent of our species. They do very well in captivity; one caught off Barnstable in 1961 is doing fine at the Atlantic Aquarium in Hull after fourteen years. However, they are best kept isolated from each other and all other turtles. Often, they take to viciously biting each other and may kill each other if not separated.

The one I chose for Marty's photographs has a remarkable history. It was caught in Sesuit Harbor, Dennis, on 12 November 1973 and sent to Sealand in Brewster. There it was tanked with other turtles, and no one quite knows what happened next, except that most of its left side got bitten away, exposing its viscera to fish and other menacing turtles. Again Curt Horton and the staff performed an amazing rescue, and the specimen, though memorably modified, is perfectly healthy today.

Ridleys thrash around and flail their flippers, making a great fuss, when turned over. For this reason they are unpopular with most turtlers who hunt with harpoons from boats and store their catch on the deck, belly up. I believe that if they can be protected where they nest, this species—certainly now rare and endangered—has real hope for survival. We here in Massachusetts should endeavor to learn about the habits of our ridleys, and other species, through a program of tagging and releasing. It is important to know whether ours travel all the way back to Texas or Mexico every year, or only every other year. There was some evidence developing up to 1961, our last major inundation and the beginning of the decline of the great *arribada*, that ridley numbers in our waters were somewhat cyclic. There is much that we can do to help the remarkable ridley here on its migration path.

The grey ridley is named for Richard Kemp, late of Key West, Florida, who sent the first scientifically described specimen up to Dr. Samuel Garman at the MCZ. Sam Garman was a most amazingly diverse biologist; he specialized in fish, but his efforts on reptiles and amphibians were also spectacular, especially for tropical forms. Although for years Mr. Kemp's turtle was not regarded as a valid species, or even mentioned in texts—like Dr. Babcock's—Sam Garman ultimately proved right when he named and officially described it. I find it by far the most interesting of the Cheloniidae.

6

The Greatest Reptile

I have seen specimens weighing over a ton.
LOUIS AGASSIZ

THE LARGEST living reptile, by weight, is the leatherback, *Dermochelys coriacea.* Although the Atlantic and Pacific populations are listed as being racially different, the distinction is dubious at best. The current weight record is held by a Pacific individual at 1,902½ pounds. Much greater lengths, on the average, have been measured on Atlantic specimens, and the record listed is ten feet three inches. (That is a total length; in most turtles, only the shell is measured.) To date no one has confirmed Louis Agassiz's claim of "over a ton," but he was not prone to misstatements of fact, and I think he will ultimately be proven correct.

Of all living reptiles, only the largest crocodiles might rival this weight. Dr. Allen Greer at Harvard has carefully studied length and weight records of the big crocodiles. He calculates that the largest specimens ever recorded would not have topped the scales over 1,500 pounds. Numerous leatherbacks have been recorded over this weight.

I have a strange and remarkable affinity for leatherbacks. Whenever I go down to the sea, or set foot in a boat, anywhere around the Cape or Islands, look out—a turtleaceous ton is likely to appear. But

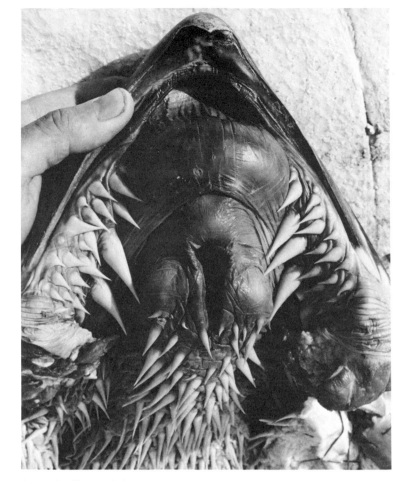

Leatherback (*Dermochelys coriacea*): the opening of the windpipe is surrounded by heavily muscled bone.

my affinity is not good for the mighty leatherback. Other people usually see them first, harpoons fly, shotguns roar, and this most wonderful creature often dies. I am proud to have saved a few; I reached them in time. But the uncanny coincidence of my presence and theirs, often leading to their deaths at others' hands, haunts me.

In 1965 Dr. J. S. Bleakney successfully disproved the theory that New England and Canadian leatherbacks were accidental strays, lost from the tropics. He examined the records and fresh specimens. They were healthy, robust individuals with bellies full of arctic jellyfish. The evidence was overwhelming: they were here on purpose, not by accident.

Like many people, they may go elsewhere in winter, but they come to the waters around the Cape and Islands, the Gulf of Maine, and Nova Scotia for the summer. Usually they stay far out at sea.

Dr. Wayne Frair, of King's College, and his colleagues in Canada discovered the first answer to the important question: how can a "cold-blooded" reptile live in the Gulf of Maine?

Leatherbacks are warm-blooded, just like mammals. Frair and colleagues found in Nova Scotian waters of about 45° F. a healthy specimen maintaining a body temperature of about 80° F. They checked their results on a badly injured Florida captive. Until she died, she could still keep her temperature up; she was very warm-blooded. How is it possible that we can have a warm turtle from cold water?

Al Greer, Marty, Numi, Peter Lynch, and I, plus a dozen others, got together in September 1972 to dissect a leatherback that had died at the New England Aquarium. We found the answer: a counter-current circulatory system. Have you ever wondered how a hot-blooded sea duck can float in the icy waters of Nantucket Sound in midwinter, with its feet bare and dangling down into the frigid sea, and not lose all its heat?

We are all accustomed to radiators. These household devices really convect heat, rather than primarily radiating it. A radiator is designed to have a huge surface area in proportion to its volume—the space it takes up in the room. The whole purpose of the radiator is to lose heat. It gives its heat up to the air in the room, and so heats the room. The leatherback's flipper, or the duck's foot, also has a huge surface area in proportion to a tiny volume. Why doesn't it lose all the heat the leatherback can generate trying to heat up the cold ocean?

The answer is in the plumbing: the blood vessels. In a counter-current system, the outgoing arteries are packed together with the incoming veins. Blood, heated in the leatherback's massive body, is pumped out to the flipper. It cannot hope to keep the flipper 80° F. and doesn't try. All it needs to do is circulate the necessary oxygen and nutrients to the living cells of the flipper. The flipper can be 45° F., like the surrounding water. Blood cooled to 45° F. returns to the body in the veins, and the incoming and outgoing blood travels side by side. So, the warm blood in the arteries loses its heat to the cold blood in the veins.

As the arterial blood goes farther out its temperature drops by heat loss to the veins. As the blood in the veins comes in toward the body, it gains heat from the arteries. Ultimately, the arterial blood at the surface of the flipper tip is little or no warmer than sea water, but rather than wastefully giving up its heat to the water, it has heated the incoming blood. The incoming blood, which would quickly kill

Leatherback (*Dermochelys coriacea*), young female, about six feet total length and 625 pounds: Gulf of Maine, about 150 miles ENE Provincetown, Cape Cod. This individual died accidentally and formed the basis for our dissections.

the leatherback if it rushed into his body at 45° F., has gained nearly all the heat of the outgoing blood and reenters the body at about 80° F. All the turtle needs to do to keep its heat is keep swimming. Muscular activity, as we all know, generates plenty of heat.

Counter-current systems are well known in birds and mammals. A beaver's tail is a classic example. Our leatherback provided the first ever described in a reptile.

It is interesting to note that more male leatherbacks seem to be caught in cold northern waters than females. Our female showed clearly the rubbery, pale scar tissue on the top of the head believed to result from bites during mating. Also, she had old, well-healed holes in her right front flipper, just where tags might have been clamped on her on the breeding beach, probably in South America. These lines of evidence suggest that she was fully mature. However, her ovaries and reproductive tract showed no sign of breeding activity, either coming in the future or recently passed. It is quite possible that leatherbacks lay their eggs only every other year. This might explain the relative scarcity of females up here each summer. About half the females, on the average, would be involved in egg-laying activities each summer. These either start their northward trip later, do not go as far, or perhaps skip the journey entirely every alternate year. I believe they come later and stay a shorter time.

Another startling feature of the leatherback is the digestive tract. It bears little resemblance to that of other animals. Huge spines, up to two inches long in our 625-pound specimen, begin in the mouth and extend down the esophagus for five and a half feet in a dense forest. (Esophageal spines are reported in the hawksbill by Steinbeck

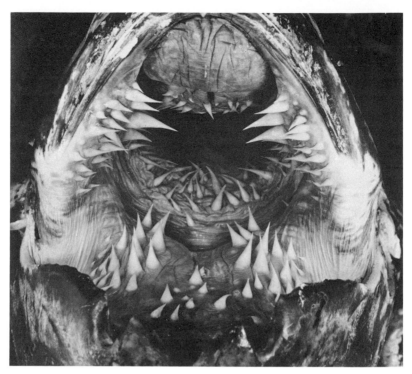

Leatherback (*Dermochelys coriacea*): a jellyfisheye view of food consumption.

and Ricketts [1941]; I have found them present in loggerheads.) This length of intestine makes more than a full circle loop on the animal's left side. There doesn't seem to be a regular stomach or a differentiated large intestine. I suppose if you eat jellyfish, you are entitled to certain peculiarities.

Leatherbacks are frequently cited as the noisiest of all turtles. When captured or attacked, they are said to emit whistles, moans, groans, and roars. No other reptile—not even some of the most vocal lizards—can match such a range of different sounds. There is no voice box or larynx, as in mammals, and no syrinx, as in birds. Apparently, the leatherback must make its noises by modifying the opening of the windpipe or trachea.

Marty and I set up a real Rube Goldberg experiment with our specimen. We hooked up a small air pump into one bronchial tube and closed off the other one. Then I "played" the windpipe opening to make all the sorts of noises I could. I got high-pitched whistles when I closed the two sides of the opening at the rear and left the front open. By closing the front, using a medial bone that is present and pushing it against the two sides, I got low-pitched noises. I have not been hailed for my musical abilities in the past, and I did not gain any points that day, but I did achieve variety.

Obviously, many things are wrong with such an experiment. The pump probably exerts more pressure than the leatherback's lungs and certainly provides much less air. The abilities of a living leatherback to coordinate movements of the opening are irrelevant to my abilities when she is dead. Most important of all, airborne noises are of virtually no consequence under water, and the leatherback's ear looks like an underwater type. It has massive fat deposits instead of a normal eardrum.

However, the windpipe opening is far more elaborate than in any other reptile I have examined. There is the normal basket of heavy bones in the throat-tongue area, as in other turtles, but the joints are quite different and the opening seems to be movable from three directions—front and both sides—with actual bones underlying the soft tissues. We will have to make a detailed study of the muscles here to determine the real possibilities open to the animal.

The several live leatherbacks I have wrangled with never made a peep or a grunt. All of these have been females. Is it possible that only the males are vocal? I am reminded of D. H. Lawrence's poem, "Tortoise Shout." In the species he saw, the male was the noise-maker. However, I have never been lucky enough to hear any turtle make any sound other than the sigh or hiss of exhalation.

Of the fifteen specimens of this species from our area which I have examined in the flesh or from photographs, *five* had their right front flippers either entangled in lobster pot lines, or showed deep cuts in and around the base of this flipper, indicating that they had been so entangled.

How and why do leatherbacks entangle their right flippers in pot lines? The answer was conjured up by Numi Spitzer, one cold and wintry October day, while she, Al and Phlyp Green, and I tried to untangle a thousand-pound female caught by the right flipper in pot lines in Buzzards Bay. The leatherback was towing four pots and Ted Spencer's catboat.

In order to understand Numi's theory, you first have to know or imagine the appearance of a floating pot buoy from *underneath*, the way a leatherback sees it. Covered with brownish algae, some of which hangs down in long streamers, it looks just like *Cyanea*, the dinner-plate-sized, brown, arctic jellyfish that leatherbacks adore and come all the way here from the equator to eat.

The leatherback swims a meter or two under the surface—*fast*. I do not know how fast, but over ten knots per hour. He sees what he takes to be a lovely big jellyfish and cants up towards it, mouth agape. As he hits it, the great basket of the hyoid bones in his chin and throat expand suddenly to draw the jellyfish into the one-way street of his gullet. The hyoid basket contracts and ten pounds of jellyfish shoot down his throat; no other way it can go. From the anatomy of the system—the spines and the muscular hyoid basket—it must be one of the most effective procedures going. The whole process, from a free-swimming jellyfish to one far down the intestine, need take only a couple of seconds.

But this time he doesn't hit a jellyfish. He hits a pot buoy that *looks* like a jellyfish. It caroms off his bony mandibles, and, straining on its line to the anchoring pot, jumps a few feet. Since the leatherback's head is immobile relative to its body, it cannot retract its head or move its neck from side to side. Instead, the whole turtle must move.

He sculls hard right (being right-flippered), backwaters left, and hits it again. The pot line is now snug in his axilla (arm pit). The buoy is dragged down a little. Sculling again with backwater and down, he hits the buoy a third time. Now the line makes one full circle around the right flipper; the leatherback is caught.

Once caught, the leatherback sculls, backwaters, and dives. He tows both pot and buoy easily in a great circle to the right. He accumulates all the pots in the circle if he keeps going long enough. Ours also accumulated seven people and a catboat. I wish lobstermen would clean the algae off their pot buoys; it would be to everyone's advantage.

It is difficult to imagine that leatherbacks are rare and endangered until you accept that at no other time in their life history, once they leave the nests they hatch in, are they so concentrated as they are in our waters. Dr. Peter Pritchard has tried to document the actual numbers and localities for nesting females. There are not many, and they are spread all the way from occasional nesters in Florida to fair numbers—dozens, anyway—on beaches in Central and South America. Thus, at their nesting season leatherbacks are widely dispersed as a species and only slightly clumped around their favorite beaches.

Up here, where they do their summer feeding, we must make every effort to conserve them. This migratory, warm-blooded, largest-living reptile, *Dermochelys*, is simply too wonderful to abandon to extinction.

7

Snakes, Order Squamata

Was it cowardice, that I dared not kill him?
Was it perversity, that I longed to talk to him?
Was it humility to feel so honoured?
I felt so honoured.
And yet those voices:
If you were not afraid, you would kill him!
And truly I was afraid, I was most afraid,
But even so, honoured still more
That he should seek my hospitality
From out the dark door of the secret earth.

* * *

And I thought of the albatross,
And I wished he would come back, my snake.
For he seemed to me again like a king,
Like a king in exile, uncrowned in the underworld,
Now due to be crowned again.
And so, I missed my chance with one of the lords
Of life.
And I have something to expiate;
A pettiness.

D. H. LAWRENCE

From "The Snake," reprinted from
The Complete Poems of D. H. Lawrence
by permission of Viking Penguin, Inc.

THE RANGE of human response to snakes is incredibly varied. To those of us who enjoy them and find them fascinating and beautiful, those who react with fear, hatred, and horror simply appear to be insane. What is it about the snake that conjures up irrational and inhumane behavior in humans?

We have no venomous snakes in the Cape-Islands region, and only a few depauperate, remnant populations left in Massachusetts. Rattlesnakes, *Crotalus h. horridus,* and copperheads, *Agkistrodon contortrix mokeson,* still survive in little colonies on the bedrock mainland. I know of no case of either of these being fatal to man, though a search of early colonial records—at a time when these species were more abundant and widespread—might turn up a few examples. Because none of our Cape-Islands species are poisonous, and since most are genuinely beneficial to man as consumers of insects, slugs, and rodents, I believe they deserve our respect and kindness.

The snakes, classified as Ophidia or Serpentes, are one of several suborders of the vast order Squamata: the squamate, or scaly, reptiles. Two other groups, the lizards, suborder Sauria, and the peculiar amphisbaenas, suborder Amphisbaenia, are widespread and conspicuous to the south of us, especially in the tropics. Neither has a native representative in our area.

It requires an astute anatomist to distinguish lizards from snakes. You cannot just count the legs—zero for a snake, four for a lizard. Quite a few lizards have no legs at all, and two families of snakes— the Boidae (boas and pythons) and the Leptotyphlopidae (tiny burrowers)—have vestigial hind legs. No snake has eyelids; in all species the eye is covered by an immobile, transparent scale. This feature is shared by lizards of a diversity of families. Similarly, snakes have no eardrum or tympanum, and are virtually deaf to airborne sounds. Most lizards do have well-developed eardrums, located (like ours) in a hole on the side of the head. A number of lizards species, in several families, have lost their outer ears—eardrums—also. Snakes are extraordinarily sensitive to vibrations in the substrate: earth, rock, tree branch, or whatever they are lying on. These vibrations are sensed by the inner ear exactly as airborne sounds, translated into vibrations of the eardrum, are sensed by our ears. So to say snakes are deaf is misleading. They simply "hear" different things than we do.

The ear is the balancing organ of both snakes and men. In snakes, especially the climbing species, it is most highly developed.

The classification of snakes is in an awful state. Dr. Herndon G. Dowling, while at the American Museum, tried hard to make headway in rationalizing snake taxonomy. He was handicapped by the fact that there are so many publications, in so many obscure journals, written in so many languages, that it is about impossible to keep track of developments. Dr. Dowling tried to set up a computerized system to monitor all this, but it was too expensive to receive support from major funding agencies. It is deplorable that chaos still reigns.

Any student of natural history should be familiar with some of the major groups of snakes, usually classified as families. I have mentioned the Leptotyphlopidae, tiny burrowers with remnant hind legs. These are largely tropical, although one species, *Leptotyphlops dulcis*, is widespread and often quite common in the southern, central United States. The Boidae includes the egg-laying pythons and the live-bearing boas. Pythons, largest of all snakes, are the only ones definitely recorded eating people. The boa constrictor of Central and South America, and a few West Indian islands, is famous for its length, but rarely grows very large, about twelve feet maximum. Pythons may triple that size, and some proponents of the anaconda, or South American water boa, claim it does too. They haven't got a specimen to prove it though. Two small boas, the rosy and the rubber, occur along our Pacific coast.

The vipers, family Viperidae, have the most highly developed venom injection system yet evolved. The maxillary bone of the upper jaw bears the only teeth in that jaw (the dentary, of the lower jaw also has small teeth). It is greatly shortened, and rotates like a bearing on the skull. When a viper strikes its victim, it rotates the maxillaries so that the long fang, normally folded up against the roof of the mouth, extends straight out. The fangs, usually just one on each side, are hollow like hypodermic needles, and connected by a tube to modified salivary glands that produce the mix of virulent digestive enzymes that do the poisoning. The purpose of the viper's poison is to predigest, as well as kill, its prey. Of course, the system works well also as a defense against potential predators, like man.

Our rattlesnake and copperhead are vipers. Some authorities separate them, and their relatives that also have a pit between the eye and nostril, as the family Crotalidae: the pit vipers. Most of us regard the difference as subfamily level at most. The pit is a heat-sensing organ, a sort of lensless eye that senses infrared light. Many other sorts of snakes have heat sensitive scale organs on various areas of the face, but only the pit vipers have such a complex, single, localized device for this purpose.

John James Audubon, master painter of birds, once depicted a rattler up in a tree attacking mockingbirds. He has often been criticized for this, as rattlers rarely climb, and feed primarily on rodents, not birds. But that is trivial. Look closely at that snake. Not only does it have a whole row of teeth in the upper jaw, it has a *round* pupil. All our pit vipers have a vertical, cat-like pupil. Audubon was a poor observer of snakes.

Another family of snakes, the Elapidae, is equipped with a fang on the maxilla. While the fang is rather short and immobile, the venom it delivers is often the most devastating of all. These are the world's deadliest snakes: cobras, mambas, coral snakes, and sea snakes. They inhabit warm to tropical climes of all continents and the Indian and Pacific Oceans.

There are several additional families, including the burrowing Typhlopidae. These little snakes are common in many tropical areas, even the Hawaiian Islands. It is blithely claimed that Hawaii has no snakes, but in addition to *Typhlops*, it has *Pelamis platurus*, the yellow-bellied sea snake—likely the deadliest of all.

None of the families I have noted above has a representative in our area, and our snakes provide a knotty problem in classification. Most herpetologists put them all in the single family Colubridae. Dr. Garth Underwood of the British Museum, however, has suggested that the water, garter, ribbon, and little brown snakes deserve a family of their own: Natricidae. I rather like this arrangement. Natricids have very peculiar vertebrae, and are obviously all very closely related. Other proposals to sort out groups from the Colubridae have met with severe difficulties. For example, a number of species have peculiar teeth. Often a fang-like tooth, in the rear of the mouth, is enlarged. Our hognose and ring-neck snakes show this condition. In some tropical forms, like the boomslang of Africa, this fang and its associated venom gland are evolved to a deadly extent. The problem is that similar rear-fanged structures seem to have been independently developed in several distantly related lineages. This is called *convergent* evolution; two or more groups, basically unrelated, look alike. Whales and fish are a blatant example.

Since the Natricidae does sort out, and is a close-knit group of related forms, I choose to regard it as a full family. Even so, the Colubridae is a huge group; most of the world's snake species belong to it.

One of the most striking features of our Cape and Islands species is extreme differential abundance. Why are kingsnakes so abundant on Nantucket, or ribbon snakes thick on Chappaquiddick, and relatively scarce elsewhere? I shall try to come to grips with possible causes and explanations.

But there is a very big question here. Just *how* do I *know* these differential abundances occur? Maybe it's just snake hunter's luck that I find a dozen green snakes in a few minutes on one island and none at all on another. Well, of course, there does exist a margin for error; sometimes I may be wrong. I must point out that I am no demographer, and have used no sophisticated techniques. There is much to be learned about population biology here by carefully planned mark and recapture studies. I hope these will soon be undertaken. I also hope that my rather raw data will jog my colleagues into studying some of these remarkable phenomena. All I have done to determine relative abundance is count. I count as many snakes in a given area as I can, and then extrapolate to a per acre figure. Then, by consulting aerial photos and topographic maps, I estimate the size of the area where my per acre figure is likely to apply. This procedure would obviously lead to horrendous errors, especially because one of the most obvious facts I know is that similar habitats often have totally unlike numbers of snakes.

So, I go and check. Using my initial figure as a prediction, I move to another region within my putative region of abundance. If I get a similar count, I figure I am guessing pretty close to the truth. By doing this over and over, I slowly build up some confidence in the figures and the map I am making.

Snakes can be readily marked by clipping scales in unique patterns, in some area—like under the tail—where a little superficial damage will not really hurt them. Also, little transmitters can be readily inserted, surgically, into a snake's body cavity. Experiments and long term studies have proven that these transmitters have no ill effect on the animals, and their travels, home ranges, and numbers will begin to emerge as the data come in.

Cape Cod and the Islands provide the finest natural laboratory known to me for studies of this type. Yet, with some of the great universities in the country close by, and some of the most high-powered biologists living today, no one has ever attempted such a study. They just left it up to an itinerant snake hunter, who simply went around and looked under things, and wrote down what he saw.

Black Racer

I am sitting on the west end of Naushon, looking across the narrowest of the Holes—Robinsons—at Pasque. Here on Naushon there are black racers, while at Pasque, and on all the rest of the islands down the chain of the Elizabeths, there are none. I am at the absolute end of a species' range. The racer, *Coluber constrictor* (misnamed by Linnaeus, for it does not constrict), stops here. Just a hundred yards or so over to port, is a clump of bayberry and poison ivy, a little miniature dump, and a morainal rock jumble. A couple of fine racers live right there. Just across the slash of blue water, straight ahead, I

Black racer (*Coluber c. constrictor*), adult male, about five-and-a-half feet total length: Edgartown, Martha's Vineyard.

can see Fred Gaskill puttering around in his skiff. He is little farther away than the racers.

Racers are fondest of eating mice, rats, other rodents, shrews, and small mammals in general. Many individuals show a taste for frogs, toads, fish, birds, other snakes—almost anything alive may be eaten by a hungry racer. Their food supply is certainly abundant on down the islands. Racers occur all the way north to Nova Scotia. Here, in the Cape-Islands region, I have records of racers up and active on the surface during every month of the year except February, and that exception is just an oversight deriving from the fact that, like the leatherback, I spend February in the tropics. Black racers certainly are cold tolerant. They absorb heat very quickly when basking in the sun, owing to their satin-sheen, black hides. A racer can warm up well over 80° F. on a 50° F. day. Racers could easily have dispersed overland to the nether Elizabeths, and Nantucket, where they simply do not exist. Racers swim very well, and often take to the water voluntarily. They could swim over to Pasque if they wanted to. They do not.

The black racer is our largest and most conspicuous snake, for it is diurnal—active by day—and travels long distances over the surface. Racers are paired, often, in late summer and fall, but usually are solitary the rest of the year. Apparently mating occurs in late summer and fall; the sperm overwinter in the female's oviducts, and egg laying occurs in June and July. Often, racers mate again in the spring, but I have never found them doing so in this region. Farther south, in New Jersey and Tennessee, for example, I have often found spring-mating racers.

I do not know how many eggs the average female lays; one from

198

Snakes, Order Squamata

Brewster laid fifteen in the first week of July at the Cape Cod Museum of Natural History. Often large clutches are found in suitable locations, like mouldering wood pulp, and I suspect several females have found the same laying site ideally suited to their needs. The little ones are about a foot long at hatching, usually in August.

Range of the black racer (*Coluber constrictor constrictor*): dots indicate where specimens have been examined. Shading indicates the probable actual range of the species. This is pretty solid. Racers are large, obvious snakes; I will be surprised by any legitimate record outside the shaded area, and expect them *everywhere* within it. The arrow indicates Robinsons Hole.

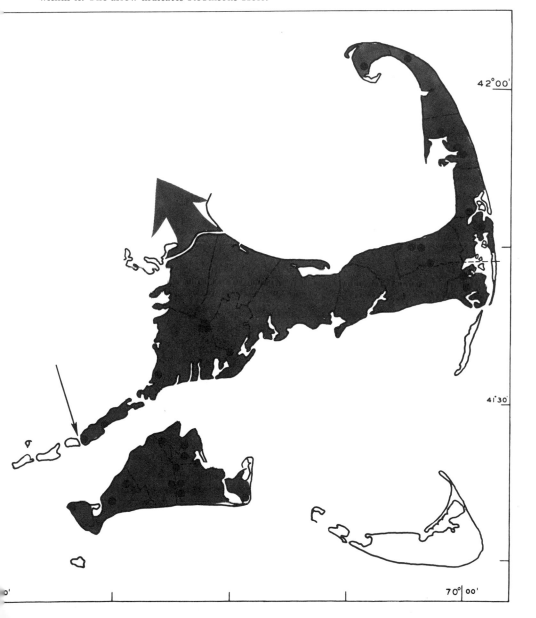

At hatching, baby racers are patterned with dark, grey-brown saddles on an ashy ground. They are often mistaken for kingsnakes—"milk snakes." It takes them about three years to reach maturity, at which time all trace of pattern is gone, except for white on the chin and throat, and sometimes light and darks spots and mottles on the slate-grey belly.

The largest racer I have ever measured was six feet and one quarter inch. A female, she was an inch-and-a-quarter longer than I am tall. She probably still lives at the Gay Head dump. On the same day I found her I turned out another, much smaller female. I pitched her behind me a few feet, and continued rooting in the heap of old boards where she lived. In just a minute or two, I received a solid blow to the back of my leg. There she was, striking away at me. I pitched her a little farther this time. Right back she came. She would open her mouth wide, rear up, and bang right into my leg. She wasn't really even trying to bite. This time I tried shooing her off. I grabbed at her, intending to miss; she retreated, still belligerent. I went after her once more; she turned and glided away. I never saw her again.

Many people have reported similar incidents with aggressive black racers. Once, in the Pine Barrens of New Jersey, I was followed for what must have been half a mile by a racer. He kept his distance, and stopped when I did. When I started up, so did he. When I turned and tried to catch him, he took off. Racers have large home ranges, frequently many acres. At least parts of their home ranges seem to be defended territories.

Racers seem to be quite intelligent as snakes go, but their wide-ranging habits, and love of basking in the sun, get them slaughtered on the roads. Few racers take well to captivity. I once had a fine one from Connecticut that lived happily for years, eating fish. One at the day camp at Wellfleet Bay in 1975 was similarly cooperative. These are exceptions to the rule, however; most are just too vigorous and active to survive in a cage.

The taxonomy of racers is confused and confusing. Many subspecies have been described and named, but in the eastern states these are often *polytopic*. Polytopy is the situation of similar-looking populations being scattered around, widely separated by different, ordinary looking populations. Thus, pale-backed racers with spotted bellies occur on the Outer Banks of North Carolina, at Cape Canaveral, and in the Everglades and upper Florida Keys. Normal black ones occur over most of the rest of the Atlantic seaboard, including the lower Florida Keys. It appears that similar colorations have evolved separately several times. Calling an amalgamation of remote populations of similar color a "subspecies" is just as illogical as lumping birds, bats, butterflies, and airplanes together in the same "family" because they all have wings.

Southern coastal plain, Florida, and Gulf coast male racers are very distinctive in having enlarged spines on their hemipenes. The females are not readily separable from northern racers, however, and the subspecies rule says that 75 percent of *all* adult individuals must be identifiable. Since at least 50 percent of racers (more from my field evidence) are females, I cannot see how the southern populations can qualify as a subspecies either, at least qualify as is presently defined. There may well be other characteristics that will aid identification of females, and bring the percentage up to a respectable level.

Paul Elias got very interested in variation in racers after a couple of trips to the Outer Banks with me. He continues his interest now, out at the University of California, Berkeley, and reports that western racers are an even bigger mess than the east coast ones. If subspecies of racers turn out to be recognizable—and I suspect some will—then ours is presumably the first named form, *Coluber constrictor constrictor*.

Racers often *rattle* loudly and well, especially when nervous or irritated. They just vibrate their tail tips. This makes a fine buzz on anything the tail hits. It is perfectly reasonable to dislike these big, aggressive snakes; they bite hard and bloodily if you give them a chance. It is terrible to kill them, however, for they are a major asset in keeping down rats and mice, and play a most important role in the overall balance of nature.

Green Snake

The smooth green snake, *Opheodrys vernalis*, which is smooth because the scales lack keels, is a pretty little relative of the larger racer. Rio Grande racers, in fact, are smaller than other sorts, often quite green, and so seem to bridge the gap between the two species. The genus *Opheodrys* includes a much larger, keeled species occurring south of us, and several Asiatic forms as well. What they have in common, aside from being green, no one has ever made clear to me. Ours should be put right back in the genus *Coluber*. I certainly hope all the people who do not believe that will get excited about it and try to tell me why not.

Adult green snakes are usually less than two feet long. Most are

Green snake (*Opheodrys vernalis*), adult female, about eighteen inches total length: Naushon, Elizabeth Islands.

The strange distribution of the green snake (*Opmeodrys vernalis*). Dots indicate single specimen records. Blackened areas, indicated with arrows, are regions of extreme abundance; here there seem to be at least four or five per acre, or more than 1000 per square kilometer. Note the big dot off the East Chop of Martha's Vineyard in Nantucket Sound.

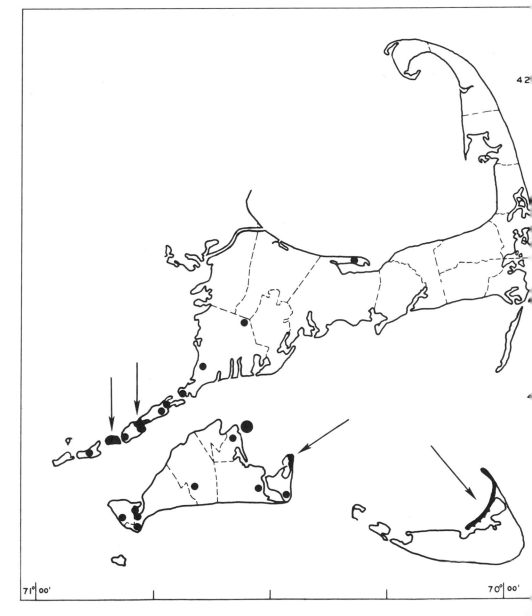

quite bright green, but those I have seen from Cape Poge, where they are very abundant, were dull olive or brownish green. Those from the Coatue-Great Point arc of Nantucket, where they are similarly very abundant, were somber grey-green with pale grey flecking on the lips and chin. Baby green snakes, from four inches or so until they grow past eight inches, are quite grey.

I have never found mating green snakes, and, in fact, infrequently find males. Only two of ten examined on Pasque were males. That percentage holds up for my totaled records: about 20 percent males. I have found eggs frequently in areas of abundance, but only in July when they were about to hatch. At Kettle Cove, Naushon, several discrete clutches of six eggs each were found. At Cape Poge a seemingly communal nest contained twenty-eight. My other clutches have been singles, four or six eggs, and have averaged about five. I have never found a clutch of five, however. Eggs are laid under planks or logs, in open, grassy situations.

Lots of people have told me what green snakes eat, but I have no first-hand evidence that they eat anything at all. The ones I have known in captivity refused insects and spiders, and dwindled to their deaths if not released. I once told this to a meeting of the Connecticut Herpetological Society. After my talk, a little boy came up to enlighten me by explaining that green snakes eat grapes. Well, I can't prove they do not, but no herpetologist known to me has recorded any species of snake not exclusively carnivorous.

I *guess* green snakes eat crickets, moths, spiders, and other soft-bodied succulent arthropods, because that is what most people who claim to know say they eat.

The distribution of green snakes is mightily peculiar. They are exceedingly abundant in *some* grassy, open, small island habitats where kingsnakes are scarce or absent. That makes sense, for kingsnakes have been caught in the act of eating green snakes, for example, by Martha Esmond on Nashawena. On some seemingly small islands, however, I can find no green snakes at all. The biggest of the Weepeckets, off the north side of Naushon, in Buzzards Bay, would seem perfect green snake habitat. Al Greer, David Bruce, and I searched that island thoroughly, and found no reptiles or amphibians at all. Penikese, with lots of garter and DeKay's snakes, should be ideal too. Maybe no snake can survive on big Weepecket, perhaps for lack of fresh water. Snakes can certainly survive on Penikese, however. Why no greens? Cuttyhunk presents a similar problem; interested residents, like Wilfred Tilton, are sure there are none there.

Green snakes are of regular occurence over Martha's Vineyard and the base of Cape Cod. On the outer, lower Cape, however, they seem downright rare.

It is generally held that there are two races of smooth green snakes: *O. v. vernalis* in the east, and a western, prairie and alpine meadow form, *O. v. blanchardi*. These two forms look pretty good, but there are some problems. The way to tell the two apart is ventral scale count. The eastern males have 130 or less; eastern females 139 or less. Western individuals have more. The difficulty is that isolated populations of low count, eastern-type snakes occur in South Dakota and Wyoming. Are these legitimate *O. v. vernalis* that arrived from the north, say Manitoba? Or are they an independently evolved population? It makes all the difference between valid races and invalid ones. Possibly, these snakes differ from both eastern and western ones in some other way, and constitute a third race. Someone really ought to consider the problem.

I have never met Fred Ginches, but should he happen to read this book, I sincerely hope he will accept my congratulations and heartfelt gratitude. You see, Mr. Ginches was out fishing in Nantucket Sound off the East Chop of Martha's Vineyard, one fine October afternoon. Along came a green snake, swimming over to Spain. Mr. Ginches snagged it and brought it to Dr. William Schroeder, the ichthyologist at Woods Hole. Bill Schroeder sent it to the MCZ, along with the whole story. That was fifteen years ago, but Mr. Ginches' snake is safe and sound. With evidence like that, explaining why green snakes are absent from some islands is difficult indeed. Obviously, they *can* go just about wherever they want; if not Spain, at least to Muskeget, or Tuckernuck.

One day in July I was walking from the east end of Naushon down to Tarpaulin Cove, via the south shore. I caught the biggest green snake I had ever seen. I carefully stretched him (it was a male) out along my turtle net handle, and scratched a mark where he came to his end. Then I let him go. When I got to Tarpaulin Cove I measured the length of net handle to the scratch—thirty-one and three-eighths inches. It was days later, when I got back to my old station wagon in Woods Hole, that I pulled out the *Field Guide* and discovered the record for *O. vernalis* is just twenty-six inches. I *would have* had a new record! I would have, but I didn't and I don't. The difference between me and Mr. Ginches is that mine is just another snake story; his is *real*.

Kingsnake or Milk Snake

Our magnificent, boldly patterned, richly colored kingsnake—just as much a kingsnake as the famous scarlet king or the chain king—is *Lampropeltis triangulum triangulum*. Most people call it a milk snake. This ridiculous name derives from the myth that these snakes milk cows, by latching onto their udders with their mouths full of needle-sharp, recurved teeth.

The milk-snake legend derives from the fact that these kingsnakes are even fonder of rats and mice than many other members of genus *Lampropeltis*, and so enjoy the environs of barns, where pest rodents abound. They are among the most beneficial species of animal life, because they are devout tunnel travelers and search out rats and mice way down in the foundations and walls, where they get the little pink babies right in the nest. A kingsnake is smaller and less active than a black racer, but it eats four or five times as many rodents, because it gets the nests, while the racer hunts primarily adults on the surface.

Our kingsnakes, like the other members of their genus, are also fond of eating other snakes. They do not seem to eat the foul-smelling, musky members of nefarious *Natrix*, and for some reason ring-neck snakes often abound with them. But green snakes really get it. It is the sheer abundance of kingsnakes on Nantucket that makes the place uninhabitable for green snakes. If the harbor closed, it would go fresh, and then slowly succeed to a swampy, red maple forest. The kingsnakes would move north, eventually to what today is the Coatue Peninsula. There, in the absence of kingsnakes—who just can't take it that open and arid—green snakes abound. The kingsnakes would gobble them up. If green snakes survived, it would probably be only at Great Point. Of course, all that would take centuries, and it will begin just as soon as people get tired of dredging out the harbor entrance.

The kingsnake situation on Nantucket is so extraordinary as to be unbelievable to anyone who has not been there. I found sixteen the first day I hunted there, and had not found six in all the previous snake hunts I had made in New England, taken together. Numi, Al and Phlyp Greer, John and Lynne Alexander, and I all went to Nantucket one spring. Nobody quite believed what I said about king-snakes. I must have just had unusual luck. By the end of the day, they were all believers. Numi summed it all up as we finished up our hunting. She turned over a board, lowered it back, walked away, and said, "Damn, only two milksnakes."

Kingsnake or milk snake (*Lampropeltis t. triangulum*), adult male, about three feet total length: Nantucket.

George Vesper, then a graduate student at the University of Connecticut and long a prominent Connecticut naturalist, became interested in the peculiar, barred, big, dark garter snakes of our Islands. He decided to do a project on Nantucket garter snakes, but had only a few cold, clammy May days for field work. He got only fifteen garter snakes, but in a few minutes in one small area he found seventeen kingsnakes.

What can account for this vast population? I can suggest several factors to put into the equation: (1) The abundance of small mammal food items. Five species in particular are meadow voles (*Microtus pennsylvanicus*), white-footed mice (*Peromyscus leucopus*), masked shrews (*Sorex cinereus*), short-tailed shrews (*Blarina brevicauda*), and common moles (*Scalopus aquaticus*). (2) The absence of a primary competitor and occasional predator, the black racer (*Coluber constrictor*). (3) The absence of native predatory mammals such as raccoons, foxes, skunks, and weasels.

Well, that's all right for a start, but there are other islands—like Cuttyhunk and Tuckernuck—with similar qualifications and no known kingsnakes at all. Also, there are predatory mammals, like feral house cats, in abundance on Nantucket today. Furthermore, hawks—such as the marsh hawk—are very common on Nantucket. They are commoner there than on the mainland. These both compete with and prey upon kingsnakes. The worst problem of all was revealed by George Vesper's work on his garter snakes; they seem to eat small mammals. The huge garter snake population is competing, on Nantucket, with the astronomical kingsnake population for the same prey species. I shall have more to say about this when discussing garter snakes, below.

The size our northern kingsnake attains is a question of debate. Wright and Wright claim they grow to fifty-four inches—perhaps much too conveniently four-and-a-half feet. They do not cite a specimen of such size. In the first edition of the *Field Guide*, Dr. Conant listed only forty-seven and one-quarter inches. Jeff Keidel caught a fifty-two inch male at Polpis, and gave it to me on 16 July 1969. It lived awhile in captivity, but probably did not grow. When it

Range of the kingsnake (*Lampropeltis triangulum triangulum*): dots indicate where specimens have been examined. The blackened area of Nantucket is an area of extreme abundance, totally unlike any other region known to me. Here there seem to be more than 10 kingsnakes per acre, or (gasp!) about 2,500 per square kilometer, or something like 6,000 per square mile.

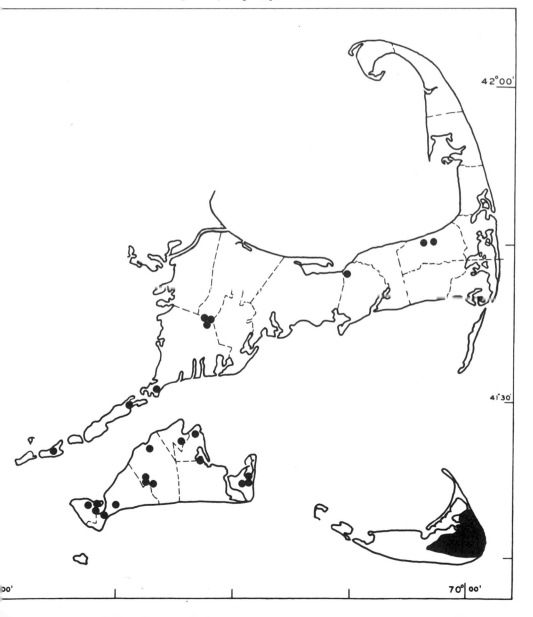

died, I put it in the MCZ. It is fitting that a Nantucket specimen should hold the record, but Jeff and the Perkins brothers, who have long hunted snakes together there, are unanimous in their belief that much larger ones occur. Frankly, I have measured so many in excess of four feet that I cannot doubt some really big fellow will turn up one day.

Our kingsnake is one of a group of spectacularly different looking subspecies of a single species. Included in this *rasenkreis*—a complex of geographic races—are the scarlet kingsnake (*L. t. elapsoides*—formerly called "*L. doliata*"), the Mexican "milk snake" (*L. t. annulata*), and the red "milk snake" (*L. t. gentilis*)—to name a few. These snakes look so different from each other in coloration, pattern, size, and head proportions, and are even so different in behavior and habitat, that the fact that they all intergrade into each other where their ranges meet seems preposterous. But, along most of their borders, they do. If we applied Dr. Highton's woodland salamander reasoning to the subspecies of kingsnakes, all would have to be declared invalid. It would then be utterly impossible to identify a specimen of *Lampropeltis triangulum*. You have to recognize the subspecies first; you only know the species secondarily.

I have no reproductive data on Cape and Islands kingsnakes. Out of more than 300 individuals examined, most of them from Nantucket, I have never found a hatchling or a clutch of eggs. This is amazing. All those Nantucket kingsnakes seem to be adults. I have never found any very young adults. Turnover, and recruitment into the adult population, must be very low, indeed. It seems that once you have become an adult kingsnake on Nantucket, you are set for life—and a very long life into the bargain. I can think of no natural population of snakes that would more fruitfully repay a detailed demographic study than the kingsnakes of Nantucket.

The average density of kingsnakes in their region of abundance on Nantucket is, I estimate conservatively, ten to twenty per acre. I *know* of acres that contain 200. As I said in my 1969 paper on Nantucket, I have never seen "so many snakes . . . anywhere outside of the tropics."

Ringneck Snake

This beautiful little creature is technically *Diadophis punctatus edwardsi*, the northeastern subspecies of a species found from coast to coast and south into Mexico. It is a *xenodontine*—strange toothed

—and very closely related to such forms as our southeastern yellow-lipped snake and the tropical members of the *Dromicus-Alsophis* complex. Its closest relative in our area, strangely enough, seems to be the hognose snake.

Our subspecies can be recognized by its rather small size—to about two feet at most—bright yellow belly with few, if any, black spots down the middle, and the *complete* yellow ring around the neck. Occasional individuals do have belly spotting. Marshal Case caught one in Harwich that has heavy ventral spotting, just like a southern ringneck. He pickled it, and put it in the American Museum, number 101375. However, it has a complete neck ring, a give-away for *edwardsi*, since true *D. p. punctatus* of the south have at least the median scale row dark on the neck, interrupting the ring.

The most interesting thing about ringneck snakes is what they eat: salamanders. In other parts of the country they may eat other things —frogs, lizards, other snakes. Here, so far as I can determine, they eat only lungless salamanders. That means, most of the time, and most places, they have to eat woodland salamanders, *Plethodon cinereus*. The members of the genus *Plethodon* produce a thick, whitish, glue-like slime that gums up every moving thing it gets on in sufficient quantities. Making a woodland salamander miserable and unhappy—for example, by trying to eat him—seems to cause a precipitous and copious secretion of this material. It has often been suggested that this secretion makes woodland salamanders undesirable prey, where a choice occurs, for small predators.

Some years ago, one of my first students, Eliza Klein, and I decided there could be no better predator to try choice experiments on than ringneck snakes. We got two of them from inland Massachusetts, and all the salamanders we could. We had three species of salamanders: woodland (*P. cinereus*), two-lined (*Eurycea bislineata*), and the lungless dusky (*Desmognathus fuscus*). We put one of each kind in a small beaker and aimed the open end at the snake. Then, we simply scored one for the species he ate first, and two for the species he ate next. We never let either snake eat the third salamander: we just scored it three. We didn't have enough salamanders, and (most of all) the snakes got so fat eating just two salamanders, at intervals as long as our patience could stand waiting, that we feared they might eat just one. If they didn't take two salamanders in each trial, we would not have a complete score. We would have to reject our data and start over. It was awfully boring work. A week's interval was about as short a time as we could wait; so, with just two snakes, it took us *months* to pile up much data.

Ring-neck snake (*Diadophis punctatus edwardsi*), adult female, about twenty inches total length: Chatham, Cape Cod.

In the end we got thirty full-score trials. The species with the lowest score was the one taken first most times; it was the two-line. The dusky and the woodland were about tied with much higher scores. A *chi*-square test revealed that our data was statistically significant; apparently ringnecks really do prefer two-lines.

The most interesting thing about all this is the fact that dusky salamanders seem to mimic the color patterns of woodland salamanders. Where red-backed woodlands are common, dusky salamanders commonly have reddish backs too. Where woodlands have red cheeks, or red legs, a percentage of the dusky salamanders do too. This tendency to mimic is best developed, apparently, in areas where ringneck snakes are most abundant: upland Massachusetts, the southern Appalachians, and similar regions. If some dusky salamanders escape predation by ringnecks because they look like woodland salamanders, that would be an immediate and obvious natural selection for mimicry.

There are lots of problems, though. Do ringneck snakes really orient to their prey by sight? I would think they mostly captured their prey *underneath* things, in the dark. If not by sight, then I cannot visualize the benefit of color pattern mimicry.

What about Naushon and Nantucket, where there would seem to be nothing to eat but woodland salamanders? Here, ringnecks are especially abundant. There must be some other feature of the environment that optimizes these island habitats. I just don't know.

A clutch of ringneck eggs found in Falmouth on 3 July contained six eggs. They ranged from 19 to 21 mm. in length (average 20), and from 8.5 to 9.5 mm. in width. They are long, thin, blunt-ended, and rather cylindrical. A clutch of five eggs laid by a Chatham female on 28 June were basically similar, but were longer: up to 23 mm., averaging 21 mm.

Within the areas of abundance on Naushon and Nantucket I have never found eggs or hatchlings. This is in direct contrast to the situation with green snakes, whose eggs and young are common where the snakes are, but fits the peculiar pattern of the Nantucket kingsnakes.

Range of the ring-neck snake (*Diadophis punctatus edwardsi*): dots indicate where individuals have been examined. Blackened areas on Naushon and Nantucket are regions of abundance; here one may find a specimen per acre, or about 250 per square kilometer. Islands indicated by arrows (Monomoy, Penikese, No Mans Land, and Muskeget) lack a food supply. Anywhere else I anxiously await specimens: the food supply (woodland salamander) occurs.

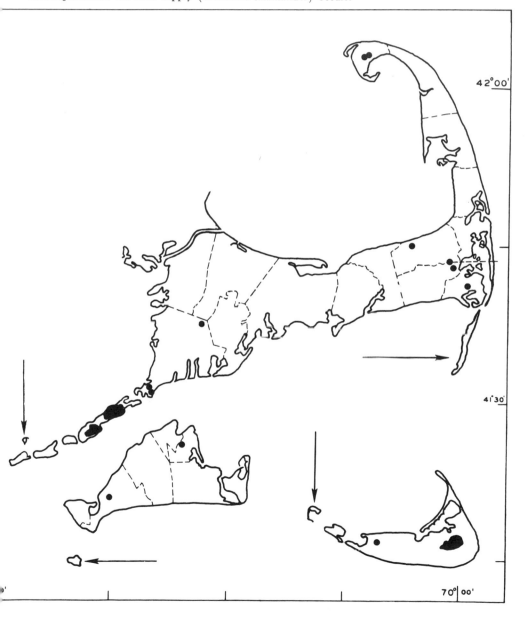

Hognose Snake

I have been a hunter all my life. My parents are, since I have known them at least, rather indoor, center-city folks; but I did not grow up exclusively with my parents. Every summer, with only a couple of exceptions, from the time I was two until I was fifteen, I went to Mississippi. There I fell into the clutches of my uncles.

My Uncle Dick was a bird hunter. He still hunts them, but now mostly with a paint brush instead of a gun. Although bird hunting was a fall and winter activity, Uncle Dick's walls were adorned with weathered trophies. At that time Uncle Dick practiced taxidermy, and gave me some of my earliest lessons in that art. I rarely went afield with Uncle Dick, but when I had got something special I would repair to his house to have it immortalized.

My Uncle Loot (a corruption of his rank of Lieutenant) and my Uncle Chick were the summertime hunters, or rather fishermen. They connived constantly to avoid the responsibilities of families and business to head out to the swamps, ox-bow lakes, and river bottoms. I never cared much for fishing, but there were always lizards, snakes, turtles, and remarkable birds. Uncle Loot has passed away, but Uncle Chick will still take a brief sojourn in the woods, and even occasionally try a shot at a squirrel. Uncle Chick has little love of snakes but he taught me all he knew about them, and much more about the lives of innumerable other creatures. It is to my Uncle Chick that I attribute my seemingly innate passion for replacing the habitat. Every log turned over must be turned carefully back again; that way, it will produce other treasures another day.

It was with Uncle Chick that I got my first all-black hognose snake. Today this color phase is known not to be rare, and I have seen quite a few of them, but back then it was a remarkable occasion. As my passion for reptiles and amphibians increased over the years, I developed a view that I hold today: hunting selected kinds of these creatures is the greatest sport of all.

A beauty of hunting reptiles and amphibians is that one always seeks to secure the specimen alive and unharmed. Only rarely is it necessary to put one in the freezer, later to be pickled and tagged as a museum specimen. Often, one can secure all the museum specimens needed by merely pickling those killed on highways (DOR, we say, for dead-on-road).

In this democratic age there are hardly enough kings to go around, but given the chance I would rank hunting of the hognose snake of Cape Cod high on their list of potential sports.

Hog-nose snake (*Heterodon platyrhinos*), young female, about fourteen inches total length. Harwich, Cape Cod.

Hognose snakes on Cape Cod are scarce enough to make finding one an exciting event, but common enough so it is likely a good hunter will get one with patience. Aside from jet black (which I have not yet seen on the Cape), these creatures come in a bold and gaudy assortment of hues and patterns. They may go in for ashy shades of grey and brown, or flashy shades of pink, orange, yellow, and black.

When first encountered, they are apt to try to terrify you with a fearsome display of hissing and puffing, complete with spreading of a grand, cobra-style hood. If that doesn't work (sometimes they never even give it a try), they will endeavor to die so completely dead that you feel elated by such an easy victory. They writhe around, belly up, tongue extended and dragging through the sand, mouth distorted and agape. It is really quite an act, but the snake is so taken with his role that he flips right back over—belly up—if you turn him rightside up. Ingrained in his DNA, and programmed into his tiny mind, is the notion that dead snakes *always* lie belly up. Put him belly down again and he will immediately correct your misconception. *He* knows what a good dead snake looks like.

Some individuals don't bother with these antics; some won't play dead; some won't try to intimidate you first and play dead right away. In captivity most give up this behavior in a few days. I had one from Falmouth, though, that never quit trying, and was the star of numerous snake talks with school children.

Most hognose snakes eat only toads, at least as adults. Young ones cannot handle anything bigger than a tiny, newly metamorphosed toad, and eat salamanders and spring peepers. This provides an important and often overlooked clue to good hognose habitat. Sheer abundance of toads is not enough to sustain a population. Smaller prey species must exist for the young snakes. If, for example, there

Probable range of the hog-nose snake (*Heterodon platyrhinos*), based on topography, habitat, and food supply (toads). Arrow indicates Monomoy, where I suspect the species occurs, but where it has not been found. The cluster of dots at Ashumet, in Falmouth, indicates a cluster of snake hunts. There is no reason to believe the species is unusualy abundant there.

really are no peepers or woodland salamanders on Monomoy, then maybe there really are no hognose snakes there. If either of these small prey species *does* occur on Monomoy, and I suspect they do, then one day we may actually get a hognose there. Certainly, there are plenty of toads.

My Falmouth specimen would eat frogs. He would even eat *dead* frogs. This made him an ideal captive, for I could freeze enough frogs to keep him going strong all winter.

If you want to keep one of these delightful snakes around as a pet, you had better quickly learn his food preferences. If he insists strictly on living toads, he won't make it through the winter. Then just keep him a few days and take him *right back where you caught him* for release. Hognose snakes show a spectacular and wildly discordant geographic variation. No subspecies can be sorted out, but the different parts of the species' range support very different variations; transport and release could be devastating to these patterns of variation.

Dr. Conant says *Heterodon platyrhinos* attains a record size of forty-five and one-half inches. Goodness gracious, I never saw one anywhere *near* that. I have seen one or two in North Carolina just over thirty inches, but the biggest one I ever saw on Cape Cod was just twenty-six inches. I have never found eggs or hatchlings of this species, so for such data you will have to check Wright and Wright.

Nefarious *Natrix*

I may, from time to time, have herein indicated a certain lack of ardor for the works—or a certain attenuation of respect for the mentalities—of a few selected colleagues in the field of herpetology. I have now before me the unparalleled opportunity to heap abuse upon virtually all of them.

You see, virtually to a one, they go right on referring to our American water snakes, on the one hand, as *Natrix*, and our garter and ribbon snakes, on the other hand, as "*Thamnophis*." I sunk the genus "*Thamnophis*" several years ago (1972) in a footnote. (I learned the trick of sinking genera in footnotes from my ex-major-professor, Dr. Ernest E. Williams of Harvard. It is a dirty trick.)

Anyway, that obvious footnote was in an obscure publication put out by Massachusetts Audubon Society. They only printed a thousand copies. A second edition, with "*Thamnophis*" still sunk in the same footnote, and with a printing of two thousand copies is now available.

My colleagues will, however, admit that it is not the obscurity of the publication, nor the format of the footnote, nor the paucity of copies that keeps them using "*Thamnophis*." They know I did it, but they ignore it. They *know* genera require definitions that work.

They *know* no such definition has ever been framed for "*Thamnophis*." They *know* all the New World *Natrix*, including "*Thamnophis*," are more closely related to each other than to the Old World *Natrix natrix*; and last of all they *know* that the deprecators of taxonomy, those other biologists who think taxonomists are neither biologists nor intelligent, are nurtured by this very sort of pig-headed stupidity. But they just don't give a damn.

The genus *Natrix* and its often-called-*Natrix* relatives are nearly cosmopolitan. There are dozens—perhaps hundreds—of species. They occur everywhere except in the oceans and on some oceanic islands, and are absent from Antarctica, Greenland, and other frigid regions. There are more than fifty different kinds in North America north of Mexico. Right here in New England we have a slender, striped extreme species, N. *saurita*—the ribbon snake—a heavy-bodied, barred species, N. *sipedon*—the water snake—and a dead-on intermediate, N. *sirtalis*—the garter snake.

Ed Malnate, of the Academy of Natural Sciences in Philadelphia, produced a revision of the nearly worldwide *Natrix* assemblage in 1960. He explicitly steered clear of the "*Thamnophis*" question, and that, among other things, got him into a bit of trouble at the hands of Dr. Sam McDowell, anatomist and reviewer of the work (1961). As McDowell says ". . . there is better evidence of close affinity between New World "*Natrix*" and *Thamnophis* and *Storeria* than there is of affinity between New World "*Natrix*" and Old World *Natrix*. . . ."

You see, the problem hinges on the relationship of any of our members of the group to the European *Natrix natrix*—grass snake—the type species of the genus. All of our *Natrix* and "*Thamnophis*" are live-bearing and their embryos develop a yolk-sac *placenta*—analogous to the placenta, or "after birth" of human embryos, and a very remarkable thing for reptiles. *Natrix natrix*, though it looks just like a garter snake, lays typical, shelled, reptilian eggs.

All of our American species belong to the same genus. (I believe *Storeria* can be validly differentiated.) But is that genus really *Natrix* at all? If someone were to provide a good definition for all our *Natrix* and "*Thamnophis*," separating them from the Old World forms, the name *Thamnophis* would become available. *All* our species might end up being "*Thamnophis*," truly; but as long as some of them are called *Natrix*, they are all *Natrix*, unless *you* can prove otherwise.

Now, the burden of proof rests squarely on anyone who would use the name "*Thamnophis*," in speech or print, to justify that usage.

216

Snakes, Order Squamata

Three characteristics have been suggested for separating out the garter and ribbon snakes: (1) *apical pits*—tiny organs on the scales; (2) *a complete and undivided anal plate*—the belly scale just before the cloacal opening; and (3) *the proportions of the quadrate bone.* I have discussed all of these in that aforementioned footnote. I state flatly that none of them works to define a group when large series of specimens from a wide diversity of the involved species are examined. But *everybody knows that.* No one has ever even hinted at disputing it. So, I maintain you have to redefine *"Thamnophis"* before you use it. No editor should allow that name to be published until it has been validated, and any lecturer who uses it should be hissed and jeered until he comes up with a definition that works.

There is among herpetologists a lunatic fringe that splits our *Natrix* into not just *"Thamnophis"* but yet a third "genus" called *"Regina".* *"Regina"* includes rather small, slender, often striped species, quite similar to many of the so-called *"Thamnophis."* Indeed, the only justification that I have ever heard or read for *"Regina"* is that it is no worse a genus than *"Thamnophis."*

Genera have to be defined, and the definitions have to hold up. If someone shows your definition to be faulty, or species in it to be interfertile with species in some other, then it is no good. That is all in the *Principles of Animal Taxonomy* (Simpson, 1961), and, if you just go by that book, things will work out just fine. The critics will dry up, and sanity will prevail. If you do not, if you just go right on ignoring facts, doing what your whimsy dictates, and justifying yourself by saying "gee, that's what lots of other guys do," then you are guilty of screwing up the works. The only reason I care is because they are *my* works too. I want a reasonable, workable, agreeable classification of known living things, and cannot see any good reason why we should not have it.

RIBBON SNAKE

Not only is this the prettiest, most active, and most agile of our three *Natrix* species, *Natrix saurita saurita* seems to be the most intelligent of all our snakes. In the Cape-Islands region, the ribbon snake is the only boldly striped species. Some Cape garter snakes are pretty well striped, but the vast majority appear somber brown, barred, or spotted. A good identification check is the pigmentation of the upper labials or lip scales. A series of large scales actually forms the upper lip of all snakes. In garter snakes the *sutures*—borders or

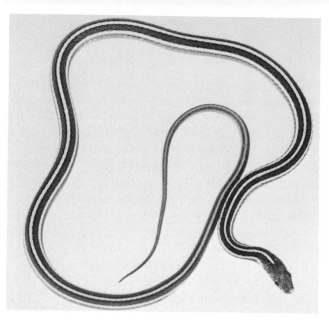

Ribbon snake (*Natrix s. saurita*), adult male, about eighteen inches total length: Chappaquiddick.

edges between each scale—are darkly pigmented. In ribbon snakes the upper labials are uniformly light.

The presence of paired spots on the top of the head is supposed to separate the western ribbon snake, billed as a distinct species—*Natrix proxima*, from our eastern forms. *Natrix saurita* has a southern subspecies also, so our northern form is the nominate race. I was not aware that other herpetologists had claimed *proxima* as a distinct species. I believe it is an older name than *saurita*, and so I used to call all ribbon snakes *Natrix proxima*: for example, in my Nantucket paper. Since paired head spots are a commonplace in Cape-Islands ribbon snakes, I remain unconvinced that I was wrong. However, I have not studied the question, and will defer to those who have.

Ribbon snakes depart significantly from the ecological regime of garter snakes, and overlap severely the food niche, at least, of the water snake: *Natrix sipedon*. Ribbon snakes in our area *never* eat birds, mammals, or earthworms—all garter snake favorites. Like water snakes, they eat fish, frogs, and salamanders. I have never found ribbon snakes abundantly in areas where water snakes occur, like Nantucket. The abundance of ribbon snakes in Provincetown is, for me, an indicator that the apparent absence of water snakes there is real. But why are there no water snakes at Wellfleet Bay Wildlife Sanctuary? Ribbon snakes are egregiously abundant there.

Ribbon snakes grow to more than a yard (or meter) in length

and produce litters of about a dozen young, usually in late summer. I have records of a heavily gravid female on 4 August and another that produced eleven young on 23 August (Falmouth); a twenty-four-inch female that produced nine young on 17 August (Harwich); newborn young with yolk-sac scars on 14 August (Wellfleet); and a similar recent arrival on 9 October (West Tisbury).

Localities for ribbon snakes (*Natrix saurita*): dots represent from one to three specimens; blackened areas are those of abundance, with concentrations of 1000 per square kilometer, or about four per acre—or even more. Shaded areas have seemingly suitable habitats, but apparently lack ribbon snakes; arrow indicates one such place: Coskata.

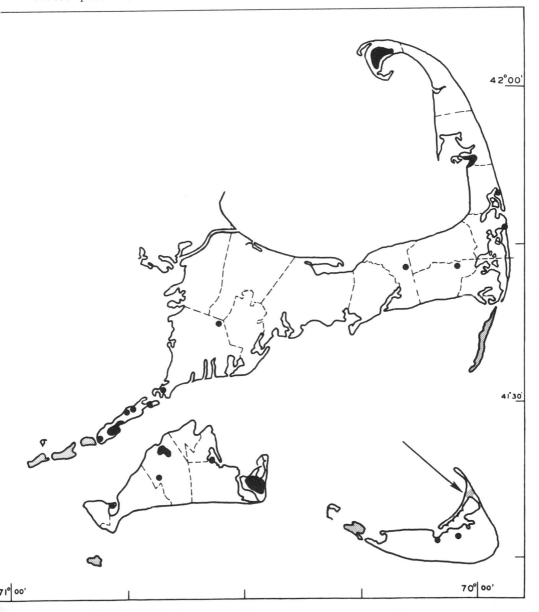

Ribbon snakes seem naturally gregarious and often occur in pairs, or even large aggregations. In captivity they do superbly on a diet of minnows or other bait fish. Their demonstrable intelligence is revealed by the ease with which they learn to recognize their feeder, feeding schedule, and associated details.

Most of our ribbon snakes combine shades of yellow or tan with coppery brown and black, but green shades are common too. Occasionally, a mutant appears that cannot make yellow pigment. As in the blue "green" frogs, these mutants appear blue in all the places they would normally have been greenish. They are quite striking snakes.

The areas of extreme abundance for this species combine several characteristics aside from lacking water snakes. They are dotted with small ponds and marshes, have extremely high green frog populations, and are not on islands smaller than Chappaquiddick. The first two features certainly fit perfectly with what we know of ribbon snake ecology, but the last one seems inexplicable.

Why are there no ribbon snakes on, for example, Nashawena—where small ponds, green frogs, and woodland salamanders are abundant?

GARTER SNAKE

This utterly ubiquitous, amazingly abundant species exhibits bizarre aberrations of appearance and behavior in our region. Here is a perfect example of the uniqueness of populations on our Islands. Dr. Ian Nisbet and I published on the tern-eating garter snakes of No Mans Land, and C. B. Floyd, in the thirties, recorded similar behavior in the Penikese population. Garter snakes are still abundant on Penikese, but the terns are gone. Weatherbee, Coppinger, and Walsh suggested that garter snakes were somehow accidental on Muskeget, dropped there by passing marsh hawks. I regard that notion as strange, and note that no herpetologist has ever had trouble finding garter snakes on Muskeget. Of course, the only herpetologists I know of who ever went there are Dr. Arthur Echternocht of Boston University and I. We went separately, years apart. We both caught garter snakes. Maybe we are both just unusually lucky, but I wouldn't bet on it. The Muskeget garter snakes were doubtlessly tern eaters generations back, when terns nested in profusion on that bizarre islet.

Ian Nisbet and I wrote, in that 1972 paper:

It is interesting that Drs. Zinn and Rankin, who reported on Penikese Island's fauna in 1947, found only one garter snake there. By this time the tern colony was down to about 1200 pairs; there were nearly as many pairs of herring gulls, and Floyd had claimed that herring gulls were vigorous predators on garter snakes.

It is too early to be sure, but garter snakes may well play a part in the complex inter-relationships between terns and gulls on these small islands. It is now well-known that the exploding herring gull populations have put severe pressure on breeding terns in Massachusetts: the gulls simply occupy the space before the terns arrive in spring, and the terns are forced to withdraw to breed on other, generally less suitable islands. On islands where high snake populations were supported by large terneries, as on Penikese in the thirties, these may actually have helped to attract herring gulls to settle there early in their period of colonization. Then, when the gulls displaced the terns, the snakes would have declined again, having lost a food source and acquired a new predator.

We know that tern colonies were very volatile in the past, even before the arrival of the gulls—they often shifted unpredictably from one island to another. In some cases these shifts were associated with human disturbance, the introduction of rats, or depredations by great horned owls, but in other cases there was no obvious cause. Perhaps in some of these cases a "population boom" of snakes had lowered the reproductive success of the terns below the self-sustaining level. When the terns left, the snakes would have suffered a "population bust," so that the island would soon have been suitable for reoccupation by the terns. Colonial sea birds are very vulnerable to predators which can become established and numerous in this way on their island colonies. The volatility of tern colonies may indicate the adaptive strategy which they have adopted to minimize the effects of the predators.

At least Muskeget Island might support this theory: garter snakes were once common there, and are now scarce. Terns are almost entirely gone from Muskeget today, though they once nested there by the thousands. Was it gulls alone that forced out the terns, or did the garter snakes play a role as well?

If garter snakes persist, as they do, on Muskeget and Penikese after the demise of the terns, they must have a rather plastic, highly adap-

Garter snake (*Natrix s. sirtalis*), adult male, about two feet total length: No Mans Land.

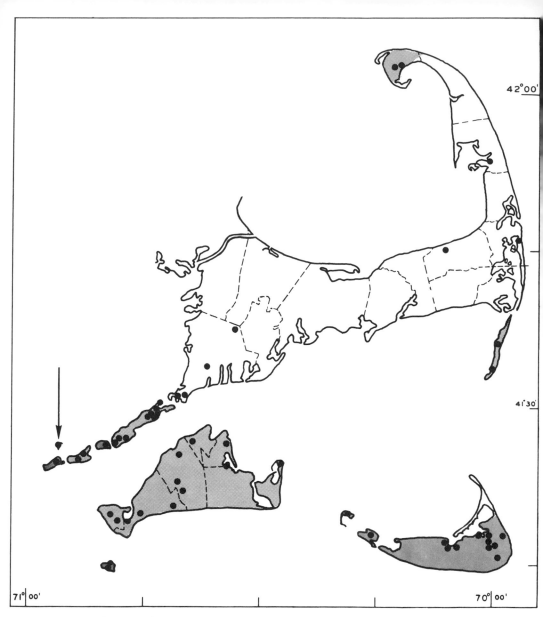

Garter snakes (*Natrix sirtalis*) occur virtually everywhere; I have searched for them unsuccessfully only on the islands in Pleasant Bay. Dots indicate records, often of dozens of individuals. In the shaded areas 75 percent of specimens I have seen were brown, barred across the back, and had obsolete mid-dorsal stripes. The arrow indicates Penikese: covered with brown, barred, stripeless garter snakes.

tive ecological strategy. Much light was shed on this by George Vesper when he was at the University of Connecticut. George abandoned his business career to pursue his interests in reptiles, amphibians, and conservation. He went back to graduate school, and, as part of his production for the Master's degree, studied the abundant garter snakes of Nantucket. He did not publish his results, but he sent me a copy; with acknowledgment and gratitude, I will present some of his conclusions.

George's garter snakes ate or had recently eaten voles(*Microtus pennsylvanicus*), shrews (*Sorex cinereus*), and laboratory mice (*Mus musculus*), as well as the more mundane earthworm fare. Dr. Echternocht's Muskeget captive took quickly to a rodent diet. So, it appears the secret of insular success for these snakes is to hunt warm-blooded —bird and mammal—prey. That is strikingly out of line for any other eastern populations of *Natrix*, but similar to the feeding strategy of some western, desert country forms.

The scarcity of garter snakes on Muskeget, as compared to Penikese, may simply reflect the fact that the common Muskeget rodent, *Microtus breweri*, is a good deal larger than adjacent, insular populations of *M. pennsylvanicus*. Muskeget sand voles may just be harder for garter snakes to subdue and swallow.

George Vesper also addressed the question of the peculiar, barred, nearly stripeless color pattern of insular garter snakes. He suggests that stripes are most effective at deluding terrestrial predators—like skunks, foxes, and raccoons—and least effective against aerial predators —birds. Against a hawk, for example, the outline breaking pattern of dorsal bars may be effective camouflage. That reads pretty well, even though Provincetown, Naushon, Nashawena, and the Vineyard certainly have *some* of the terrestrial, predatory mammals. These areas also have primarily barred garter snakes.

The whole issue of geographic variation in garter snakes needs much more work. Dr. J. Sherman Bleakney, of sea turtle fame, redefined the northern New England and eastern Canadian garter snake subspecies *pallidula* in 1959. This is a somber, barred form, quite like our Cape-Islands individuals in pattern. Our specimens seem to have scale counts like the striped garter snakes of our mainland. Does their color pattern reflect isolation of northern adapted snakes on our islands during the colder climate immediately following glacial retreat? Or is it, as George suggests, an anti-predator camouflage of present survival value? Or, perhaps, a combination of the two?

Our garter snakes do not fit the diagnoses of either the nominate *Natrix sirtalis sirtalis* or the boreal *N. s. pallidula*. Until someone does something about the problem, I can only call them simply *Natrix sirtalis*—subspecies undetermined.

Incidently, "*Thamnophis*" is masculine and *Natrix* is feminine.

So, when I transferred the ribbon snake *"Thamnophis" sauritus* to *Natrix*, the name changed to *saurita*. The name *sirtalis*, I thought, should change similarly to *"sirtala,"* but apparently I was wrong. Dr. Dowling at that time had his Herpetological Information Search System working at the American Museum. He checked and assured me the name remains *Natrix sirtalis*. I hope he is right.

WATER SNAKE

This species, *Natrix sipedon sipedon*, seems to be the one capable of inspiring the greatest fear in New Englanders. Although absolutely nonpoisonous, water snakes—often miscalled moccasins—will bite savagely, and do attain large size. Wright and Wright note that the famous mammalogist W. J. Hamilton, Jr., measured a fifty-five-inch specimen near Ithaca, New York. Apparently he did not save it, for Conant admits nothing larger than fifty-three inches. Females grow considerably larger than males, and when gravid with young attain enormous girth. Females *are* gravid most of the spring and summer, when we generally hunt them. A three-foot specimen may have a three-inch diameter.

The biggest water snake of this species I ever saw, and the record for its subspecies—a Carolina salt marsh snake—was caught by Numi Spitzer at Ocracoke, North Carolina. Numi was just fourteen at the time, and a gangly, wispy fourteen-year-old at that (you should see her now). Anyway, in the spring of her ninth grade year, she begged me to save her from export to a summer camp for group-grooving guru grovellers. Numi had heard the tales of my field trips—great chunks and joints of game meat roasting over the coals, coffers of rattlers and cottonmouths, encounters with alligators, wild boars, and bobcats. Numi wanted to go hunting. She wanted to hunt things that *mattered*, things scientists knew little or nothing about, things that didn't even have names yet. Numi wanted to go hunting with *me*. And so she did.

I was apprehensive about taking so young and tender a girl on a long field trip through the South with a gaggle of much older, experienced, swamp-stomping boys and two salty, hard-drinking old men. Sure enough, Numi took hell and abuse from everyone and survived.

One of the first days out in the field we set out to get Carolina salt marsh snakes. This race of *Natrix sipedon* occurs in the *Spartina* and *Juncus* (black rush) marshes along the Outer Banks. We had hunted them there in previous years, and *believed* there were no cottonmouths, at least in the stretch below Cape Hatteras and above Cape Lookout, where Ocracoke lies. We still believe that, because we have never found a cottonmouth there. But I wouldn't bet much on it. Cottonmouths are common at Cape Hatteras, and well-known to enter brackish and salt marshes farther south. A cottonmouth can kill you.

All of us—John Alexander (who had abandoned his wife to teach school so he could go on this snake hunt), Paul Elias, Mark Merrill, and the other boys—knew cottonmouths first hand and in the field. Numi had never seen one, or even a wild water snake.

We all fanned out into swampland of broad marshes ridged with live oak, red cedar, and stemless palmetto. We moved under the nests of night herons and startled squirrels. We soon lost each other quite completely, and each continued to work generally eastward towards the Sound. Emerging from the woods and swamp into a grassy edge, John and I first came upon each other. Luckless, we had not caught a thing.

A far-off, high-pitched voice barely carried towards us: something about a big snake. We bellowed in concert, "Don't try to catch it! Stand there and keep it in sight! We're coming!" John was off like an antelope, clearing the bayberries and old boat hulls with his long-legged stride. My short, stumpy legs propelled me, bear-like, through what John went over.

Water snake (*Natrix s. sipedon*), adult female, about three feet total length: Nantucket.

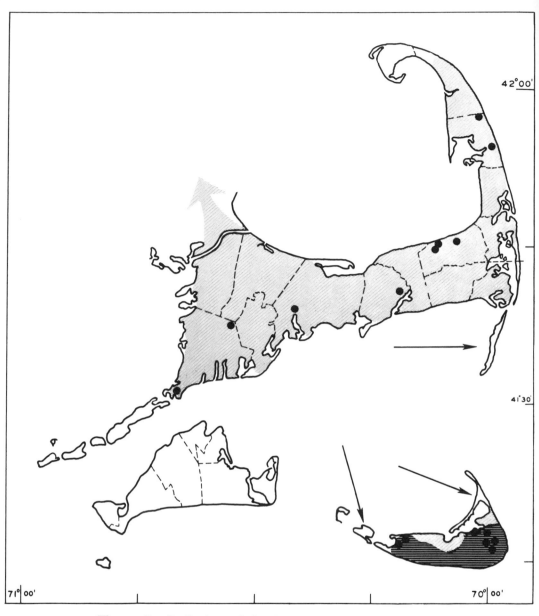

The peculiar distribution and abundance of the water snake (*Natrix s. sipedon*). Dots indicate recorded specimens (often several). Light shading indicates a sort of minimal potential range based on available habitat and topographic features. The barred region of Nantucket is an area of relative abundance: I estimate at least one per acre, or better than 250 per square kilometer. Arrows indicate Monomoy, Coskata, and Tuckernuck, where the species might occur, but there are no records.

Numi's voice drifted back on the wind, but we could not make out the words over all the racket of breaking brush. "Just keep it in sight. We're coming!"

She called again, but we weren't listening. Barrelling past a clump of redcedars, we broke out into a little sand road, curved hard left, and there was Numi. She was standing in the middle of the road, hands on hips, dwarfed by a big snake bag that obviously contained a huge snake.

"I've already caught it," she said quietly. "It's a water snake."

It was four feet long. A couple of years later Dr. Conant and I got around to naming the Carolina saltmarsh snake, *Natrix sipedon williamengelsi*, for Dr. Engels at the University of North Carolina. This remarkably blackened form should have been described and named more than three decades before, but the issue had become confused, and there were very few specimens to base an evaluation on. So, Numi had her first unnamed animal. No one has ever caught one nearly as big since.

But the boys couldn't let it go at that. "Better just commit suicide now," they advised. "You'll never do anything like it again, you know. You've got your world's record, so life will just be a downward spiral for you from now on. It's too bad to have reached the pinnacle at fourteen and have to realize there's nothing left to live for. . . ."

All I wanted to know was how she knew it was a water snake, and not a cottonmouth. I didn't ask, though, until years later. "Oh," she said, "I could see quite a bit of it in the grass—almost the whole middle of it. It just didn't look like a cottonmouth."

Here in New England there are no cottonmouths to fear. They occur only as far north as southeastern Virginia. Calling the northern water snake a "moccasin" only confuses the issue, for that is a common name for both the cottonmouth and the copperhead in the South. I have had long arguments with Yankees who swore they knew Massachusetts "mocassins," only to discover that was what they were calling harmless water snakes.

Water snakes are not very common on Cape Cod, but they are abundant on Nantucket. Since they take readily to salt water, at least temporarily, and eat any sort of fish, frog, or salamander, their peculiar distribution seems inexplicable. At one time I believed they somehow reached Nantucket via Monomoy, and just had not made it to the western islands. That intriguing notion founders for the lack of a Monomoy water snake. I cannot imagine why they are not there.

I have no breeding data for this species in our region. Wright and Wright give extreme litter sizes as eight to ninety-nine. Both figures seem incredible. The bulk of their figures are over ten and under fifty. I think about two dozen is a fair average for a big mother. The time of birth is late summer, August and September, with a few October records.

Water snakes, though aggressive with both bodily extremes—biting, defecating, and musk-slinging—when first caught, usually tame down to make fine exhibit specimens. A big water snake is a most impressive animal.

There are two mightily peculiar Cape Cod specimens of the species that I feel compelled to point out. Both are pale, uniform brown without the characteristic bands across the back. Their bellies are pale, lacking the usual dark-bordered, reddish crescents or any other prominent markings. Their bellies are just vaguely mottled with grey brown, becoming denser posteriorly. I have never seen living *Natrix sipedon* like them, although they certainly sound like the peculiar, insular subspecies from the Put-in-Bay Archipelago of Lake Erie—*N. s. insularum*. But they are darker than examples of that race that I have seen.

One of them is AMNH 6420 from Woods Hole. It is an old specimen, a juvenile, and may be faded. When I first saw it I sincerely questioned that it was a *Natrix sipedon*. Could it be some exotic brought home by a wandering oceanographer that just by chance fit the scale characters of our water snake? But then I saw the second, one of a litter of young born at Brewster on 7 October 1965. Marshal Case preserved the plain brown one, and another typical specimen. Both are in the collection of the Connecticut Audubon Society.

The Little Brown Snakes, Genus *Storeria*

When I was a small boy, growing up in the city of Philadelphia, I firmly believed that God loved not just the poor, but little brown snakes, and for the same reason: he made so many of them. I later learned that God had nothing to do with it. First of all, both the poor and the little brown snakes made themselves in a veritable frenzy of fecundity. Ecological awareness, even later, brought the realization that people in general—not just the poor—but *quantities* of people, are responsible for the abundance of both.

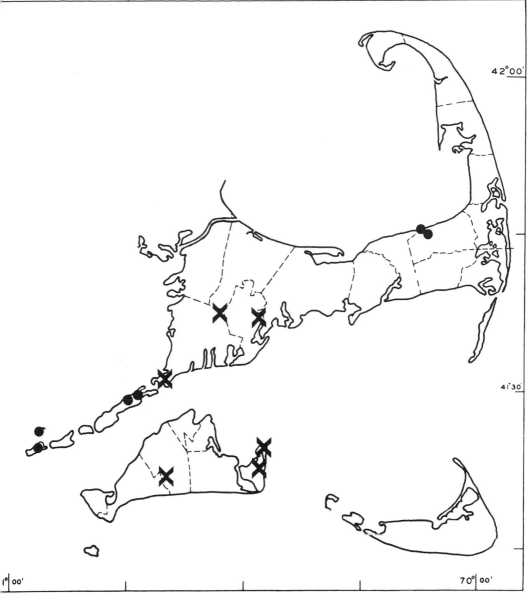

Locality records for the little brown snakes. Dots indicate specimens of Dr. DeKay's snake (*Storeria d. dekayi*) examined; except for Penikese and Cuttyhunk, represented by series, these are single specimens. X's indicate specimens of red-bellied snakes (*Storeria o. occipitomaculata*) examined; all are single specimens.

Where I grew up the city had been densely settled for more than two hundred years. Little brown snakes were one of the commonest vertebrate animals in the city; I could always zip out into the back yard and find one in short order—if the temperature was above freezing. (If it was below, the task was harder but not impossible.) I couldn't have got a rat, or a pigeon, or an English sparrow nearly so easily.

Every summer I went off to visit my relatives in Mississippi, and there the commonest snake was another little brown fellow: *Virginia* (it used to be *"Haldea"*) *striatula,* the rough earth snake. It has a lovely lime-green belly.

When I went off to the University at Sewanee, Tennessee, I came to know two more egregiously abundant, little brown snakes: *Virginia valeriae,* smooth earth snake, and *Carphophis amoenus,* the worm snake. The latter has a bright pink belly (the former is nondescript).

I am at a loss to explain why the snake taxonomists separate the so-called genus *Virginia* from *Storeria.* All the species involved are incredibly similar and obviously each other's closest relatives. They are live-bearing, dimunitive Natricidae.

The worm snake, however, is no relation; rather it is a miniature first cousin to the big and gaudy rainbow and mud snakes—of "hoop snake" fame—that occur to the south of us. Worm snakes reach Massachusetts in the Connecticut River Valley. I wish they had made it east to Cape Cod because I have lots of good worm snake stories.

Anyway, when I took up my disjointed study of Cape Cod and the Islands I discovered a remarkable fact. Little brown snakes— apart from baby garter snakes—are just plain rare here.

RED-BELLIED SNAKE

I have elsewhere called this, *Storeria o. occipitomaculata,* a brilliant little gem of a snake. Not only is it lovely to look at, but it further endears itself by eating slugs. Hardly anybody else loves slugs. Some red-bellies, I will admit, also eat worms, but most that I have known ate nothing but slugs.

These snakes vary in color from fawn-brown to ashy grey, on the back and sides, to an occasional plain black. If the belly is not bright coral red, as it almost invariably is, it will probably be black also. Wright and Wright note other belly color aberrations: blue, yellow, or even white. There are usually three orangish blotches on the neck, one in the middle, one on each side. It was these blotches that made Mark Merrill think he had a ring-neck snake when he caught the Ashumet specimen whose photograph appears here. So be careful—ring-necks are fairly common; red-bellies are really rare.

I have examined only six specimens from our region. Mark's

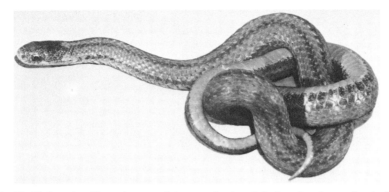

Red-bellied snake (*Storeria o. occipitomaculata*), adult female, about nine inches total length: Falmouth, Cape Cod.

Ashumet specimen was a female; we released her after photographing, in the same spot of course. Another big female was on exhibit at Cape Cod Museum of Natural History in the summer of 1973. It came from near Cotuit in Mashpee. A preserved specimen, AMNH 2703, from Woods Hole is very dark. Whether this is natural or due to preservative, I cannot now determine. There are said to be additional preserved specimens from Woods Hole in the USNM and Carnegie Museum.

Andrew Woodruff caught the first Vineyard specimen at New Lane, West Tisbury, in April 1970. But the strangest one of all is the Cape Poge specimen caught by Peter Rabinowitz in mid-July 1971. Lest you fear he endangered a rare population, let me assure you that Peter saw others he did not collect. In any case, there is no worry of wiping out these secretive little burrowers. Any one we can find must represent a thousand we cannot ever hope to see. In 1975 we got another record from the main part of Chappaquiddick.

Dr. Conant gives the record size for this species as sixteen inches, but I never saw one over a foot long. Wright and Wright say they produce from one to twenty-one young from late June through September. The Mashpee female was obviously gravid on 14 August.

DR. DE KAY'S SNAKE

It was one of those grey, overcast, drizzly days, the 23rd of October 1972, that is a sure harbinger of winter. Ted Spencer, of Woods Hole, along with his neighbor Edie Bruce and her son David, loaded our gear into his catboat. We were determined to go to the nether island of Penikese, despite the weather. We were Al and Phlyp Greer,

Dr. DeKay's snake (*Storeria d. dekayi*), adult female, about twelve inches total length: Naushon, Elizabeth Islands.

Numi, and I, bent on herpetological exploration. I asked Ted how anyone ever manages to *sail* out of the Woods Hole eel pond; it opens to the sea through a tiny channel under a drawbridge. "Oh," said Ted, "it's easy. You just toot your horn."

The Hole was a surging rip of current and the little boat dug in to gain passage into Buzzards Bay. The bulk of the leatherbacks had gone on south, I guess, for that day we only found one—a big female right off the East End Gutter of Naushon. We hung onto her for a while, and Al and Phlyp took photographs. She was too much for us, and we had to let her go, which she did at probably ten knots.

When we got to Penikese the sun was peeking through the scudding clouds just a little bit. There were snakes all over the place. The garter snakes came as no surprise, for we knew they were there, and had already seen museum specimens. It was Al who came up with the surprise. Under planks and wrack right along the water he found one of those little brown snakes—and then another. Both were *Storeria dekayi*, the snake named in honor of Dr. James Ellsworth DeKay, author of the *Natural History of New York*, one of the great nineteenth-century works of American biology.

I grew up with DeKay's snakes, and always called them by that name. Roger Conant, however, finally got fed up with explaining it, and changed the common name to northern brown snake.

Here's how it goes. The phone rings and the distraught housewife says, "My little boy has found a *snake* in our backyard!"

"Yes, madam, that is not unusual."

"Is it poisonous? It's about a foot long and brown."

"No, madam, it sounds like the perfectly harmless DeKay's snake."

"Oh no, you don't understand! This snake is still *alive*."

"Uh-hmm. Yes, madam. I did not mean *decayed*, as in dead and rotten. You see it is a species of snake named for the late Dr. James Ellsworth DeKay, the nineteenth-century naturalist who. . . ."

Well, you can see the rub.

Now, rather than give up a most honorable patronym, I propose we just call it *Dr.* DeKay's snake. Then the conversation will go like this —taking up after the "is it poisonous."

"No, madam, it sounds like the perfectly harmless Dr. DeKay's snake."

"Well, I certainly wish he hadn't let it out in *my* backyard. I'm scared to death of it. What's his number? I'll have him come get it at once!"

Like its red-bellied relative, this nondescript, little brown snake eats slugs, and sometimes worms. Since it is incredibly abundant in urban and suburban lots and backyards, and on far-flung islets like Cuttyhunk and Penikese, it seems strange that it was not discovered, described, and named until the mid-nineteenth century.

That seems strange at least until you realize one important fact: both the common garden slug and the standard lawn earthworm are European imports. They were not here for Dr. DeKay's snakes to eat much further back than Dr. DeKay himself. What they ate before we brought them what they love today I hardly know, but if it was *native* slugs and worms, they must have been very rare snakes.

The two principal ingredients in DeKay's snake abundance are plenty of European slugs and earthworms, and an absence of predators like kingsnakes. That is just what city lots and far-flung islets have in common.

Dr. Conant gives the record size for this species as 18⅜ inches, and that seems quite reasonable to me. In the Cape-Islands region they often exceed a foot. Wright and Wright say they produce three to twenty-four young, but while the ones I kept as captives in Philadelphia often produced litters, they never numbered more than a dozen. Young are produced in late July and August, as a rule.

8

Zoogeography

$$S = CA^z$$

MAC ARTHUR AND WILSON

I HAVE STUDIED the animals of islands by hunting them where they live. This I can tell you: you will never know until you go to see, and even then you will not find all.

The animals of islands—their numbers, their species—are known only by hunting. Of course they fluctuate, and there will be better hunters than you or I. Choosing between real history and a good hunter is often hard indeed.

Krebs (1972: 500-539) has summarized the most cogent views of workers interested in answering the compound question, "How many species, and how many individuals of each, live in place X?" Krebs shows that no theoretical approach yet devised accurately answers that question, and suggests that out of all the approaches may yet emerge a general theory: a sort of "unified field theory" of zoogeography.

I have previously (Lazell, 1972) labeled mathematical approaches to island zoogeography "pseudoscience." I do not believe the practitioners of the art understand the relationship of mathematics to natural science, or the purpose and values of applied mathematics. All of that is, of course, philosophy, but it is worth explaining.

Mathematics, from arithmetic through the calculus, is a body of invention. Man invented math. The inventors did not (and rightfully do not) care if their inventions were applicable to the real world, as long as they are true. Mathematics is ultimate truth, because it is internally defined. Its processes, axioms, symbols, etc., are stated to begin with. Then, anything goes, and what you invent will be true as long as it does not run amuck of the defining statements. Otherwise it will be untrue, or wrong.

An equation—a mathematical statement—is either true or untrue. If it is true, it is true in an absolute, not relative, sense. Correct mathematical relationships are ultimate truth. Mathematics has proven enormously useful in science. Are there some aspects of science for which mathematics is useless?

Before developing the idea that a mathematical theory of zoogeography (or biogeography, if you include both plants and animals) is useless in actual practice, let me first give an example of the way mathematics is supremely useful. Physics and chemistry are full of such examples.

Consider a volume of gas—any gas. The early physical scientists, especially Robert Boyle, noted in repeated experiments that the volume of a gas increased as the temperature was increased. Also, if the volume was held the same, the pressure increased as the temperature was increased. The converse of each was experimentally true: decrease of temperature would cause decrease of volume, and/or decrease of pressure, depending on which (or both) was allowed to vary. Boyle's measurements were accurate, and he devised a set of formulas, or equations, that ultimately led to a Universal Gas Law. This law predicted the relationship between temperature, pressure, and volume of a gas; and it predicted it correctly every time. Thus, it was no longer necessary to set up the apparatus of an experiment to determine the volume of a gas at some desired temperature and pressure; you could calculate it, and be sure you would be right (if you did your arithmetic right, of course).

Zoogeographers have long noted the rather obvious fact that small land areas have fewer species (and of course fewer individuals) than large land areas. Darlington (1957) noted of reptiles and amphibians on islands (in the West Indies) that one island ten times as big as another had about twice as many species. Of course, this is "about" —there were numerous exceptions known even then, and many more are known today. You can think of dozens of things that might affect this simple relationship—distance between islands, distance to mainland, time lapse since island separation, rainfall, hurricane frequency, volcanic activity, and the pockets of little boys, just to name a few.

Of course, people like MacArthur and Wilson (1967) are fully aware of all the variables and complexities involved. In fact, beginning with Darlington's little rule-of-thumb, cited above, they have generated a book-length treatise on the animals of islands, or rather, on the theoretical numbers of animals of theoretical islands. I imagine they had fun, and they certainly gained in fame and fortune; but is such a thing a useful endeavor?

Certainly their results are quite unlike the Gas Law: their formulas cannot accurately predict anything; if you want to know how many of what lives on an island you will have to go and see. Many islands may fit the formulated patterns, but you cannot predict which will be different, or how different. Perhaps most important, you may come up with a number of species to expect on an island, but you can never predict what species they will be.

What a mathematical theory of zoogeography is like is this: the mathematical theory of rocks. I have compiled, let us say, bushels of facts about rocks. Every time I see a rock, I measure its length, width, circumference, weight, and so on. Pretty soon I begin to notice some correlations. As a rule, for example, longer rocks are heavier than shorter rocks—not always, but on the average—most of the time. Similarly, I noted that wider rocks are heavier, as a general rule. Also, most of the time, heavier rocks were bigger around. I even compounded some of these generalizations. As a rule, and more often than not, the heaviest rocks were also the longest, the widest, and had the greatest circumferences. Boy! Was I getting to know a lot about rocks.

Pretty soon I entered the predictive stage. Whenever I found a short rock, I'd predict it was going to be light. I'd usually be right. Of course, when I got more detailed, and tried to predict just how light a rock of a certain length was going to be, I started getting some pretty wide discrepancies; but, hell, sometimes I was fairly close, even so.

Then I combined prediction and experiment. I took a rock of known length, smashed it, counted the pieces, and predicted the average weight. Well, you know . . . a lot of the time I wasn't so far wrong as you might think. If I weighed the rock, then I could sort of predict, a lot of times, about how long the average piece would be. I really did have rocks awfully well figured out.

The only trouble with my mathematical theory of rocks was that it really didn't tell me a thing about the next rock I was going to encounter. Nothing, that is, that did not absolutely require to be checked out on that next rock. You see, I didn't *really* know anything more about the next rock than I had known about the very first rock I ever encountered, long before I developed my theory.

What is wrong with the mathematical theory of island zoogeography is the same thing that is wrong with my theory of rocks; it's useless.

MacArthur and Wilson used the term *equilibrium* to describe the relationship between loss and gain of species from islands. Loss, or extinction, and gain, colonization, are *not causally related*, of course. However an island may be colonized—over water, through the air, or by some temporary land bridge—the potential colonizers no more know what is going on there before they set out than MacArthur and Wilson do. What's more, of course, islands are colonized by accident—almost never on purpose—by animals, at least. (I'm not a botanist; maybe plants colonize islands on purpose. I doubt it, though.)

The extinction of species A on a given island might, or might not, make it easier for species B to survive there, if it were lucky enough to wash up on shore. Sometimes you might try to *guess* what might happen. Lambs might do better colonizing an island on which lions had just become extinct, but, for a thousand complex ecological reasons, they might do worse.

When MacArthur and Wilson called this purely happenstance, at best loosely probabilistic, relationship an "equilibrium," they immediately made their theory appear to be a predictive tool such as those found in physics and chemistry. Literally hundreds of young aspirants were sucked into the "new" biogeography because now it seemed a quantitative, predictive, *real* science. That is not so.

There is one other sort of useful scientific prediction; the class of predictions exemplified by a weather forecast. A weather forecast is an educated guess. It may be wrong, but it is a lot better than nothing. Dr. Jared Diamond, remarkably a professor of physiology at a medical school, has picked up the MacArthur-Wilson package and found a use for it. Weather forecasters would never be so stupid as to use their gauges, machines, tables, and formulas to attempt to determine what the weather *was* on 15 August 1973. They would just look it up. So, rather than use MacArthur and Wilson to try to determine what lives on any real island, you go and see. But what can we guess—in educated fashion—may become of animal species already known to occur in areas that will *become* islands in the future? What will happen to the faunas of our National Parks when those Parks are just relatively tiny islands of suitable habitat in a sea of man-devastated, uninhabitable terrain? Jared Diamond set out to forecast.

Well, Diamond hardly needed MacArthur and Wilson to do that. Darlington's rule-of-thumb is perfect for the purpose. The smaller and more isolated the "island," the fewer species it is likely to support. But, you say, surely that is because small, remote islands are harder to colonize. We are dealing with a National Park that already has a thousand species; they don't have to run a gamut to get there. True, but probably species that become extinct on our National Park "island" will not be replaced. The sea of human devastation will be harder to cross than any real, unpolluted ocean. Once our National Parks, and other preserves, are rendered biological islands, their species composition will simplify, their species numbers decline, their diversity diminish. You can make that generalization, as Diamond did, but if you try to get more specific your predictions are going to be more prone to error.

Let us return to real islands that exist today, and rocks. Just as it may be extremely useful to know the actual length, width, or weight of a particular rock, so it is useful to know about the actual species composition of islands. At least useful to me as a naturalist, trying to understand animal distributions. Let us try to understand not some theoretical, as yet unvisited island, but our own real islands, as they are.

Sometimes a bigger island has less species than a smaller one, or two islands of similar size have radically different numbers of species. It is perfectly legitimate and scientific to ask the question why—and to try to answer it.

Reptiles and amphibians are incomparably valuable subjects for zoogeographical study. They are large enough so that the practiced hunter may actually hope to collect a sample of the bulk of species in any given locality. A good hunter may write history. If things change, we may reasonably elect to believe a good hunter and evaluate the changes that seem to have occurred.

Land, Freshwater, and Saltmarsh Forms

All species but the marine turtles (true sea turtles and the leatherback) are tied to the land of Cape Cod or the Islands. The saltiest forms— diamondback terrapin, snapping turtle, and, of course, the garter and green snakes—are unable to really *live* at sea. The land and its marshes are their home. They may cross sea water, but they cannot live there. They will die if they do not soon reach another shore.

The basic notion of terrestrial zoogeography of Cape Cod and the Islands is simple. Northern forms can be expected on the remote islands, because they could have walked or crawled there before those land areas became islands. Southern forms can be expected on Cape Cod because it remained connected to the mainland until just a few decades ago and has a mild, equable climate. This basic plan may be modified by several other factors, of which the most obvious is ground temperature stability. This varies directly with island size. The larger the island, the more stable its ground temperature. We should also consider human extirpations, as of the toads on Nantucket. Of course, these extirpations open up a vacant niche for some other species, or the same one to reinvade, in theory at least. Thus, one toad species has replaced another, through direct human intervention, on Cuttyhunk.

We may sort distribution patterns into eight general categories. I have noted, with abbreviations, which of these each species belongs to on the table of species and islands. Garter snake and snapping turtle are omitted from the table and my figures because they are ubiquitous. They both fit into the first category.

Northern forms found everywhere there is suitable habitat (NH). Along with garter snake and snapping turtle, two other species fit this pattern: woodland salamander and painted turtle. Woodland salamanders occur everywhere except Monomoy, Penikese, No Mans Land, and Muskeget. Their absence from Monomoy may be an artifact, for there exist some wooded thickets on moist, low ground; a few might actually live there, but the habitat is severely limited. Penikese and Muskeget have no suitable habitat for this species. No Mans Land probably once had woodland salamanders, but the clearing of the forest wiped them out. A few might have survived in stone fences or foundations, and, if they did, the species might recover and reappear in the future as woodland comes back.

Painted turtles are absent from Monomoy, Penikese, Tuckerneck, and Muskeget. Of these islands, only Monomoy and Tuckernuck might possibly support this species. Monomoy is the best bet; it has extensive fresh water ponds and marshes. On Tuckernuck the habitat is marginal, at best. The one fresh marsh has little open water and is far better habitat for spotted turtles—which do live there—than painted.

Northern forms restricted to large islands (NL). There are seven species in this category, one of the most puzzling of all. The green frog is absent from Monomoy, Pasque, Cuttyhunk, No Mans Land, Tuckernuck, and Muskeget. It is said to have lived on Cuttyhunk prior to the great insecticide era, and to have been extirpated there. The smallest island it occurs on today is Nashawena. If it did live on Cuttyhunk, its absence from the larger Tuckernuck requires explanation. Once again, insecticides probably did it. Then we are left with Pasque and No Mans Land, both with plenty of good habitat, and Penikese and Muskeget, with marginally suitable habitat.

Pickerel frogs occur on no island smaller than Nantucket, no matter its history. They are just as absent from pristine, undisturbed Naushon as they are from raped and pillaged No Mans Land or Cuttyhunk.

The wood frog, most boreal of all species, lives on nothing smaller than upper Cape Cod. The American toad is confined to the upper Cape and the Vineyard, as a native species, but survives abundantly on the small island of Cuttyhunk to which it was introduced.

The spring peeper is not known from any island smaller than Chappaquiddick, but this is surely a collecting artifact. They are said to have lived on Cuttyhunk prior to aerial spraying, and are claimed to still live on Nashawena and possibly Pasque. Since we have no idea how and where they live, we may as well discount them from our reckonings.

Ring-neck snake and ribbon snake are very similar in distribution. Both eat salamanders, but only the ring-neck might be limited by this fact; ribbon snakes eat lots of other things too. The apparent absence of ring-necks on Chappaquiddick is probably just the result of faulty collecting.

Of all these species, only the wood frog can be compellingly argued to be limited by ground temperature instability. It is easy, for me at least, to see how this creature of the cool, damp forest floor might simply be unable to take the late summer high temperatures of small islands. It would certainly be easy to test this hypothesis on adults, but it may be at other stages in life that temperature is critical.

It is very difficult to see how any reptile could be limited by high ground temperatures, and these northern forms should be able to take the late winter lows. The ribbon snake, in its amazing abundance, with its ease of maintenance in captivity, and its colossal fecundity, would be an ideal subject for experimental ecology. Somebody really ought to try to find out what is going on.

Temperate form with a reasonable range (TR). The only species in this category is the kingsnake, and it really isn't so reasonable at all in close detail. Kingsnakes are very rare, if they occur at all, on the lower Cape. None has ever been reported at Wellfleet Bay Sanctuary, and the snake is unfamiliar to the staff there. I have a verbal report of one in Provincetown many years ago. Trying to reconcile this with the situation on Nantucket is going to be very difficult.

Temperate form with a range deviant from that expected (TD). The only other temperate form is the two-lined salamander. Its deviant range may reflect poor collecting. It is also possible that high ground water temperatures may limit it, and, in any case, its habitat is in short supply. I expect it is more widespread in upper Cape streams. Its absence from the Vineyard may be due to insecticides. Its absence from Naushon is perhaps a little strange.

Southern forms with restricted ranges (SR). Four species fit this pattern, one we might most confidently have predicted. The bullfrog, musk turtle, diamondback terrapin, and hognose snake all occur right where they are supposed to, and nowhere they are not. Bless them.

Southern forms remarkably widespread (SW). Two species of definite warm climate affinity, that reach the northern limits of their range in our area, are found on Nantucket and (in the past, at least) other islands. These are the spadefoot and spotted turtle. Both are amazingly tough and highly salt tolerant. Both obviously just crossed sea water to get where they are today.

Artificial (A). Three species are definitely known to have suffered wholesale destruction by the hand of man. Fowler's toad, chemically poisoned off of Nantucket, Muskeget, Cuttyhunk, and probably Tuckernuck, would have gone in the SW category above; like those species, it is a tough, salt-tolerant southerner that obviously just crossed sea water.

The red-bellied turtle is common and conspicuous in Indian midden remains. The few that survive uneaten are shy and wary; they cannot tolerate close encroachment by humanity.

The pathetic box turtle has had just about everything perverted and unnatural the human imagination can conjure up done to it.

Last of all, we come to the biggest of my categories: *Bizarre* (B). Nine species have ranges that just don't fit any pattern. These are the most interesting of all, of course. Spotted salamanders and newts should be more widespread. Both can take cold climate, and both have suitable habitat in places where they have not been found. The absence of newts on Naushon is particularly galling. Insecticides may have extirpated these two over many other areas where they are seemingly absent. Tantalizing sight records of the spotted salamander on Martha's Vineyard remain unsubstantiated.

	Spotted Salamander	Newt	Woodland Salamander	Four-toed Salamander	Two-lined Salamander	Green Frog	Pickerel Frog	Wood Frog	Bullfrog	Spadefoot	Fowler's Toad	American Toad	Grey Treefrog	Peeper
UPPER CAPE	X	X	X	X	X	X	X	X	X	X	X	X	X	X
LOWER CAPE	X	X				X	X		X	X	X			X
MONOMOY											X			
NAUSHON	X		X	X		X					X		X	X
PASQUE			X								X			
NASHAWENA			X		X						X			
CUTTYHUNK			X								X	X		
PENIKESE											X			
VINEYARD		X	X	X		X	X				X	X		X
CHAPPAQUIDDICK			X			X					X			X
NO MANS LAND														
NANTUCKET			X			X	X							X
TUCKERNUCK			X											
MUSKEGET														
PATTERN	B	B	NH	B	TD	NL	NL	NL	SR	SW	A	NL	B	NL

Four-toed salamanders, and red-bellied and DeKay's snakes, are just too rare. They are so rare you cannot figure what their real distributions might be. As records trickle in, some sensible patterns might emerge.

The grey treefrog is a salt-tolerant, temperate climate form that should have made it to at least the Vineyard. Insecticides would have surely set it back severely, as they have on Cape Cod (compared to Naushon), but it should have survived, one might think. To say something *should* occur where it apparently does not is sad folly.

The black racer, the green snake, and the water snake are real stumpers. Their presences and absences, although inexplicable, are among the most ecologically important features of the entire Cape-Islands region. Here is where one longs to say, "Stop the world. Don't let anything move or change until we figure out these peculiar distributions, absences, and abundances." Something very important has happened out there, or goes on happening. If only we could see what it is. If only we could understand.

	Musk Turtle	Diamondback Terrapin	Painted Turtle	Red-bellied Turtle	Box Turtle	Spotted Turtle	Racer	Green Snake	Kingsnake	Ring-neck Snake	Hognose Snake	Ribbon Snake	Water Snake	Red-bellied Snake	DeKay's Snake
UPPER CAPE	X	X	X		X	X	X	X	X	X	X	X	X	X	X
LOWER CAPE		X	X		X	X	X			X	X	X	X		
MONOMOY															
NAUSHON			X	X	X	X	X	X	X		X				X
PASQUE			X			X		X							
NASHAWENA			X			X		X	X						
CUTTYHUNK			X			X								X	
PENIKESE														X	
VINEYARD			X		X	X	X	X	X			X		X	
CHAPPAQUIDDICK			X			X	X	X	X			X		X	
NO MANS LAND			X												
NANTUCKET			X		X	X		X	X	X		X	X		
TUCKERNUCK						X									
MUSKEGET															
PATTERN	SR	SR	NH	A	A	SW	B	B	TR	NL	SR	NL	B	B	B

If we plot island size against number of species present, the large islands work out very well. Cape Cod, Martha's Vineyard, Nantucket, and Chappaquiddick form a pattern where the species number decreases by one for every decrease of about twenty-two square miles. Naushon has more species than it should on this scale, but that is understandable because of its relatively undisturbed state. Chappaquiddick has less species, but that is a result of poor collecting and, possibly, some human extirpations.

If you graph these islands, the line of best fit proceeds right along to where an "island" with no land area at all would still have eight or ten species. That is ridiculous, and shows you the sort of trouble playing with numbers can get you into.

If you graph the small islands, beginning with Chappaquiddick and descending through Monomoy, Nashawena, Tuckernuck, Cuttyhunk, Pasque, No Mans Land, Muskeget, and Penikese, the whole thing makes chaos. Penikese has more species than Monomoy, Pasque more than Tuckernuck. It makes too much chaos, in fact. I am convinced that much of this is artifact and poor collecting; a lot of the rest of the mess is insecticide spraying extirpations. One fact does emerge, however: MacArthur and Wilson's "equilibrium" just does not exist.

A great effort should be made to correct the artifacts of poor collecting. Some consideration should be given to ecosystem restoration: bringing species back to places they once demonstrably lived—*but not yet*. First we have to find out what really does live where, how and why it is restricted in range or limited in population size. I have crawled through a lot of brush and green briar, waded a lot of swamps, hiked a lot of miles, and—finally—pushed this pen a long way to reach this point; the point where I tell you we don't know nothin' yet.

Marine Forms

The marine turtles are not constrained by the size of land areas, their distance from a source, or the formulas of MacArthur and Wilson. They can go wherever they damn well please. We know almost nothing of their actual movements, but some fragments exist. There are clues, and one may speculate. We know a great deal more than we used to.

Our only green turtles seem to be youngsters in their highly carnivorous stage. They are not lost and benumbed, but vigorous feeders in water over 50° F. They obviously come up here on purpose, to get good things to eat, and then go back to the tropics again when cold weather arrives. Once they grow up to the age when they begin to graze turtle grass, they are stuck with the tropics. It just doesn't grow up here. Where hatchling greens go no one knows. They do not stay near the shores where they hatched, and do not go to the flats where their parents graze. They just disappear. As yearlings, or two-year-olds, perhaps, they reappear in coastal waters. One of the standard places to find them is Nantucket Sound off Chatham and Monomoy. This seems to be a regular summer feeding ground for young green turtles. Specimens are often caught here, in pound nets, and sold to commerical aquaria. They do very well, but do not grow appreciably. Whether their lack of growth is because of low temperatures or the fact that they are unable to switch to their normal turtle grass diet is a good question. Kept in New England, they remain small and carnivorous, even after five years in captivity.

The hawksbill probably does not travel far from its birth place. Hawksbills of all sizes, and presumably all ages, may be found around the same reefs near shores where they nest. Because of this, they have been more severely decimated even than the green. I believe some hawksbills may have naturally wandered up our way, and returned to the tropics without ill adventure, back in the days when they were more common. I doubt if many do so today.

Loggerheads are common in the North Carolina Sounds by the end of March, and nest as far north as New Jersey today. The young seem to disappear like baby greens, but the evidence is that they go out into the Sargasso Sea area of the middle North Atlantic, and do not return inshore until they are about ten pounds or more. In summer, loggerheads just naturally push northward into the Gulf of Maine, where the eating is good. Like leatherbacks, they love jellyfish. Like ridleys, they tend to travel in groups. Drowning in fish trawls is a major cause of death, especially to females coming inshore to lay their eggs. I have seen loggerheads make perfectly successful nests on St. Catherine's Island, in Georgia, where raccoons and pigs are unmercifully abundant. The secret is to come in after midnight on a rainy night. The 'coons and pigs are not then abroad, and when they come out next morning all the evidence is gone.

Ridleys nest on the coast of Mexico and migrate regularly across the Gulf to Florida, and then on up to the Gulf of Maine. No one knows where the hatchlings go. Ours are regularly subadults, travelling in bunches. They come right into harbors and creeks, and are about the easiest of our species to see. They go back to Florida in the autumn. Apparently, adult ridleys lose their wanderlust, and take up residence in the Gulf of Mexico.

About eight years ago, when I knew even less than I know now, I met a pilot at Hyannis airport. He said he had once, for some reason or another, spent several hours flying around way out east of Nantucket and Georges Bank. It was mid-June. He saw a huge marine turtle swimming north, underwater, fast. A few minutes later he saw another one, same direction, speed, etc. Pretty soon, here came yet another one. He began to realize that not long after he lost sight of one, another appeared, coming up from the south.

It has taken me eight years to decide I want to believe that story. If he made it up, he invented just exactly what I now think must be going on out there. All the leatherbacks in the Atlantic swim past us every year, far out to sea, headed north to the arctic jellyfish they love so well. If there are several thousand of them, and they spread their passage over fifty days of passing us, then a hundred or so must go by each day. That's several every hour, or more if they only travel by day. I want to go out there and see them pass. It must be one of the greatest sights on earth.

In late summer and fall they come back. Coasting now, they follow the passive schools of jellyfish brought down by the current into the Gulf of Maine. Some probably go east, and so down the coasts of Europe. Lots hunt the quiet waters of Cape Cod Bay, Nantucket and Vineyard Sounds. By November they have passed us again, going back to the tropical Caribbean and equatorial Atlantic. I wonder if they go on southward with the summer to the Southern Hemisphere. I bet they do. I bet the greatest reptile travels from the Arctic to the Antarctic, with the seasons, and only slows down a little early each spring for courting and nesting in the tropics. Somebody ought to find out. I'll go, if no one else wants the job.

CHAPTER

9

Accounts of the Absent and Oddities

＝＝＝＝＝

Aonumber of species occur in the general area of south-eastern New England that have not been found—at least by me or anyone else who kept a specimen—on Cape Cod or the Islands. It is worthwhile to give brief accounts of those that really might be here, in hopes that someone will discover them and document their existence. It is necessary in any such case to *save the specimen*. Sight records are not valid in herpetology.

The marbled salamander, *Ambystoma opacum*, probably really does occur on the Cape, at least on the base in Bourne, Sandwich, or Falmouth. Bill Haas, currently at Harvard, says he found marbled salamanders in Sandwich some years ago. It was this report that led to the discovery of the two-lined salamander here, but the two species are utterly dissimilar in appearance and habitat, so he could not have been confused. Marbled salamanders are short, stock fellows, three or four inches when adult. They begin their terrestrial life as slate-grey salamanders with lighter grey speckles, but rapidly attain a striking pattern of silver or pearly grey, roughly hour-glass-shaped bars across the back, on a black ground color. Unlike other members of *Ambystoma* (like the spotted), they lay their eggs in autumn in the then-dry beds of temporary ponds. The female remains with her clutch, under a log or rock on the pond bottom, until the rains of winter flood the site. The larvae must lose their gills and leave the pond before it dries up the next summer. Marbled salamanders once occurred widely in Plymouth, Norfolk, Middlesex, and Essex Counties, but today are known to survive only in Bristol and Worcester Counties. Insecticides may have wiped them out, or the acid rain.

The blue-spotted salamander (*Ambystoma laterale*) is well-known and widespread in Essex and Middlesex Counties. Bill Haas says he once found these in Sandwich also. They are proportioned like spotted salamanders, but do not grow so large. They are slaty to black with blue—often great big sky blue—irregular spots, blotches, and flecks along the sides. In many individuals the spots are rather small; these can be mistaken for dusky salamanders or even lead-phase woodland salamanders. Young spotties may not show good, clear, yellow spots, and may have light lateral flecking. For this reason identification of the blue-spot is tricky, and claimed sight records are really dubious. There is a population of this species on Long Island, New York, so precedent exists for their occurrence on glacial moraine land.

The dusky salamander (*Desmognathus fuscus fuscus*) is widespread and often abundant in small, clear brooks and rocky marshes on the bedrock mainland. No one has ever claimed seeing one on Cape Cod, but after finding two-lines—a species of similar habitat—I would be remiss if I did not point out the possibility of finding them here.

I have included in this book accounts of two species that I believe are not native: the leopard frog (*Rana pipiens*) and the wood turtle (*Clemmys insculpta*). Several other exotics have been introduced, but fortunately seem not to have survived, and are not represented by actual specimens.

The red-eared turtle (*Chrysemys scripta elegans*) is the standard baby turtle of the pet trade. People buy the little, green, red-head-

striped infants and—of course—often dump them in local ponds
when they tire of them. Although their native home is the Cumberland region of the central South, some do survive our winters and
grow to adulthood. The old adults are somber-colored and might be
mistaken for red-bellied turtles. They retain the stripe on the side
of the head, although it turns ultimately dull, brick-brown. Marshal
Case photographed a wild-caught adult at Orleans some years back.
Others are bound to turn up, but I do not believe they will establish
populations in our area, so far from their natural habitat and climate.
Most of them die a slow death.

A pine snake (*Pituophis m. melanoleucus*) was released on Nantucket in the early 1960s and is said to have been seen around the
Polpis area for several years thereafter. Pine snakes are great, massive
creatures, predominantly whitish with black or grey markings. They
are harmless, but hiss and puff quite a bit. The species is native to
the southeast, and occurs as far north—in an isolated population—
as the Pine Barrens of New Jersey. I am confident that a severe
winter tortured this poor creature to death.

A speckled kingsnake (*Lampropeltis getulus holbrooki*) was released on Martha's Vineyard in 1969. I know about this sad snake
because I caught it, in its natural habitat in Mississippi. I gave it to
an ex-student of mine who begged me for it. She wanted a pet snake
for a graduation present. Doltishly, she gave it to her brother when
she got tired of it. He let it go and it no doubt died a gruesome death
in this cold and foggy land. I wish she had just given it back to me.
It was a lovely specimen, jet black peppered with pale green spots
and a sulfur-blotched belly.

No doubt other people have released a long list of exotic pets here
also. I can only hope that something will happen to these people to
make them regret their stupid actions. If you can tell me who they
are, I have a long list of things I would like to help happen to them.
Perhaps just pointing out that they are practicing extreme cruelty to
animals will persuade them to desist in the future. If you do not
want an animal, and cannot release it exactly where it came from,
give it to a museum, zoo, or the Massachusetts Herpetological Society.
Unless you have a real reason for capturing an animal—say you are
a biologist studying that species, or the animal represents a new
record—please just leave it alone. Enjoy animals in their natural
habitat, wild and free. As the sign says at Ashumet Holly Reservation: "Leave only footprints. Take only pictures."

This is not quite the end.

After delivering a lecture on the solar system, philosopher-psychologist William James was approached by an elderly lady who claimed she had a theory superior to the one described by him.

"We don't live on a ball rotating around the sun," she said. "We live on a crust of earth on the back of a giant turtle."

Not wishing to demolish this absurd argument with the massive scientific evidence at his command, James decided to dissuade his opponent gently.

"If your theory is correct, madam, what does this turtle stand on?"

"You're a very clever man, Mr. James, and that's a good question, but I can answer that. The first turtle stands on the back of a second, far larger, turtle."

"But what does this second turtle stand on?" James asked patiently.

The old lady crowed triumphantly, "It's no use, Mr. James—it's turtles all the way down."

BERNARD NIETSCHMANN

PHOTOGRAPHER'S NOTE

by Martin C. Michener

SEVERAL special techniques were used to make the illustrations of the animals in this book. Generally, close-up photography suffers from a severe lack of depth of field. That is, one part of the animal is in sharp focus, while another part, closer or farther from the lens, is fuzzy. This parameter depends on only two variables: magnification of the subject on the film (the ratio of the size of the subject to the size of the image) and the "F stop setting" (numerical aperture). If the subject is small (less than three inches) and the size of the film is fixed (say, 35 mm.), the best a photographer can do is to use the smallest aperture (largest "F stop") on his lens. On the other hand, for a given size of animal subject, the best depth of field can be had with the smallest film format which still affords good resolving power in the film. For these reasons, all the illustrations of animals in this book were made on Eastman Panatomic X, 35 mm. film with a Pentax camera at F/16 to F/32 aperture. This procedure was found to maximize both depth of field and resolution, as well as possible. Because the aperture greatly restricts the passage of light and because the film is very slow the procedure requires huge amounts of light.

The photography of wet, living amphibians under strong light conditions is almost impossible, as long as the light delivers heat as well. Frogs and salamanders show extreme discomfort under either sunlight or photoflood lights. A few such trials convinced us that electronic flash lighting was essential. Strobes allow sudden pulses of high intensity light which does not heat the subjects. The short pulse duration also allows extreme close-ups with hand-held cameras, since the exposure, 1/2000 second, effectively stops wiggle and blur.

Strobes only supply the light when the camera is triggered, so composing each picture is made more difficult when looking through the camera viewfinder. One strobe light forms harsh shadows. Two strobes form more interlocking harsh shadows. Three lights are better, but, even with a white surface below the animal, many strange shadows appear around the animal. To eliminate these shadows we used two special techniques. Each subject was placed on white plastic sheeting, about ⅛ inch thick. Below the plastic was another, fourth, strobe light. The subject was thus illuminated from all sides and almost all shadows were eliminated. After the film was enlarged, the final print was painted with a silver-dissolving bleach to remove the last traces of grey shadows from the finished illustration.

Turtles were immobilized by placing them on small juice glasses so their legs could not reach the support point. The bleaching then was used to make the glass disappear in the finished print. Thus, some of the pictures show the turtles reaching with their legs to find some support so they can walk away. This produces a rather foolish pose, but has the advantage of showing a great deal of the turtle to the viewer.

Also, some of the prints were reversed, left for right, to show all the turtles in the same position. For this reason, some of the top and bottom views do not agree with the side view of the same specimen, since they are merely mirror-images of each other.

BIBLIOGRAPHY

Babcock, H. L. 1919. The turtles of New England. *Memoirs, Boston Soc. Nat. Hist.* 8(3): 323–431.

———. 1937. A new subspecies of the red-bellied terrapin *Pseudemys rubriventris* (LeConte). *Occ. Pap. Boston Nat. Hist. Soc.* 8: 293.

Barbour, T. 1936. A salamander new to Cape Cod. *Bull. Boston Soc. Nat. Hist.* 78: 9.

———. 1942. New records for ridleys. *Copeia* 1942(4): 257–258.

Bishop, S. C. 1943. *Handbook of Salamanders.* Ithaca: Comstock, Cornell Univ. Press.

Bleakney, J. S. 1959. *Thamnophis sirtalis sirtalis* (Linnaeus) in eastern Canada, redescription of *T. s. pallidula* Allen. Copeia 1959(1): 52–56.

———. 1965. Reports of marine turtles from New England and Canadian waters. *Canadian Field Nat.* 79(2): 120–128.

Brodie, E. D. 1973. Defensive mechanisms of plethodontid salamanders. Abstract. *HISS News-Journal* 1(2): 55.

Bumpus, D. F. 1973. A description of the circulation on the continental shelf of the east coast of the United States *in*: Warren, B. A., Ed., *Progress in Oceanography* 6: 111–157.

Bumpus, D. F., and L. M. Lauzier. 1965. Surface circulation of the continental shelf off eastern North America between Newfoundland and Florida. *Serial Atlas of the Marine Environment,* Am. Geog. Soc. 6.

Carlquist, S. 1974. *Island Biology.* New York: Columbia Univ. Press.

Carr, A. 1952. *Handbook of Turtles.* Ithaca: Comstock Publ.

———. 1956. *The Windward Road.* New York: Alfred A. Knopf.

———. 1967. *So Excellent a Fishe.* New York: Anchor Books, Doubleday.

Chamberlain, B. B. 1964. *These Fragile Outposts.* Garden City, N.Y.: Nat. Hist. Press.

Colton, J. B., and R. R. Stoddard. 1972. Average monthly sea-water temperatures: Nova Scotia to Long Island: 1940–1959. *Serial Atlas of the Marine Environment,* Am. Geog. Soc. 21: xviii.

Conant, R. 1951. The red-bellied terrapin, *Pseudemys rubriventris* (Le Conte), in Pennsylvania. *Ann. Carnegie Mus.* 32: 281–290.

———. 1957. *Reptiles and Amphibians of the Northeastern States.* Third Edition. Zool. Soc. Philadelphia: 41 pp.

———. 1958. *A Field Guide to Reptiles and Amphibians.* Boston: Houghton Mifflin Co.

———. 1975. *A Field Guide to Reptiles and Amphibians of Eastern and Central North America.* Boston: Houghton Mifflin Co.

Darlington, P. J. 1957. *Zoogeography: The Geographical Distribution of Animals.* New York: John Wiley & Sons.

Davis, D. D. 1964. The giant panda. *Fieldiana: Zoology Memoirs* 3: 339 pp.

DeKay, J. E. 1842. *Natural History of New York*, Part 3, Reptiles and Amphibia. New York.

Diamond, J. M. 1972. Biogeographic kinetics: estimation of relaxation times for avifaunas of southwest Pacific Islands. *Proc. Nat. Acad. Sci.* 69(11): 3199–3203.

———. 1973. Distributional ecology of New Guinea birds. *Science* 179: 759–769.

Dolbeer, J. A. 1969. A study of population density, seasonal movements and weight changes, and winter behavior of the eastern box turtle, *Terrapene c. carolina* L., in eastern Tennessee. Master's thesis, Knoxville: Univ. of Tennessee.

Douglas, M. E. 1975. A study of three sympatric ambystomid salamanders in Bernheim Forest, Bullitt County, Kentucky. *Abstracts, Am. Soc. Ichthyologists and Herpetologists*: 38.

Drury, W. H. 1974. Rare species. *Biol. Conservation* 6(3): 162–169.

Drury, W. H., and I. C. T. Nisbet. 1973. Succession. *J. Arnold Arboretum* 54(3): 331–368.

Dunn, E. R. 1926. *The Salamanders of the Family Plethodontidae.* Northampton, Mass.: Smith College Anniv. Publ.

Edwards, J. L., and M. K. Hecht. 1975. Further evidence concerning the relationships of the proteid salamanders. *Abstracts, Am. Soc. Ichthyologists and Herpetologists*: 39

Ernst, C. H. 1972. Temperature-activity relationship in the painted turtle, *Chrysemys picta. Copeia* 1972 (2): 217–222.

Ernst, C. H., and R. W. Barbour. 1973. *Turtles of the United States.* Lexington: University of Kentucky Press.

Ewer, R. F. 1973. *The Carnivores.* Ithaca: Cornell Univ. Press.

Floyd, C. B. 1932. Strange disappearance of nesting Penikese Island terns. *Bird-banding* 3(4): 173–174.

———. 1933. Further notes on Penikese Island terns. *Bird-banding* 4(4):200–202.

Frair, W., R. G. Ackman, and N. Mrosovsky. 1972. Body temperature of *Dermochelys coriacea*: warm turtle from cold water. *Science* 177: 791–793.

Gibson, C. D. 1948. *Sea Islands of Georgia.* Athens: Univ. of Georgia Press.

Goin, C. J., and O. B. Goin. 1972. *Introduction to Herpetology.* Second edition. San Francisco: W. H. Freeman & Co.

Greer, A. E. 1973. The color phases of the red-backed salamander in New England. *Man and Nature*, March, 1973: 27–32.

Greer, A. E., J. D. Lazell, and R. M. Wright. 1973. Anatomical evidence for a countercurrent heat exchanger in the leatherback turtle (*Dermochelys coriacea*). *Nature* 244: 181.

Healy, W. R. 1973. Life history variation and growth of juvenile *Notophthalmus viridescens* from Massachusetts. *Copeia* 1973(4): 641–647.

———. 1975. Terrestrial activity and home range in efts of *Notophthalamus viridescens. Am. Midland Nat.* 93(1): 131–138.

Hellman, L. 1973. *Pentimento.* Boston: Little, Brown & Co.

Highton, R. 1959. The inheritance of the color phases of *Plethodon cinereus. Copeia* 1959(1): 33–37.

Bibliography

————. 1962. Revision of the North American salamanders of the genus *Plethodon. Bull. Florida State Mus.* 6(3): 235–367.

Hildebrand, H. H. [no date] Hallazgo del área de anidación de la tortuga marine "lora," *Lepidochelys kempi* (Garman), en la costa occidental del Golfo de México (Rept., Chel.). *Ciencia, Méx.*, 22(4): 105–112.

Hoff, J. G. 1972. The introduction of diamondback terrapin, *Malaclemys terrapin* Schoepf, from southern New Jersey into Buzzard's Bay, Massachusetts [*sic*]. *Bull. New Jersey Acad. Sci.* 17(1): 21–22.

Krebs, C. J. 1972. *Ecology.* New York: Harper and Row.

Larsen, J. H., and D. J. Guthrie. 1974. Parallelism in the Proteidae reconsidered. *Copeia* 1974(3): 635–643.

Lazell, J. D. 1968. Mr. Fowler's Toad. *Mass. Audubon* 52(2): 4 pp.

————. 1969. Terrapin terminals. *Mass. Audubon* 53(4): 3 pp.

————. 1969. Nantucket herpetology. *Mass Audubon* 54(2): 32–34.

————. 1970. Nantuckete gnome. *Mass Audubon* 55(4): 4 pp.

————. 1972. Painted turtle. *Aquasphere* 6(2): 3–5.

————. 1972. The anoles (Sauria, Iguanidae) of the Lesser Antilles. *Bull. Mus. Comp. Zool.* 143(1): 115 pp.

Lazell, J. D., and I. C. T. Nisbet. 1972. The tern-eating garter snakes of Nomans Land. *Man and Nature* 1972(2): 27–29.

Le Conte, J. 1830. Description of the species of North American tortoises. *Ann. Lyc. Nat. Hist.* 3: 89–131.

Lynch, J. D. 1971. Evolutionary relationships, osteology, and zoogeography of Leptodactylid frogs. *Misc. Publ. Mus. Nat. Hist. Univ. Kansas* (53): 238 pp.

Lynn, W. G., and J. N. Dent. 1941. Notes on *Plethodon cinereus* and *Hemidactylium scutatum* on Cape Cod. *Copeia* 1941(2): 113–114.

MacArthur, R. H., and E. O. Wilson. 1967. *The Theory of Island Biogeography.* Princeton, N.J.: Princeton Univ. Press.

Malnate, E. V. 1960. Systematic division and evolution of the colubrid snake genus *Natrix*, with comments on the subfamily Natricinae. *Proc. Acad. Nat. Sci. Phila.* 112(3): 41–71.

Mayr, E. 1942. *Systematics and the Origin of Species.* New York: Columbia Univ. Press.

Mayr, E., E. G. Linsley, and R. L. Usinger. 1953. *Methods and Principles of Systematic Zoology.* New York: McGraw-Hill.

McDowell, S. B. 1961. Systematic division and evolution of the colubrid snake genus *Natrix*, with comments on the subfamily Natricinae: Review. *Copeia* 1961(4): 502–506.

————. 1964. Partition of the genus *Clemmys* and related problems in the taxonomy of the aquatic Testudinidae. *Proc. Zool. Soc. London* 143(2): 239–279.

Mecham, J. S. 1967. *Notophthalmus viridescens. Cat. Amer. Amphib. Rept.* 53.1–53.4.

Morris, R. and D. Morris. 1966. *Men and Pandas.* New York: McGraw-Hill.

Nantucket, Town of, *et al.* 1966. *An Inventory and Interpretation: Selected Resources of the Island of Nantucket.* Coop. Extension Service, U. Mass., and U.S.D.A. Publ. 4.

Neill, W. T. 1963. *Hemidactylium* and *Hemidacylyium scutatum. Cat. Amer. Amphib. Rept.*: 1–2.2.

Nietschmann, B. 1974. When the turtle collapses the world ends. *Nat. Hist.* 83(6): 34–44.

Noble, G. K. 1931. *The Biology of the Amphibia.* New York: McGraw-Hill, Dover reprint, 1954.

Oliver, J. 1955. *The Natural History of North American Amphibians and Reptiles.* Princeton: D. Van Nostrand Co.

Phillips, V. T., and M. E. Phillips. 1963. Guide to the manuscript collections of the Academy of Natural Sciences of Philadelphia. Spec. Publ. 5, Acad. Nat. Sci. Phila.: xxvi + 553 pp.

Pough, F. H. and M. B. Pough. 1968. The systematic status of the painted turtles (*Chrysemys*) in the northeastern United States. *Copeia* 1968(3): 612–618.

Pough, F. H., and R. E. Wilson. 1975. Acid precipitation and reproductive success of *Ambystoma* salamanders. *Abstracts Am. Soc. Ichthyologists and Herpetologists*: 58.

Pritchard, P. C. H. 1967. *Living Turtles of the World.* Jersey City: T. F. H. Publ.

Redfield, A. C. 1953. Interference phenomena in the tides of the Woods Hole Region. *J. Marine Res.* 12(1): 121–140.

———. 1967. Postglacial change in sea level in the western North Atlantic Ocean. *Science* 157: 687–692.

———. Tide and time on Cape Cod. *Cape Naturalist* 1(2): 22–26.

Redfield, A. C., and A. R. Miller. 1957. Water levels accompanying Atlantic coast hurricanes. *Meteorological Monographs* 2: 23 pp.

Ritchie, W. A. 1969. *The Archeology of Martha's Vineyard.* New York: Nat. Hist. Press.

Schoop, C. R. 1974. Yearly variation in larval survival of *Ambystoma maculatum.* *Ecology* 55: 440–444.

Simpson, G. G. 1961. *Principles of Animal Taxonomy.* New York: Columbia Univ. Press.

Smith, H. M. 1953. The generic name of the newts of eastern North America. *Herpetologica* 9(2): 95–99.

Smith, H. M., and F. N. White. 1956. A case for the trinomen. *Systematic Zool.* 5(4): 183–190.

Soler, E I. 1950. On the status of the family Desmognathidae (Amphibia, Candata). *Univ. Kansas Sci. Bull.* 30: 189–232.

Steinbeck, J., and E. F. Ricketts. 1941. *Sea of Cortez.* New York: The Viking Press.

Strahler, A. N. 1966. *A Geologist's View of Cape Cod.* Garden City, N. Y.: Nat. Hist. Press.

Teal, J., and M. Teal. 1969. *Life and Death of the Salt Marsh.* Boston: Little, Brown and Co.

Thoreau, H. D. 1864. *Cape Cod,* in Krutch, J. W., ed. 1971. *Thoreau: Walden and Other Writings.* New York: Bantam Books.

Tihen, J. A. 1958. Comments on the osteology and phylogeny of ambystomatid salamanders. *Bull. Florida State Mus.* 3: 50 pp.

———. 1969. Ambystoma. *Cat. Amer. Amphib. Rept.*: 75.1–75.3.

Underwood, G. 1967. A contribution to the classification of snakes. *Publ. British Mus. (Nat. Hist.)*: x + 179.

Walford, L. A., and R. I. Wicklund. 1968. Monthly sea temperature structure from the Florida Keys to Cape Cod. *Serial Atlas of the Marine Environment,* Am. Geog. Soc. 15: ii + 16 plates.

Bibliography

Waters, J. 1964. Subspecific intergradation in the Nantucket Island, Massachusetts, population of the turtle *Chrysemys picta*. *Copeia* 1964(3): 550–553.

Wetherbee, D. K., R. P. Coppinger, and R. E. Walsh. 1972. *Time Lapse Ecology, Muskeget Island, Nantucket, Massachusetts*. New York: MSS Educational Publ. Co.

Wilbur, H. M. 1975. The evolutionary and mathematical demography of the turtle *Chrysemys picta*. *Abstracts Am. Soc. Ichthyologists and Herpetologists*: 67–68.

Wilson, E. O., and W. L. Brown. 1953. The subspecies concept and its taxonomic application. *Systematic Zool.*: 2: 97–111.

Wilson, H. C. 1973. *Those Pearly Isles*. Falmouth: Kendall.

Wright, A. H., and A. A. Wright. 1949. *Handbook of Frogs and Toads*. Ithaca, N.Y.: Comstock Publ.

———. 1957. *Handbook of Snakes*. Ithaca, N.Y.: Comstock Publ., 2 vols.

Zinn, D. J., and J. S. Rankin. 1952. *The Fauna of Penikese Island*. Falmouth: Kendall.

INDEX